First
Word Book

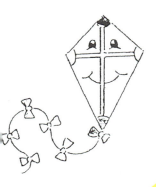

To Parents

About this word book

The *Hamlyn at Home First Word Book* is a fun and practical way to introduce your child to letter sounds and letter shapes. For each letter there is a picture of a lively scene illustrating a selection of words that begin with that letter, plus a selection of these pulled out and labelled around the outside.

The composite pictures will help your child to become confident at hearing and recognizing the sounds of letters of the alphabet. Where a letter has more than one sound, the small labelled pictures include only words that begin with the sound your child will learn first at school. For example, the pages illustrating the letter "**a**" include words like **apple** and **acrobat** (which begin with a short "a" sound). Words that begin with a different "a" sound, like **accordion**, are included only in the main scene. When you use these pages with your young child, refer to the sound that is illustrated and help your child to point out the things that begin with that sound. There are many more examples for your child to find in the main picture in addition to the ones labelled around the outside.

Helping your child

• When your child starts to attempt his or her own writing you will find the *First Word Book* a very useful first spelling aid. It can be used for stories, poems, scrapbooks, letters, notices, cards, lists and to complement *The First Dictionary*, also in the *Hamlyn at Home* series.

• Keep the *First Word Book* somewhere at hand – as your child becomes more interested in words and spellings, you'll find it useful to refer to on all sorts of occasions.

• Concentrate on one particular letter sound at a time. Ask your child to describe what is going on in the main picture.

• See if your child can find all the items labelled in the small pictures in the main picture. Helping children *to look carefully* encourages important early reading skills.

• Emphasize the first *letter sound* of all the labelled words then ask your child if he or she can point out more things beginning with this sound in the main picture. Learning letter sounds is another important part of learning to read.

• Look for things in your home beginning with a particular letter or play a game of I-spy. Don't go on for too long, though, or try to correct your child. Always praise your child's good guesses.

• Learning to recognize the shapes of the individual letters is important, too. Use the alphabet at the top of each page to point out the coloured letter. You could look for other examples of a particular letter – when you are out shopping or in the kitchen together, for example.

• Again, only do one letter at a time. Young children can't concentrate for long so don't go on if your child is losing interest or becoming tired!

   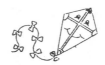

First Word Book

Educational adviser
Jane Salt
Advisory Teacher for the Early Years, Merton

This book belongs to

Illustrated by
Kate Jaspers

a b c d e f g h i j k l m

apple

acrobat

animal

ankle

alligator

axe

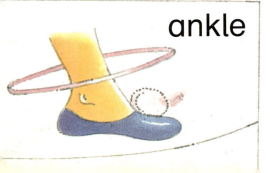

n o p q r s t u v w x y z

astronaut

admiral

ant

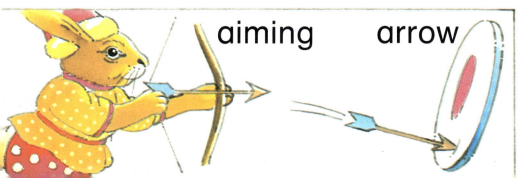

aiming   arrow

anchor

a b c d e f g h i j k l m

bath

ball

book

bird

bucket

balloon

bottle

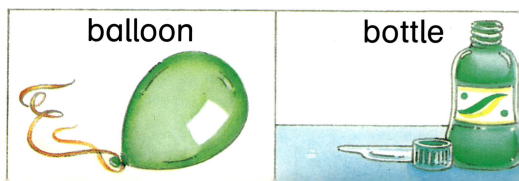

n o p q r s t u v w x y z

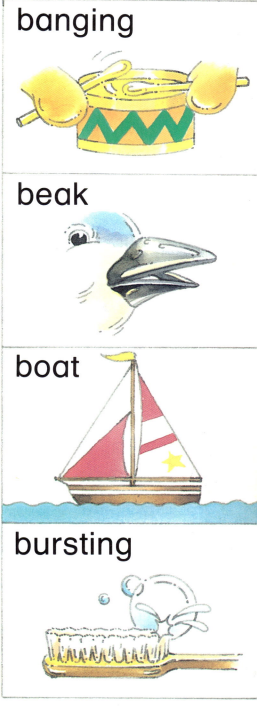

banging

beak

boat

bursting

button

bubble

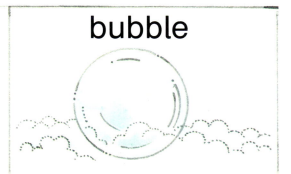

bear

a b c d e f g h i j k l m

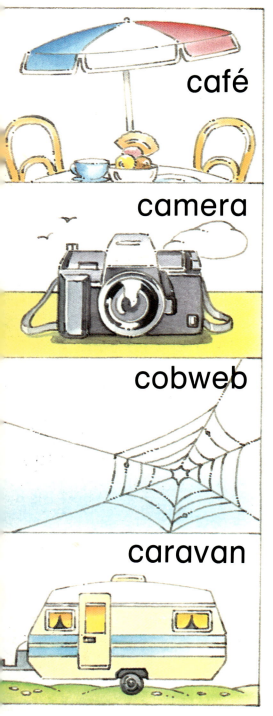

café

camera

cobweb

caravan

counting

car

comic

n o p q r s t u v w x y z

castle

cow

cake

cat

cup

catching

cave

a b c **d** e f g h i j k l m

dog

dirt

duck

ditch

door

diving

dish

n o p q r s t u v w x y z

dove

dandelion

digging

donkey

daffodil

deer

daisy

a b c d e f g h i j k l m

elephant

elephant

elbow

exit

explorer

engine

engine

exploring

exploring

n o p q r s t u v w x y

envelope

enjoying

eight

edge

entrance

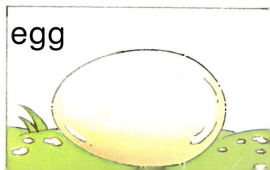

egg

a b c d e **f** g h i j k l m

fox

face

fighting

frog

foal

fire

feather

n o p q r s t u v w x y z

fish

field

fence

farm

fruit

fern

fishing

a b c d e f g h i j k l m

goldfish

garage

garden

guitar

giggling

game

goat

n o p q r s t u v w x y z

gorilla

guard

geese

goggles

gate

gift

giving

a b c d e f g **h** i j k l m

hippo

hill

head

house

hosepipe

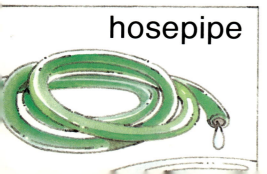

hut

hook

n o p q r s t u v w x y z

hammering

helicopter

hand

hole

helmet

hammer

holding

a b c d e f g h i j k l m

insect

juice

jug

jelly

jacket

jumping

n o p q r s t u v w x y z

invitation

juggling

instrument

jewellery

ill

igloo

a b c d e f g h i j k l m

kangaroo

kicking

kettle

kite

koala

kitten

n o p q r s t u v w x y z

kingfisher

keyhole

key

kilt

kissing

king

a b c d e f g h i j k *l* m

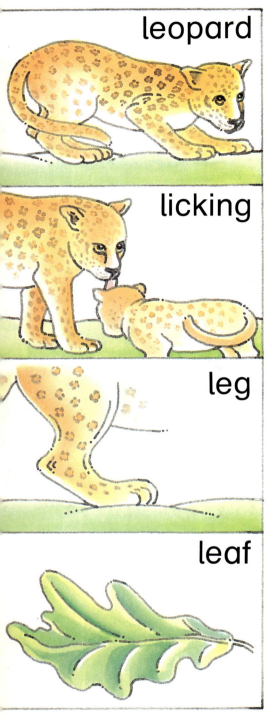

leopard

licking

leg

leaf

light

lizard

log

n o p q r s t u v w x y z

lamb

ladybird

lake

litter

lion

lying

ladder

a b c d e f g h i j k l m

mushroom

mat

melon

mug

milk

meat

mask

n o p q r s t u v w x y z

measuring

meeting

monkey

mirror

money

mouth

magazine

a b c d e f g h i j k l m

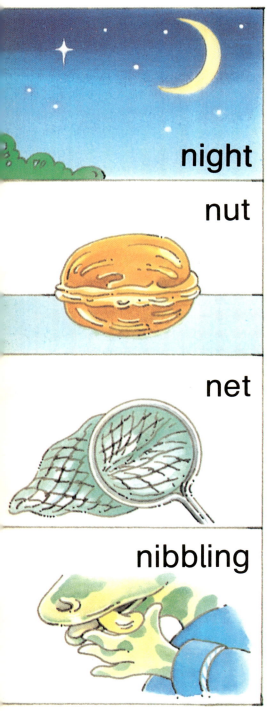

night

nut

net

nibbling

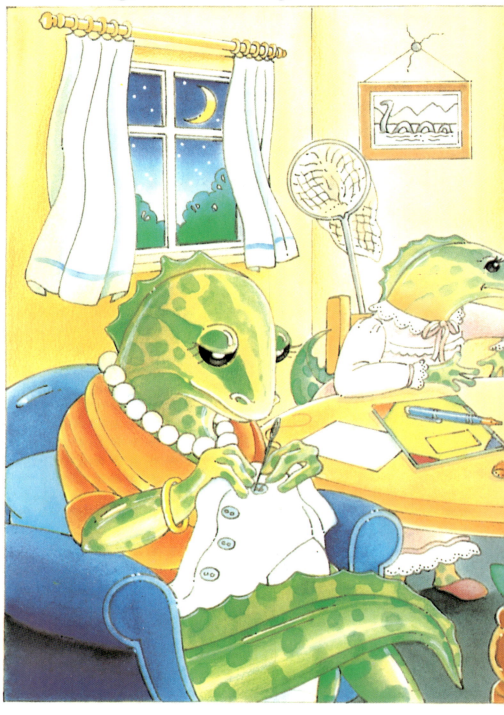

needle

necklace

nail

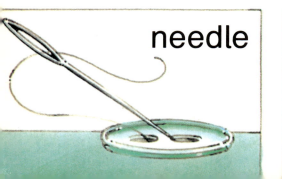

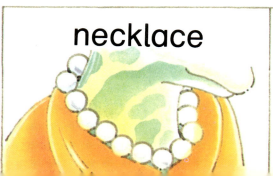

n o p q r s t u v w x y z

nudging

notebook

nose

nine

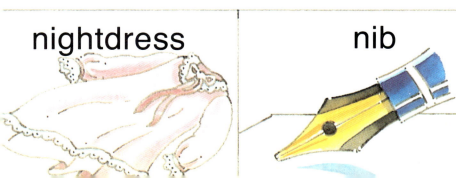

nightdress

nib

newspaper

a b c d e f g h i j k l m

owl

panda

parrot

pond

ostrich

pig   pony

n o p q r s t u v w x y z

pizza

otter

pushing

orange

oar   pulling

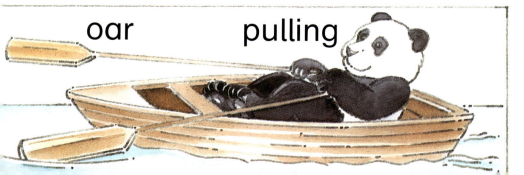

penguin

a b c d e f g h i j k l m

rabbit

queen

reading

quarrelling

robot

rug

radio

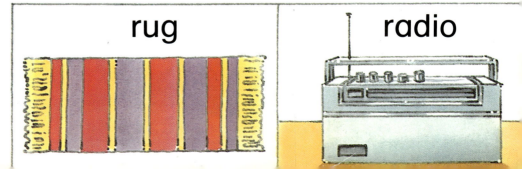

n o p q r s t u v w x y z

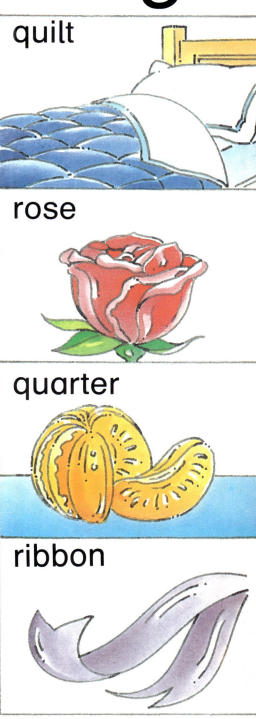

quilt

rose

quarter

ribbon

rainbow

rocket

rollerskate

Skills and objectives

3 Language

Samuel Taylor Coleridge – a Romantic poet who lived from 1772 to 1834 – defined poetry as 'the best words in their best order'. English is a superbly rich language, so a writer's choice of words can be very precise to create a very specific effect on the reader.

- To read, understand and respond to poems (AO1)

- To analyse language using suitable subject terminology (AO2)

Activity 1

a The pairs of words below are very similar in meaning, but try to explain to a partner the subtle differences between them. Explain when you might use one, and when the other.

- grieve/mourn
- shriek/laugh
- ominous/sinister
- brogues/shoes
- beckon/call

b The *first* word in each pair is used in one of the following poems:

- 'Before You Were Mine'
- 'Neutral Tones'
- 'Climbing my Grandfather'
- 'Eden Rock'
- 'When We Two Parted'

Find the poem in which each of these words is used. What would be the effect of using the second word in each pair instead?

In poetry, as well as prose, language can be **formal** or **informal**, can suggest **accent** or **dialect** (or both) and can be **lyrical** or emotionally flat. When talking about the type of language a poem uses, we often use the term **diction** to describe the arrangement and choice of words the poet has selected and the effect that this has.

Read the extract opposite from one student's description of the diction in 'Singh Song!' by Daljit Nagra. Notice how key points are supported by examples from the poem itself.

Key terms

Formal language: language that has strict grammatical structures and generally uses standard or technical vocabulary

Informal language: the opposite of formal; everyday, casual language that uses the grammar and vocabulary of conversation

Accent: a distinctive way of pronouncing words, usually associated with a particular area, country or class

Daljit Nagra

Daljit Nagra's use of diction strongly suggests the accent of British Indian speech. He frequently replaces the 'th' sounds of standard English with 'v' or 'd':

'Ven I return vid my pinnie untied'

He also indicates an Indian pronunciation of the word 'warned' by writing 'vunt'.

Activity 2

How would you describe the diction of each of the poems listed below? Write one or two sentences summing up the language used in each. Remember to provide examples to support the points you make.

- 'I think of thee!'
- 'Neutral Tones'
- 'Porphyria's Lover'

Sound effects in poems

Poets also rely on the sounds of words to create particular effects. By putting similar sounds together, they use **alliteration** and **assonance** to enhance a reader's enjoyment of a poem and to underpin its meaning. Sometimes a poet will use a word or words that create the sound made by a person, animal or event. This is known as **onomatopoeia**.

Activity 3

a What phonological (sound) effects are the poets using in the lines from the three poems below?

> **1** You out there in the cold, seeing the seasons turning, me with my heartful of headlines feeding words onto a blank screen.
> ('Letters from Yorkshire')

> **2** Since then, keen lessons that love deceives,
> And wrings with wrong, have shaped to me
> Your face,
> ('Neutral Tones')

> **3** Cha cha cha! You'd teach me the steps on the way home from Mass,
> Stamping stars from the wrong pavement.
> ('Before You Were Mine')

b What effect does the sound have in each case? Try to explain how the sounds might capture a reader's attention, help to enrich the experience of reading and bring greater depth to the meaning of a line or stanza, or indeed a whole poem.

Key terms

Dialect: a particular form of language, using words and structures that are specific to a place or region and considered non-standard English

Lyrical: expressing feelings and emotions in an imaginative and beautiful way, often associated with music or song

Diction: the choice of words used by a writer; the arrangement of these words in particular ways to create an effect

Alliteration: the use of the same letter or sound at the beginning of adjacent or nearby words, for example, _pickled pepper_

Assonance: the repetition of similar vowel sounds within nearby words, for example, _stone cold_

Onomatopoeia: the use of a word that sounds like what it is naming or describing, for example, _cuckoo_, _sizzle_

Key terms

Rhyme: the use of the same sounds in words or syllables or at the endings of lines of poetry, for example, *cry* and *dry*

Rhythm: a strong, regular, repeated pattern of beats (long and short stresses in words) created by words in a poem. Some words or syllables are emphasized more than others, for example, <u>bro</u>ken <u>hear</u>ted (the long stresses are underlined).

Rhyme and rhythm

Two particular patterns in language occur frequently in most poetry (although not in free verse). These are **rhyme** and **rhythm**.

Rhyme usually occurs at the ends of lines, but sometimes poems have internal rhyme, where words within a line rhyme, perhaps with the word at the end of the line, or on the next line. As with all ideas about sounds, you need to listen to the sounds the words make when you read them aloud. Rhyme links things together.

'The Farmer's Bride' uses rhyme at the ends of lines, as you can see in the extract below.

Extract from 'The Farmer's Bride'

'out 'mong the sheep her be,' they s**aid**

Should properly have been ab**ed**;

But sure enough she wasn't th**ere**

Lying awake with her wide brown st**are**

Activity 4

Quickly look through the poems in the Love and relationships cluster and sort the titles into two columns headed 'Rhyming' and 'Unrhymed'. Try to hear the words of the poem in your head as you read them. Remember that a poem does not have to rhyme all the way through to count as rhyming.

There are several aspects of rhyme that we can look at and write about. A poet may choose to use a rhyming pattern, where the rhyme scheme repeats itself in every stanza:

Extract from 'When We Two Parted'

When we two p**arted**

   In silence and t**ears**,

Half broken-he**arted**

   To sever for y**ears**,

Pale grew thy cheek and c**old**,

   Colder thy k**iss**;

Truly that hour foret**old**

   Sorrow to th**is**.

The correct way to describe a regular rhyming pattern is to give a rhyming syllable a letter of the alphabet, starting at 'A'. In this example from 'When We Two Parted', we can assign the letter 'A' to *arted* (line 1). Then, any rhyme in the stanza that uses the same sound is also 'A' (*earted*, line 3). A different sound is given the letter 'B', then 'C' – and so on. Thus we can describe the rhyme scheme of 'When We Two Parted' as ABABCDCD. Each stanza in the poem follows the same pattern.

However, you need to be aware that simply 'spotting' and describing the rhyming pattern in this way is just a starting point (and earns very little credit in the exam). It is vital that you go on to comment on the *effect* of the rhyme. What does this rhyming pattern tell us about the poem?

Activity 5

a How would you describe the rhyme schemes of 'The Farmer's Bride' and 'Love's Philosophy', using the lettering system described opposite?

b What effects do the poets create using these rhyme schemes?

c Is the rhyme scheme the same in every stanza of the two poems? Note down any slight variations that you can find.

d Choose one of the variations and explain why you think the poet used the variation at this point.

 Support Think about why a poet may have chosen particular rhymes or rhyme schemes. Think about how rhyme draws attention to the words themselves, and how when we read we enjoy the patterns that we notice.

You might write about the effects like this (this student is talking about rhyme in 'When We Two Parted'):

> The regular rhyming pattern (ABABCDCD) in each stanza suggests that things will not change and that the poet will always feel the same about his lover and the way she left him.

Poets don't only use **full rhyme**. Sometimes a rhyming pattern is established and then deliberately changed for a few lines. Many poems also feature **half rhyme**, perhaps to draw a reader's attention to a line or group of lines, or to indicate that not everything is perfect in what the poem describes.

Activity 6

a With a partner, work carefully through 'Porphyria's Lover', looking at how Browning uses both full rhymes and half rhymes.

b Choose two examples of half rhymes and explain why you think Browning chose to use this technique in this particular poem. Support your answer with reference to the examples you have found.

 Stretch Analyse Browning's use of rhyme in 'I think of thee!' What does the rhyme add to our appreciation of the poem? How do the rhymes join ideas together here, do you think? Remember that repetition is a sort of rhyme, too.

Poets often use a mixture of full rhyme, half rhyme and no rhyme at all. The rhyming pattern (or lack of it) is deliberately varied. Remember that a poet chooses words with great care, so the presence or absence of rhyme doesn't happen randomly. Exploring rhyme is just one aspect of how a poem 'works', but it can be very useful in considering how a poem creates meaning.

Words, as we know, are made up of syllables, and when we pronounce a word some syllables are stressed and some are unstressed. In the same way that we can identify rhyme and rhyming patterns, we can mark stressed syllables in words like this:

/ language   / diction   / alliteration   / evoke

Sometimes, the syllable that is stressed actually determines the meaning of a word, as in the example of two words that are spelt the same below:

/ conduct   / conduct

Lines of poetry will often put stressed and unstressed syllables together to create a particular rhythm or rhythmic pattern. This rhythm can be the same through, for example, to suggest a kind of movement (which might be being described at that point in the poem). However, it is very important to remember that identifying stresses and how they are used (rhythm) is not enough. You must always think about the *effect* that this creates.

As an example, in 'Follower' the poet describes how he would be carried on his father's back:

> **Extract from 'Follower'**
> Sometimes he rode me on his back
> Dipping and rising to his plod

Here the use of a regular pattern of stressed and unstressed syllables (a regular rhythm) reinforces the picture of the steady tread of the father carrying the boy.

Activity 7

a Look at the stressed and unstressed syllables in 'When We Two Parted'. How would you describe the rhythm of the poem? Why do you think the poet chose to use this rhythm – what is its effect?

b Can you find any rhythmic effects in 'Follower'? (Look particularly at the last stanza.) What do these rhythmic effects add to the way a reader might respond to the poem?

Support

a Copy out the first four lines of 'Neutral Tones'. Mark the stressed syllables in each word. Here is the first line, marked up:

   /   /   /   /
we stood by a pond that winter day

b Now say the lines aloud, emphasizing the stressed syllables more than usual. Can you hear (and see) a rhythmic pattern?

In this unit you have looked in detail at poets' choice of words (diction), and the sounds, rhymes and rhythms of these words. Taken together, these aspects help us to describe and analyse a poem's language.

Remember that simply spotting language features is not enough. You must always explain the effects of these language features and how they relate to the reading and meaning of the poem.

Key questions to ask yourself are:

● Why might the poet have chosen to use this feature?

● What is the effect of using this feature? Does it have more than one effect?

● How does the feature enhance your understanding of, and your response to the message of the poem?

Activity 8

Use what you have learned to write a full analysis of the language of 'Singh Song!'

Comment on the:
● diction
● sound effects
● rhythm.

4 Creating images

- To read and respond to extracts from poems (AO1)
- To analyse how poets use imagery to create different effects (AO2)

What is imagery?

The word 'image' has several different definitions, although all are concerned with pictures. When discussing poetry, 'image' has a very specific meaning.

Activity 1

a In pairs, use a dictionary or search online to find as many different definitions of the word 'image' as you can. Which do you think is the most helpful when it comes to looking at poetry?

b Share your definitions with another pair and agree on the best one. Be prepared to explain your choice to the rest of the group or class.

When poets create imagery (word pictures) through their language, they don't just focus on how things look. They may also describe how things smell, taste, sound or feel. Imagery can appeal to all of the reader's senses, not just sight.

Activity 2

Consider the following extracts from poems in the 'Love and relationships' cluster. All of them contain images. What senses does the poet appeal to in order to help the reader see and understand the image in their mind?

1 … your ghost clatters towards me over George Square till I see you, clear as scent, under the tree, ('Before You Were Mine')

2 … her cheek once more Blushed bright beneath my burning kiss, ('Porphyria's Lover')

3 The horse strained at his clicking tongue, ('Follower')

4 … his knuckles singing as they reddened in the warmth. ('Letters From Yorkshire')

5 … the moonbeams kiss the sea ('Love's Philosophy')

When writing about several individual images in a poem we can use the word 'imagery'. For example, 'the imagery in this poem all relates to the natural world'.

Imagery is often built up using **figurative language**, which means that the images are created by comparing something with something else. This sort of comparison is not to be taken literally. If you say 'A flood of invitations arrived' you don't mean a literal flood, you mean a large quantity that seemed like a flood. This type of expression is sometimes called a 'figure of speech'.

So, why do poets use imagery and figurative language rather than simple, literal descriptions? Poets want to help readers to see the world in a different way, to interpret it more imaginatively, and to suggest new ideas and meanings in what they see around them.

This means that reading poetry isn't always easy. One of the keys to appreciating poetry is a willingness to work hard to make sense of images that might at first seem difficult to understand.

Read the lines below from 'Winter Swans':

> **Extract from 'Winter Swans'**
>
> the waterlogged earth
>
> gulping for breath at our feet

Here are one student's comments on the imagery in this extract:

This description conveys the way that rain-soaked ground squelches when it is trodden on. The image compares the ground to a drowning man who gasps for breath as he surfaces. It uses our senses of sight, sound and touch to help us see and understand walking over soggy ground in a new and different way. It also conveys a sense of panic or being trapped, which echoes the feeling of a relationship in trouble — which the poem hints at as it continues.

Key term

Figurative language: language used to describe someone or something by comparing it with something else, using words that are not meant to be taken literally

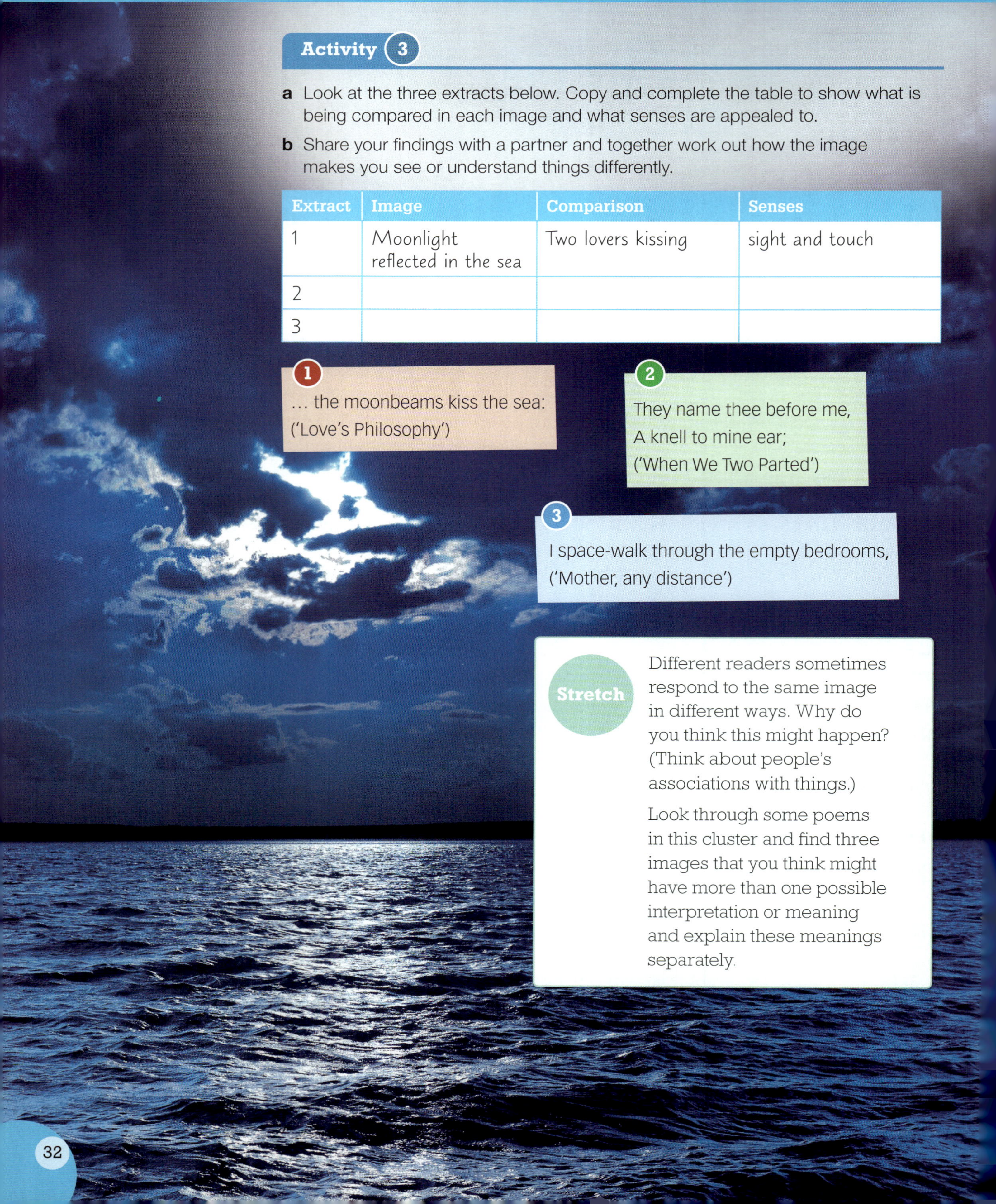

Activity 3

a Look at the three extracts below. Copy and complete the table to show what is being compared in each image and what senses are appealed to.

b Share your findings with a partner and together work out how the image makes you see or understand things differently.

Extract	Image	Comparison	Senses
1	Moonlight reflected in the sea	Two lovers kissing	sight and touch
2			
3			

1

... the moonbeams kiss the sea:
('Love's Philosophy')

2

They name thee before me,
A knell to mine ear;
('When We Two Parted')

3

I space-walk through the empty bedrooms,
('Mother, any distance')

Stretch

Different readers sometimes respond to the same image in different ways. Why do you think this might happen? (Think about people's associations with things.)

Look through some poems in this cluster and find three images that you think might have more than one possible interpretation or meaning and explain these meanings separately.

Similes, metaphors and personification

Many images rely on the use of **similes** and **metaphors** to make comparisons. In everyday speech and writing we often use common similes and metaphors, for example, *He's as skinny as a rake* or *She absolutely nailed it*. Poets, however, try to create original, new comparisons to make their images surprising, striking and effective.

Activity 4

a With a partner identify the similes in 'The Farmer's Bride' and discuss the images they create. Consider these questions:

- What does the comparison say or suggest about the person or thing being described?
- Does it make you see them or it differently?
- How does the use of the simile help the reader interpret the poem as a whole?

b After your discussion, choose the simile that you feel is most effective (has most impact or is most unusual). Write a short paragraph, explaining the effect of the imagery and why you think it is powerful.

An example student response is:

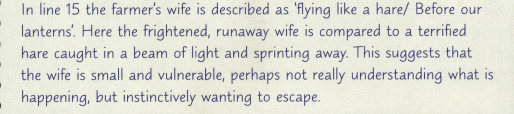

In line 15 the farmer's wife is described as 'flying like a hare/ Before our lanterns'. Here the frightened, runaway wife is compared to a terrified hare caught in a beam of light and sprinting away. This suggests that the wife is small and vulnerable, perhaps not really understanding what is happening, but instinctively wanting to escape.

Support

a Look through 'The Farmer's Bride' and list the similes that you can find.

b For each simile, note down the two objects that are being compared and what this suggests.

Activity 5

a Read the metaphors numbered 1–5 below, and find them in the poems they appear in. Explain what is being described and how the metaphor makes an effective comparison. The first one has been done for you.

b Once you've worked out a possible meaning for each of the metaphors, try to think of another meaning. Share your thoughts with a partner.

> The poet pictures her lover as a palm tree, tall and straight with arms (leaves) providing welcome shelter. This is highly effective because the qualities she admires in her lover (being tall and protective) are also key characteristics of a palm tree.

1
Yet, O my palm-tree…
('I think of thee!')

2
my thoughts do twine and bud
('I think of thee!')

3
The touch-lines new-ruled
('Walking Away')

4
a half-fledged thing set free
Into a wilderness,
('Walking Away')

5
to fall or fly
('Mother, any distance')

Key term

Extended metaphor: a series of images within one text or poem that all relate to the same central metaphor

When several images in the same poem share a common idea, we often refer to it as an **extended metaphor**. Using an extended metaphor is a way of building up an overall picture for the reader as they progress through the poem.

Activity 6

Explore the ways in which the poet uses an extended metaphor in the poem 'Climbing My Grandfather'. Consider:

- what is the overall image presented?
- how is this reflected in the title?
- which individual words and separate images in the poem help to build up a consistent overall picture?
- what does this extended comparison suggest about the poet's grandfather?

Stretch

What does this extended metaphor suggest to the reader about the boy/poet and his relationship with his grandfather? Think about the younger generations and how they follow and build on the older generation.

Stylistic links

As well as comparing and linking themes in two poems, you will also need to consider the stylistic techniques that the poets have used and how these might form further links. Remember that you need to explore both *what* the poets wrote about and *how* they wrote.

Look back at the work you have already done on Language (Unit 3), Creating images (Unit 4) and Form and structure (Unit 5). These are all part of the stylistic techniques employed by poets, and you need to think carefully about them in your comparison.

Activity 4

a Re-read 'The Charge of the Light Brigade' and make some quick notes about its form and structure, for example, the stanzas, rhyme scheme and repetition.

b Choose another poem about war to compare with 'The Charge of the Light Brigade'. Write similar notes on your chosen poem.

c Use your notes to write a paragraph about how the poems have similar or different form and structure.

Here is an extract from one student's response:

> Although both 'The Charge of the Light Brigade' and 'Bayonet Charge' are about war, their forms give a different message to the reader. Tennyson has used stanzas of varying lengths with an irregular rhyme scheme, which duplicates the sound of horses' hooves as they gallop, whereas Hughes has used a single stanza of free verse, which perhaps represents the continuous nature of the fear the soldier feels as he runs.

Activity 5

Now compare the poets' use of language and imagery in the two poems. First write a list of points that you wish to cover, then write a complete paragraph.

Key terms

Lyrical: expressing feelings and emotions in an imaginative and beautiful way often associated with music or song

Political: to do with government or public affairs of a country

Historical and cultural links

Another point of connection between poems is the time at which they were written, and (possibly) the cultural backgrounds of the poets. Knowing this information will help you to meet some of the requirements of AO3 where you need to talk about the contexts of the poems. In the Power and Conflict cluster, poems fall roughly into time categories: Romantic poets, Victorian poets and 20th- and 21st-century poets.

Romantic poets

These poets lived mainly during the 18th and early 19th centuries and wrote more about the natural world and emotional, personal themes than had been common previously. This type of poetry was often also described as **lyrical** (song-like). Shelley, Blake and Wordsworth would be considered Romantic poets.

Some Romantic poems were also quite **political**, particularly when the poets disagreed with decisions made by the government of that period.

Activity 6

Look again at the three poems written by the Romantic poets: Shelley, Blake and Wordsworth.

a What connections can you identify in their themes?

b How have the poets allowed their emotions to show in the poems?

c In what ways can the poems be described as 'lyrical'?

d Can you identify any political views in the poems? What do those appear to be?

e What view of the world do you think these poets were trying to show their readers?

Percy Bysshe Shelley

Victorian poets

Tennyson and Browning lived and wrote during the reign of Queen Victoria in the 19th century. They were both well known for writing dramatic poems. During Victoria's reign, Britain was consolidating an empire, with British soldiers and businesses being established all over the world

Activity 7

a The poems by Tennyson and Browning appear to have quite different topics. Write down any common themes you can identify. (Hint – think about the aspect of power in relation to this question.)

b Look at the form and structure of the Victorian poems.
  - What similarities are there?
  - What differences are there?

c Consider whether either of these poems contains a political message. Explain your answer.

d What other message might each poet be trying to give their readers?

20th- and 21st-century poets

With the exception of Owen, who died in the First World War, and Hughes, who died in 1998, all the other poets in this cluster still live and work as poets. They have been influenced by the effects of different conflicts around the world seen through film and TV, as well as by the changes to society brought about over the past 50 years.

Agard and Dharker write from a more individual perspective as they are from backgrounds that are classed as 'ethnic minorities'. Dharker was born in Pakistan, but brought up in Scotland. Agard was born and grew up in Guyana before moving to the UK in 1977. Both of these poets draw on their heritage and cultural background in their writing.

When responding to the question in the exam, you do not have to choose a poem from the same era as the one given in the exam. This means that you may well be comparing poems that have been written many years, even centuries, apart.

Here is an extract from a student's response comparing how two poets present their ideas about power:

> Shelley and Agard have a shared theme to their poems, although they were writing 200 years apart. Both deal with the effects of a power which believes itself to be permanent; both poems show that this is not the case. Agard explores the effect of an imposed education system based on a country that is not his native country, and reflects on the impact that had on his own identity. Shelley speaks about the effect of authority being imposed on a country and reflects on the fact that it has faded away over time so that 'nothing... remains'.

Activity 8

a Choose two poems from different time periods which you think share a theme, as in the example student response above.

b Write at least one paragraph comparing the different views of the poets that are presented in the poems.

c Share your writing with a partner. Discuss your own views about what the poets are saying to their readers and how they are saying it.

Skills and objectives

- To read, understand and respond to texts (AO1)

- To analyse language, form and structure, using suitable subject terminology (AO2)

- To show understanding of the relationships between texts and the contexts in which they were written (AO3)

7 Writing about poetry in the exam

All of the units in this section so far have helped you to explore different aspects of the poet's craft and the connections between the poems in this cluster. This unit focuses on how you can use all of these skills most effectively in the English Literature exam.

Writing an effective answer in a short space of time requires organization and skill. You need to:

- understand the question
- plan your response
- use quotations and textual references
- make detailed comparisons between two poems.

This unit takes you through all of these stages.

Understanding the question

The AQA exam board will set a different question on poetry every year, but some elements will always be the same. This means that whatever the question is, your answer should:

- always refer to *two* poems only: the one that is printed on the exam paper and one chosen by you

- always compare the two poets' treatment of a theme or idea that will be stated in the question

- always write about poetic techniques and language features.

It is important to read the question carefully, so that you are clear about exactly what you have to do. You may be asked to write about 'power' or 'conflict' in your answer, or the question might direct you to write about something more specific, such as 'war', 'the power of nature' or 'powerful emotions'.

Look at the exam question below and the annotations, which comment on the main features.

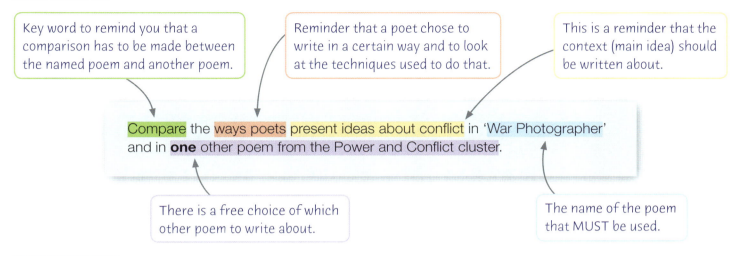

Key word to remind you that a comparison has to be made between the named poem and another poem.

Reminder that a poet chose to write in a certain way and to look at the techniques used to do that.

This is a reminder that the context (main idea) should be written about.

Compare the ways poets present ideas about conflict in 'War Photographer' and in **one** other poem from the Power and Conflict cluster.

There is a free choice of which other poem to write about.

The name of the poem that MUST be used.

Activity 1

a What aspects of conflict can you identify in 'War Photographer'?

b Which poem would you choose to write about to compare with 'War Photographer'?

c Discuss with your partner your choice of poem to compare and explain why you think it a good choice.

Planning your response

You will only have about 40 minutes to produce an answer in the exam, so you need to be well organized and to plan your answer carefully.

The aim of a plan is to help you generate the ideas that you will need to complete the task set in the question, and to put those ideas in order so that your answer is full and well-shaped.

There are many different ways of planning a response, such as drawing a mind map or jotting down the first sentence of each paragraph. You need to experiment with different ways of planning to find the one that suits you best. Here is just one possible method that you could use.

Create a table to check that you address all the correct assessment objectives for the exam and to give yourself some prompts about what to write. The following table is a sample plan in response to the question on the previous page.

Focus: Conflict	'War Photographer'	'Charge of the Light Brigade'
What? (meanings and ideas)	Job role; photos of war zones; witness terrible events; people not really caring	Obey commands even knowing they're wrong; fight against huge odds; deserve praise
How? (form, structure, language, imagery)	Single stanza; some rhymes; similes/metaphors; Bible reference; short sentences; five sections; like snapshots	six stanzas; some rhymes; metaphors; repeats for emphasis; alliteration; images of destruction; three sections; numbers used for effect
When/Where? (context)	20th century; refers to different war zones; awful events witnessed – death, maiming	19th century; refers to specific battle in Crimean War; believes in glory of battle; problems not mentioned much

Activity 2

a Draw up another table in the same format as the one on page 98 and complete it with brief notes and ideas as if you were going to answer the question below.

> Compare the ways poets present ideas about conflict in 'My Last Duchess' and in **one** other poem from the Power and Conflict cluster.

You need to think about:

- aspects of conflict in the named poem
- which other poem has areas of conflict or themes that you are confident to write about.

The opening paragraph of your answer is very important. It tells the examiner a huge amount about how successful you are likely to be in tackling the question. Key ideas from your plan should be briefly noted in your opening, and your writing must be firmly focused on the theme in the question and on the two poems you are going to write about.

Here's an example of a good opening, based on the question above:

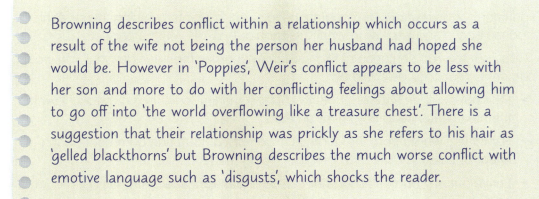

Browning describes conflict within a relationship which occurs as a result of the wife not being the person her husband had hoped she would be. However in 'Poppies', Weir's conflict appears to be less with her son and more to do with her conflicting feelings about allowing him to go off into 'the world overflowing like a treasure chest'. There is a suggestion that their relationship was prickly as she refers to his hair as 'gelled blackthorns' but Browning describes the much worse conflict with emotive language such as 'disgusts', which shocks the reader.

Activity 3

a Write the opening paragraph of your answer to the question we looked at on page 97.

b Swap your opening paragraph with a partner. Comment on your partner's paragraph by indicating two things they have done well and one thing that might be improved. Remember that the focus of the writing must be on the original question.

c Re-draft your own opening paragraph in the light of the remarks made by your partner and compare both versions you have written to see the improvement in your response.

How to use quotations and textual references

As time in any exam is limited, you will need to make sure that everything you write is useful and helps you to progress towards answering the question as fully as possible. It is important to use quotations to support your points. Try to select a few words that have real impact rather than using a long quote, unless it is really necessary.

Look at the example of a student response below and an examiner's comments.

> Clear addressing of the task. Sound point being made about the narrator.

> Long quote which links to the point, but unclear how this supports what has been said.

> Short explanation of the long quote which says something similar – no new point is made.

> Shorter quote which links better with the parts of the sentence before and after it, and introduces a fresh insight.

Armitage describes the way that the narrator was involved in conflict and the effect this has on him. 'Then I'm home on leave. But I blink/ and he bursts in again through the doors of the bank./ Sleep, and he's probably armed, and possibly not./ Dream, and he's torn apart by a dozen rounds.' This shows that even when he tries to rest, the image of the shop looter comes back to haunt him. The conflict has stayed with him even when he is now far away from it: 'he's here in my head when I close my eyes' which suggests there's no escape from what he has done.

Activity 4

Experiment with ways of using quotations to support points by using the student response above and improving what the candidate wrote. With a partner:

a Copy out the first sentence of this student response, then decide what you would do next. Your choices could be:

- Pick out another, shorter quote to support the first point being made. Rewrite the next sentence to comment on that.
- Select key words from the quote (a maximum of four) and comment on the effect of those in relation to the point being made.
- Leave out any quotes altogether here and **paraphrase** what has been quoted, adding comments of your own about the conflict and its impact.

b Choose another poem as if you were still writing about conflict. Write a paragraph about the conflict, using suitable short quotes to support your points.

c With another pair, share your writing and discuss your ideas about how you chose suitable extracts.

d Discuss any difficulties you find with using quotes – either in their selection or their length. Be ready to provide advice, support and suggestions to your peers to help them feel more confident about the process.

Key term

Paraphrase: explain what something means without using the exact same words; rewording an idea to make it clear

Making comparisons

One of the requirements of the Poetry Anthology question is that you compare two poems. You will therefore need to use words and phrases to introduce those comparisons. Remember that to 'compare' means to find both similarities and differences between things, so you need words for both types of observations.

Activity 5

a Divide a page into two columns. At the head of one write 'Similarities' and for the other write 'Differences'. Sort the words and phrases below into the relevant columns.

b Experiment with creating sentences using some of these terms. You might write for example:

- 'The Emigrée' refers to a half-remembered city, whereas the city in 'Ozymandias' has completely disappeared.

- The power of nature is explored in 'The Prelude' and 'Storm on the Island'. Both deal with strong impressions...

c Memorize some of these words and phrases as part of your revision and regularly practise comparing different poems using these terms.

as well as   moreover   whereas   furthermore   in addition to   alternatively

both   however   also   different   alike   in contrast   similarly

on the one hand... on the other hand...   although   likewise   not only... but also...

Read the extract from a student answer below. It is a response to a question about comparing how poets represent conflict in 'Bayonet Charge' and 'Exposure'.

Although both poets Hughes and Owen write about an experience of conflict linked with the army, the experiences of the persona in each one is different. Hughes suggests that the soldier has been sleeping at his post by starting with the words 'Suddenly he awoke...' implying he has been startled into action, into the conflict, whereas although Owen describes being weary he does not say the soldiers sleep, as the wind is too cold and seems to cut through them.

Owen is writing about first-hand experience of being in the First World War. He describes the boredom of being in the trenches when 'nothing happens' but also refers to the fear of dying — not on the battlefield but due to the extreme cold. Hughes does not make it clear whether the soldier in his poem is actually at war. The conflict seems to be more about himself and the fear he has while he runs across the field. This becomes so extreme that at the end he discards his feelings of 'honour, human dignity' just to escape from being shot. Owen, on the other hand, seems to have already lost all his faith in what they are doing and even suggests his faith in God is no longer strong. His experience of the external conflict seems worse.

Activity 6

With a partner, identify the language that the student uses to compare the two poems. Discuss how effective it is, and why (or why not).

Over the course of the unit you have looked at a range of techniques to help you compare poems from this cluster. It is now time to combine all of these skills to write a complete, detailed answer.

Activity 7

a Go back to Activity 2 on page 99, where you wrote the plan for your response about conflict in 'My Last Duchess', and another poem of your choice. In the exam you will not have a copy of the second text you select to refer to.

b Continue your response to the question to write a more developed answer. Allow yourself about 25 minutes to do this. Remember to:

- use quotes and paraphrasing
- include your ideas from the 'What? How? When/Where?' plan
- use linking words and phrases to introduce your comparisons.

Progress check

Now that you have completed this section on your Anthology poems, it is time to assess your confidence in responding to the poetry question in the exam.

With a partner, discuss how confident you feel about:

- understanding the overall themes and ideas in the cluster
- writing about the meaning and context of the individual poems
- exploring the way that poets use language
- explaining how poets create imagery, and its effect on the reader
- commenting on form and structure
- identifying links and connections between poems
- responding to an exam question (including planning, choosing a poem for comparison and using quotations).

Now identify two or three areas or poems that you are less confident about. In particular, be honest with yourself about any of the cluster poems that you find difficult to read and understand. Note down both the areas and the poems and decide how you might target them for improvement.

Unseen poems

Introduction

In your literature exam, as well as responding to a question on the Anthology poems you have studied, you will also have to answer questions on two 'Unseen' poems. This means that the poems will be completely new to you. You will not have prepared to write about them through discussions in lessons or through practice questions.

However, this does not mean you will be unprepared for these questions. You will find that the skills you have developed while studying your chosen cluster from the Anthology are the same skills that you will need to write about the unseen poems. One advantage of this section is that you will not have to memorize any quotations because both unseen poems will be printed in full in the exam paper.

There will be two questions for you to answer on the unseen poems. You must answer them *both*. There is *no choice*. One question will ask you to explore an aspect of the first poem; the second question will ask you to compare that first poem with another poem, linked by theme. The first question carries 24 marks. The second question carries 8 marks.

Assessment Objectives

The skills that you will be tested on are grouped into two Assessment Objectives (AOs). These are two of the same AOs that are tested in the Anthology questions.

AO1 Read, understand and respond to texts. Students should be able to

- Maintain a critical style and develop an informed personal response
- Use textual references, including quotations, to support and illustrate interpretation.

AO2 Analyse the language, form and structure used by a writer to create meanings and effects, using relevant subject terminology where appropriate.

Activity 1

a Use the Assessment Objectives above to create a poster to remind yourself about the areas being assessed. Write the objectives in your own words and check the meanings of any terms that you are not sure about.

b Share your poster with a partner and discuss any areas that you found hard to explain.

Below are some of the questions that students commonly ask about the unseen poems – and the answers.

Should I prepare for the exam by reading as many poems as I can?

You should try to read a range of poems to help you get a clear understanding of the ways that poets use language and structure to create different effects for the reader. This will improve your critical skills.

If I don't understand the unseen poems, can I choose to answer another question?

No – the unseen section is a compulsory part of the exam. You should make every effort to respond to the questions after reading both poems carefully. If you do not write anything you will be throwing away a large percentage of the marks on this paper.

Should I refer to the Anthology poems if I can make a comparison with one of them?

No – absolutely not! You will get no marks for making that type of comparison.

Will I be able to answer the questions?

Yes. The questions will be clear and 'open' so that everyone can respond to them. It will be possible to write about the poems on different levels. For example, a literal interpretation of the text will be possible, but in order to access higher marks you will need to refer to metaphorical interpretations too (things that the poet may not state explicitly, but may imply through figurative language and imagery).

How will I know what to write about?

You will have practised reading and responding to different poems before the exam. You will know what the examiner is looking for because you will understand the Assessment Objectives. You will have learned the necessary vocabulary to explain what you think and you will have the ability to express your ideas thoughtfully.

Are the unseen poetry questions worth a lot of marks?

The unseen poetry questions appear on Paper 2 of your exam. Paper 2 as a whole is worth 60% of your marks, with a total of 96 marks, and the unseen poetry question is worth 32 of them. There are 24 marks for the first question and 8 marks for the second (comparison) question. This section will provide up to 20% of your final English Literature GCSE mark.

Will I get marked down for spelling mistakes?

No. It is very important that you write as correctly and fluently as possible, but spelling and grammar are not tested in the unseen poetry questions.

By working through this part of the book you will practise all of the skills that you need to tackle the unseen questions in the exam. Also, and most importantly, you will improve your confidence and enjoyment when reading poems for the first time.

Skills and objectives

- To explore ideas and meanings (AO2)
- To read and respond to unseen poems (AO1)

1 Meaning and context

The unseen poems in the exam will be the same for all students, regardless of which Anthology cluster has been studied. You need to be confident in tackling these questions as they will provide a significant percentage of your final mark.

Activity 1

a With a partner, think about the work you have done on the poems from the Anthology cluster you have studied. List the skills and strengths you have developed which you think may help you to address the unseen poems.

b Note down any weaknesses you feel you may have, or areas that you are not confident about. Discuss these with a partner, and set yourself a target to improve on them.

In the exam, you will be given two poems to read that you are unlikely to have read previously. These will be linked by theme. They may be chosen from any period of time.

You have to answer one question on the first poem. This will carry 24 marks, so you will need to be able to consider a number of different features of the text.

You will then have to answer a comparison question about the first poem and another that will be provided. This question carries 8 marks. It will focus on comparing the ways that the poets present their ideas.

After completing Activity 1, you will have realized that the skills you have already practised for the cluster poems are the same skills you will need for the unseen poems. This means that you will need to write about the language used, images, form and structure, as well as meanings.

As the Assessment Objectives at the beginning of this section state, you will have to show that you have read the poems and responded to the ideas they contain (AO1). You will also have to explore some of the ideas presented in each poem as well as comparing some aspects of each text (AO2).

However, in this unseen poetry section you will *not* need to write about context (AO3), as you will not know anything about the background to the poems or the situation the poet was in when writing.

Activity 2

a Read the titles of the poems below.

'Remember'   'As Luck Would Have It'   'Tall Nettles'

'A Green Song'   'Growing Up'   'A Child's Sleep'

b Make quick notes about what each title suggests to you. You may want to consider some of these ideas:

- What could the poem be about?
- Does it suggest any circumstances you know about?
- What sort of emotions might the poem explore?
- Does the title carry any **connotations** for you?

c Share your ideas about each title with a partner.

Stretch

How important do you think the title of a poem is? Explain your reasoning carefully, and with examples.

Support

a Look at the example below of a mind map developed from the title of one poem. Copy and complete it.

b Choose another poem title and draw a mind map showing the ideas you can link with it. These ideas can be based on personal memories, visual descriptions, connotations or other sensory perceptions.

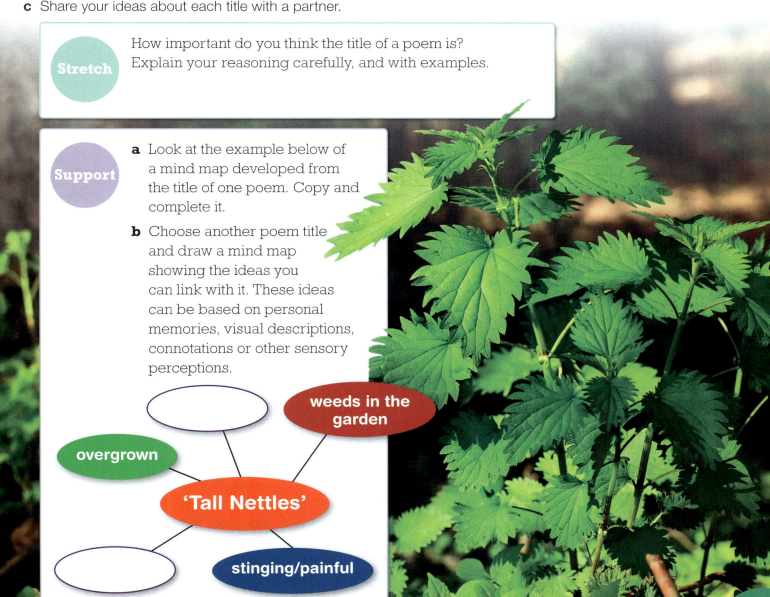

weeds in the garden

overgrown

'Tall Nettles'

stinging/painful

In your exam, you will need to spend some time reading and thinking about each poem before you start writing. It may be useful to annotate sections of the texts to remind yourself what you want to write about.

Read the poem 'Tall Nettles' by Edward Thomas below.

Tall Nettles

TALL nettles cover up, as they have done
These many springs, the rusty harrow, the plough
Long worn out, and the roller made of stone:
Only the elm butt tops the nettles now.

This corner of the farmyard I like the most:
As well as any bloom upon a flower
I like the dust on the nettles, never lost
Except to prove the sweetness of a shower.

The question about the first poem may focus on the feelings of the poet about a particular object, circumstance or event. For example, a question about 'Tall Nettles' might be:

> How does the poet present his feelings about the nettles?

Activity 3

a With a partner, discuss what the poet is saying about the nettles.

b Identify three words or phrases that you think show the feelings of the poet.

c Discuss your chosen words or phrases with a partner, explaining what feelings you believe your extracts show.

d Read the start of a student response that follows, then use your chosen words or phrases to complete the response.

> Thomas knows that the nettles have been there, undisturbed for a long time '... these many springs', which suggests he does not care that they grow so long as they cover up old machinery which may make the farm look run down.

e Share your written response with your partner. Check that the response you read by your partner makes reference to the feelings of the poet about the nettles.

Poets often reveal mixed feelings in their poems. In looking at unseen poems, you need to be aware that the emotion you first identify may not be the only one that is shown. In responding to a question about feelings, you may have to refer to the changing emotions being described by the speaker.

Read the poem 'I Am Very Bothered' by Simon Armitage below and consider the following question:

> How does the speaker present his feelings about the incident in the chemistry lab?

Clearly, the speaker has done things which prey on his mind a good deal. These worry him.

The speaker believes there are a number of things he has done which others would regard as being wrong. He still thinks about what he has done even though it was a while ago.

I Am Very Bothered

I am very bothered when I think
of the bad things I have done in my life.
Not least that time in the chemistry lab
when I held a pair of scissors by the blades
and played the handles
in the naked lilac flame of the Bunsen burner;
then called your name, and handed them over.

O the unrivalled stench of branded skin
as you slipped your thumb and middle finger in,
then couldn't shake off the two burning rings. Marked,
the doctor said, for eternity.

Don't believe me, please, if I say
that was just my butterfingered way, at thirteen,
of asking you if you would marry me.

This phrase suggests the speaker has been careless about something, rather than inflicted quite a serious injury. He seems to be regarding it in a more light-hearted way than originally.

The last phrase seems flippant. It's unlikely that a 13-year-old would ask their girlfriend to marry them, so the whole phrase now seems a bit like a joke. It adds to the impression that the speaker may not really be worried about what he did.

Now read the annotations, which pick out the ways that emotions are expressed in the opening and closing lines (in response to the question).

Activity 4

a With a partner, discuss what you think is the main emotion being shown by the speaker in 'I Am Very Bothered' by Simon Armitage. Try to support your idea with a quote.

b Look at the other lines of the poem and try to identify two other feelings that the speaker appears to be suggesting through what is said. (Consider whether any regret or remorse is shown.)

c Write out the lines you have chosen from the poem. Annotate them in the same way as the example above to explain how you think the poet has shown the different feelings.

d Share your selected lines and annotations with another pair. Discuss the different feelings the poet suggests.

When you write your response to the unseen poems, you will need to focus on particular parts of the text. There will not be enough time to write about everything in the poem. For this reason it is very important that you identify the features which *answer the question being asked*. In the example above, the question asked about the feelings of the speaker.

Read the student response below, based on the Armitage poem. Read the teacher's annotations, which show how closely the student is responding to the question.

> Develops ideas – makes a link between the meaning of the chosen word and what the connotations could be. Shows the student is still trying to focus on the question of feelings.

> This shows an alternative view – based on the connotation, the student is able to suggest different feelings from the most obvious one they started with. This shows they are considering alternative ways to interpret the views of the speaker.

The speaker in Armitage's poem seems to be apologizing to someone for burning their fingers in chemistry '... the unrivalled stench of branded skin.' It appears that the person is sorry for the pain they have caused as they have made a permanent mark on the other person's fingers. However, 'branded' is similar to what used to be done to cattle to show who owned them so maybe this person was trying to put a mark on his girlfriend to show he owned her. That makes him seem possessive and thoughtless rather than sorry.

> First response – student shows they are not sure about the feelings in the poem but suggests what they first think.

> Reinforces the idea – focuses on the fact of being sorry, which links with apologizing, but still keeps an aspect of uncertainty by writing 'It appears...'

> Support – picks out just one word to show a possible different view of events.

Activity 5

a Read the poem 'The Pond' by Owen Sheers opposite, and respond to the following question:

> How does the speaker present his feelings associated with the pond, as he grows up?
>
> Follow the steps below, as you did in the activities above:
>
> - Make some notes or annotations on the poem to highlight different feelings that you can identify.
> - Use the student answer as a model for your response.
> - Make a point about each feeling and support it with a quote.
> - Comment on what you think the quote suggests.
> - Include any connotations which you think show more than just the obvious feelings.

b Read through your response before sharing it with a partner.

c Discuss ways that your response might be improved if you were to do a similar activity again.

Support

a List three main events that the speaker remembers associated with the pond.

b Next to each event, write at least one feeling that the speaker has about that event.

c Now pick a word or phrase from the poem which shows the feeling you have identified, and write it next to the feeling.

d Use the notes you have made to help you write an answer to the question on the previous page. You could use the opening below to help you get started.

> Sheers refers to a number of events in the speaker's life which made him want to go to the pond, 'the place where I took things'. He mentions the speaker's grandfather dying and shows that he felt...

The Pond

This place where I took things,
sunk shallow in the middle of the field,
a secret bruise hidden by trees.

Where I brought my grandfather's death,
sucking squash from a shrinking carton,
while the tears dried to slug lines over my cheeks.

And my first kiss, in the arched iron cow-shed,
gum-stitched and tense,
as the light faded and the farms lit up.

Where I carried my arguments,
vowing never to return, hunching under the oak,
only to slink back

through the long grass, brushing up to my knees,
when the cold had dug deep in my bones
and my anger had evolved into hunger.

2 Looking at language and imagery

Skills and objectives

- To analyse how language and imagery can create impact on the reader, using relevant terminology to describe techniques and effects (AO2)

- To develop a personal response to texts (AO1)

In this unit, you are going to think about how the language and imagery chosen by a poet can be explored and analysed. You will also consider what type of technical vocabulary you will need to use in order to explain your ideas about language and imagery clearly.

The poems you are going to read in this section both deal with attitudes towards children. However, the words used by each poet give different impressions of their feelings associated with the events described. In the first poem some of the adjectives used are *peaceful, sacred, good, maternal, wise*; in the second poem the adjectives convey something stronger – *raw, fierce, fallen, sharp*.

Activity 1

a Looking at the vocabulary above, what type of **mood** do you think may be created in each poem? Discuss your ideas with a partner.

b Write a couple of sentences about the possible mood of each poem.

You could start your response:

I think that the adjectives in the first poem all create a sense of...

So, from just looking at a few words from each poem, you can see how much impact and information can be given to the reader through the careful choice of vocabulary.

Key term

Mood: the tone or atmosphere conveyed in a text

When writing about a poet's use of language, you will need to use some technical terms.

Activity 2

a Revise your knowledge of the six technical terms below by writing a definition for each.

1 **connotation** 2 **lyrical** 3 **diction** 4 **emotive language**

5 **imagery** 6 **evocative language**

b Challenge a partner to identify the correct terms from the definitions you provide. If there are any disagreements about the definitions, look them up and discuss them as a class.

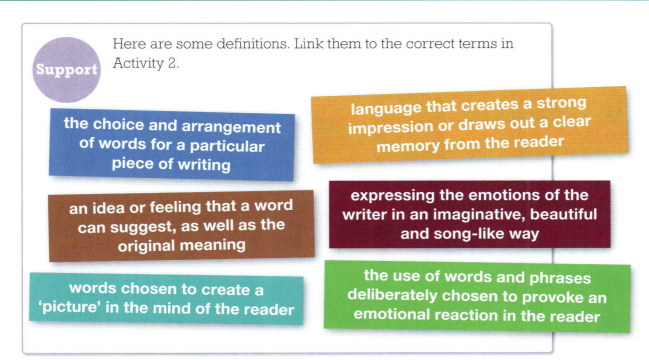

Support Here are some definitions. Link them to the correct terms in Activity 2.

the choice and arrangement of words for a particular piece of writing

language that creates a strong impression or draws out a clear memory from the reader

an idea or feeling that a word can suggest, as well as the original meaning

expressing the emotions of the writer in an imaginative, beautiful and song-like way

words chosen to create a 'picture' in the mind of the reader

the use of words and phrases deliberately chosen to provoke an emotional reaction in the reader

By using **concrete** examples of events or incidents, poets create clear images in the mind of a reader. Some of the poems you have already studied enable a reader to visualize what is being described as if they were actual physical events. However, some poems focus more on **abstract** matters. An 'attitude' is an abstract idea but may very often be linked to a specific event.

When analysing a poem, you will need to identify the language used to explore the attitudes and reactions of the poet to what is being described.

Read the poem 'A Child's Sleep' by Carol Ann Duffy below.

> **Key terms**
>
> **Concrete:** something that exists as a solid or material physical form
>
> **Abstract:** an idea or concept rather than something that has any physical properties, for example, beauty, love

A Child's Sleep

I stood at the edge of my child's sleep
hearing her breathe;
although I could not enter there,
I could not leave.

Her sleep was a small wood,
perfumed with flowers;
Dark, peaceful, sacred,
acred in hours.

And she was the spirit that lives
in the heart of such woods;
without time, without history,
wordlessly good.

I spoke her name, a pebble dropped
In the still night,
and saw her stir, both open palms
cupping their soft light;

then went to the window. The greater dark
outside the room
gazed back, maternal, wise,
with its face of moon.

Activity 3

a What are the concrete events that Duffy is describing?

b Pick out three examples of what the persona (speaker) does in the poem.

c What abstract ideas can you identify? Discuss your findings with a partner.

d What attitudes to the child are suggested by Duffy? Choose two from the selection below and write a short paragraph about each one. Use quotes to support your points.

| protective | loving | admiring | amazed | repetition | fearful |

e Share your writing with a partner. Discuss your responses to the text.

When writing about poems, you need to show that you can use the correct technical vocabulary to explain what you mean. Look at the extract from a student response below where the student has started to explore connotations in the poem. The examiner has added some comments to the response.

Student shows awareness of how their expectations build up towards one idea, but are then surprised by a twist.

Student uses the same phrase as the poet to draw attention to the misdirection experienced.

Duffy refers to being '... at the edge of my child's sleep'. This misleads the reader to a certain extent as at the start of the line it might be expected that she would be at the edge of the child's bed. Referring instead to 'sleep' has connotations of Duffy being included in the dreams her child might be having, as well as perhaps implying that her child is vaguely aware of her being there.

Uses appropriate technical vocabulary to explain impact of chosen word.

Student explores more than just the obvious meanings and extends the idea of the connotations.

As you continue to read through the poem, you can see how Duffy uses **metaphors** to continue describing her thoughts as the child sleeps. For example, she says: 'Her sleep was a small wood' and goes on to extend that idea by referring to the sleep as being 'perfumed with flowers' and 'peaceful'.

These images suggest that the child is quiet and restful, smells sweet and is also somehow quite private. The speaker cannot see into the mind of the child, in the same way that you cannot see through woods. The images that Duffy chooses have a common theme, which together create a powerful picture in the reader's mind.

There are other metaphors in this poem. In an exam response, it is important to explore all the imagery in detail, as this demonstrates your skills in explaining attitudes, feelings and the effects of the language chosen. This is an area which can be improved with practice, even if it seems daunting at first.

> **Key terms**
>
> **Metaphor:** a form of words in which one object is described as if it really is another (rather than just being like it), for example, *the news was a bombshell; her iron will was obvious in her face*
>
> **Theme:** a subject or idea that recurs frequently in a work or selection of writing

Activity 4

a Re-read the fourth stanza. Write a short paragraph exploring the images that the metaphors create, and suggest how they are effective.

Two poems may contain similar **themes** (for example, the protective feelings that a parent has for a child), but they are likely to be presented in quite different ways by different poets.

Read the poem 'Nettles' by Vernon Scannell that follows.

Nettles

My son aged three fell in the nettle bed.
'Bed' seemed a curious name for those green spears,
That regiment of spite behind the shed:
It was no place for rest. With sobs and tears
The boy came seeking comfort and I saw
White blisters beaded on his tender skin.
We soothed him till his pain was not so raw.
At last he offered us a watery grin,
And then I took my hook and honed the blade
And went outside and slashed in fury with it
Till not a nettle in that fierce parade
Stood upright any more. Next task: I lit
A funeral pyre to burn the fallen dead.
But in two weeks the busy sun and rain
Had called up tall recruits behind the shed:
My son would often feel sharp wounds again.

Activity 5

a With a partner, discuss the 'story' behind the poem, 'Nettles'. Outline a sequence of events based on the concrete information the poem contains.

b Discuss the attitude(s) shown by the speaker in the poem. What causes for these can you identify?

>
> **Stretch** What is the overall mood of the poem? Note that this may not be the same as the mood or attitude of the speaker.

Poets sometimes choose to use words that are likely to trigger a strong emotional response in the reader. They may evoke powerful feelings or memories that are common to most people, such as sympathy, happiness or anger. When you are identifying 'emotive language' in a poem, it is also important to explain what effect or emotion it is creating for the reader.

Activity 6

a Copy and complete the table below, showing the ways that emotive language is used in the poem 'Nettles', and its impact on the reader. The first one is done for you. Find five other examples of emotive language.

Example of emotive language	Impact on the reader
My son aged three fell...	Stating the age makes the reader feel sorry for the child who is very young, therefore small and vulnerable, and has clearly hurt himself.

b Choose two of your own examples from your completed table and write a short paragraph explaining how the poet uses emotive language to create a specific reaction in the reader.

In 'A Child's Sleep', Duffy creates caring, nurturing images associated with woodland scenery, but Scannell uses imagery to give a very different impression of nature. He uses many words and phrases that you might associate with the army or battles, for example, he refers to the nettles as 'spears'.

Activity 7

a Re-read the poem, 'Nettles' on page 115 and identify other words and phrases that link to the idea of battles or an army. Write them down.

b What effect do the words you've chosen have on the reader? What impression is Scannell trying to give of the nettles?

c This poem could be described as an **extended metaphor**. Explain how this might this be true. (Hint: start by focusing on the last line.)

Stretch Comment on how and why the poet presents images of a bed and a funeral pyre. How are they related?

Key term

Extended metaphor: a series of images within one text or poem that all relate to the same central metaphor

Part of the unseen section is about comparing the two poems. (There is more detail about this on pages 126–131). However, it is useful at this point to consider how these two poems are similar:

● both poems are written from the viewpoint of a parent
● both show deep love and concern for their child
● both poems describe an actual concrete event
● both speakers use metaphors to make the reader understand their feelings
● both poems use images from nature
● both poems share the theme of looking after their child.

Activity 8

a Now consider how the language and imagery of the poems differ. Complete the following sentences:

• The mood of each poem is different — one is calm and quiet, and the other is...

• The diction of each poem is different — one uses military language and the other uses...

• The metaphors in each poem suggest different outcomes — one accepts the fact that the child is outside the control of the parent; the other tries to...

When responding to a poem in the exam, it is important that you express your personal response. This means that you should explain what effect it has on *you*, as a reader. You must back up what you say, using close reference to the text, including quotations.

Activity 9

a Which of the two poems you have read in this unit do you prefer? Write a paragraph explaining your personal response to your chosen text.

b Share your ideas with a partner. Pick out one phrase from your chosen poem and explain to your partner why you think it is effective.

3 Looking at form and structure

Poems, as you already know, come in many different shapes and sizes. These different **forms** are chosen by the poet for specific reasons, in the same way that language is chosen in order to create specific effects for the reader.

There are some traditional forms of poetry that you probably already know and can recognize. However, not all poets stick to traditional forms. Many select a basic form, but then elaborate on it in order to convey their poem in the most appropriate way for what they want to say.

In the unseen section of the exam, you will need to comment on the form and structure of the poem, as well as on other aspects such as language and imagery. You will need to be able to suggest reasons for the poet's choice of form and also comment on the impact that it has on a reader.

- To read, understand and respond to texts (AO1)
- To analyse form and structure, using relevant subject terminology (AO2)

Key term

Form: how a poem is organized on a page; its physical shape

Activity 1

a With a partner, revise some of the technical terms used when describing the form of poems. Take it in turns to challenge each other to explain one of the terms below.

Ballad   Haiku   Shape poem   Blank verse

Rhyming couplet   Sonnet   Ode

b When you have agreed on the definitions, write them down for use in your revision.

Support Here are some definitions of poetic forms. Link them to the correct forms from the list in Activity 1. Note that there isn't a definition for every form. You will have to write the missing ones yourself.

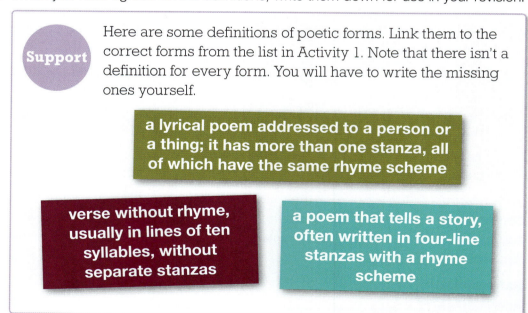

a lyrical poem addressed to a person or a thing; it has more than one stanza, all of which have the same rhyme scheme

verse without rhyme, usually in lines of ten syllables, without separate stanzas

a poem that tells a story, often written in four-line stanzas with a rhyme scheme

Poets sometimes choose a form of poem to make a point, to give a message about what they are saying. For example:

- a haiku may be used to describe a single, small aspect of nature.

- a sonnet is often chosen as the form for love poetry.

- a ballad may be chosen to present an heroic or tragic story as a narrative, which follows a sequence of events.

Many poems lead up to a significant idea at the end, so that the last few lines may summarize a key part of what the poet is trying to say. As a reader, you need to consider the impact of closing lines on your understanding of the 'message' of the poet, and then ensure that you can write about this.

Read the poem 'Remember' by Christina Rossetti.

Remember

Remember me when I am gone away,

    Gone far away into the silent land;

    When you can no more hold me by the hand,

Nor I half turn to go yet turning stay.

Remember me when no more day by day

    You tell me of our future that you plann'd:

    Only remember me; you understand

It will be late to counsel then or pray.

Yet if you should forget me for a while

    And afterwards remember, do not grieve:

    For if the darkness and corruption leave

    A vestige of the thoughts that once I had,

Better by far you should forget and smile

    Than that you should remember and be sad.

Activity 2

a What form do you think Rossetti has chosen for this poem? Explain your answer.

b How many syllables are there on each line? What effect does that have on the reader?

c What do you notice about the **rhyme** as the poem progresses?

d Why do you think Rossetti chose this form? What message does it give to the reader?

e How do the last two lines provide a significant idea about what the poet wants to say?

Key term

Rhyme: the use of the same sounds in words or syllables, or at the ends of lines of poetry, for example, *cry* and *dry*

However, choosing a particular form may also be used to **subvert** an expectation of what is 'normal', in order to make readers reconsider an opinion or rethink an established view. Sometimes these forms may be humorous or may make fun of a poem that is well known.

Wendy Cope is a poet who uses poetry to make comments about modern life. Her writing often appears light-hearted but it usually has a serious side too.

Read the poem 'A Green Song – to Sing at the Bottle Bank' by Wendy Cope.

A Green Song – to Sing at the Bottle Bank

One green bottle,
Drop it in the bank.
Ten green bottles,
What a lot we drank.
Heaps of bottles
And yesterday's a blank
But we'll save the planet,
Tinkle, tinkle, clank!

We've got bottles –
Nice, percussive trash.
Bags of bottles
Cleaned us out of cash.
Empty bottles,
We love to hear them smash
And we'll save the planet,
Tinkle, tinkle, crash.

Activity 3

a Discuss with a partner what you think 'A Green Song – to Sing at the Bottle Bank' is based upon.

- How does this version differ from the original?
- Why do you think Cope gave the poem this title?

b Look again at the first, third and fifth line of each stanza. What do you notice about the way Cope describes the bottles?

c What is the effect of the rhyme on each alternate line?

d Does the poem have serious messages for a reader as well as being humorous? Explain your answer with support from the text.

Stretch Write at least one paragraph explaining how you think this poem subverts the expected form.

Structure: how a piece of writing works internally; how the choices of language, punctuation and form affect the message being conveyed, and how contrasting images or chronological events are presented

Observational poem: a poem that looks at the details of the ways people behave or interact; it may present a viewpoint about the events as well as providing an account of them

Selecting the best words to convey ideas is what a writer strives to do. When you read good poetry, it is like listening to good music: there are pleasing patterns of sounds and rhythms. When you analyse poetry, you need to look in detail at how the poet makes this 'music' work.

Some poets write about events in such detail that the effect is almost like describing a photograph. The details provide a clear image in the mind of the reader. This is achieved by building up a careful **structure** within the poem.

Edwin Morgan was a poet who was born, educated and who worked in his home city of Glasgow. He wrote **observational poems**. One of his poetry collections was entitled *Instamatic* – named after a type of camera that was popular at the time. His poems in that collection create a 'still-life' effect in the minds of readers. The city of Glasgow had a reputation for violence when Morgan was growing up, and this is reflected in some of his poems.

Read Morgan's poem 'Glasgow 5 March 1971' below. The poem focuses on an attack by two thieves who pushed a couple through the window of a shop in order to rob it. Look at the annotations, which show how Morgan has structured the first part of the poem for particular effects.

Glasgow 5 March 1971

With a ragged diamond
of shattered plate glass
a young man and his girl
are falling backwards into a shop window.
The young man's face
is bristling with fragments of glass
and the girl's leg has caught
on the broken window
and spurts arterial blood
over her wet-look white coat.
Their arms are starfished out
braced for impact,
their faces show surprise, shock
and the beginning of pain.
The two youths who have pushed them
are about to complete the operation
reaching into the window
to loot what they can smartly.
Their faces show no expression.
It is a sharp clear night in Sauchiehall Street.
In the background two drivers
keep their eyes on the road.

Annotations:

Adjectives to show how the glass in the window is smashed beyond repair and emphasizing how dangerous it now is.

Repeated nouns reinforce the image of where the people are falling, and how the scene is changing, for example, the 'plate glass' becomes 'fragments of glass'.

Nouns highlight how the couple's bodies are affected by the fall and suggests that no part of them, from top to toe, escapes some sort of serious injury. Linking the blood with 'arterial' suggests it is life-threatening.

Verbs explain the aggressive nature of the movement and the results of being pushed. Each word indicates a different impact of the sudden movement. The verbs indicate increasing danger for the couple.

Activity 4

a Read the poem again. Copy and complete these sentences about other structural features that Morgan uses:

- The poem is written **chronologically** so the effect is...
- Morgan writes the whole poem using **enjambment**. This means that the reader's attention...
- The phrase 'their faces' is used twice. Morgan contrasts...
- Alliteration is used... which gives the impression that...
- Morgan uses the adverb 'smartly' to emphasize...
- The effect of describing the assault as an 'operation' is...

b Discuss the following questions with a partner:

- What is the effect of using the word 'starfished' to describe the fall?
- Why has Morgan used only simple punctuation?
- How do the final two sentences alter the mood of the poem?
- Does the shape of the poem have any significance?
- What message do you think Morgan is trying to convey?

c Based on your discussions with a partner, write down your own observations about the structure of the poem.

Key terms

Chronological: written in the order that things happened; in the correct time sequence

Enjambment: where lines of poetry are not stopped at the end, either by sense or punctuation, and run over into the next line; the completion of the phrase, clause or sentence is held over to extend the image or to build tension

Having looked at three poems in this section, you have explored different aspects of form and structure and how the poets have crafted them in order to create specific effects for the reader. In your exam, you will need to consider the form and structure of the poems, as well as their language and imagery.

Read the opening section of a student response to 'Remember' by Rossetti and the examiner's annotations. The response is to the question:

> How does the poet present the speaker's feelings about being remembered?

Clear opening and candidate recognizes the form.

Candidate gives reason for choice of form which is accurate and starts to address the question.

Starts to use subject, specific terms. Shows the candidate is starting to analyse the detailed structure of the poem.

Rossetti has written the poem in the form of a sonnet. It has 14 lines and each line has ten syllables and they rhyme in couplets. I think it is written like this because a sonnet is a love poem and Rossetti is writing to someone she loves about the fact that she will soon die and so will not see them again. She is trying to help them see that she does not want them to be sad but to remember her with happiness and love. She says 'do not grieve' which means she does not want them to be sad. Rossetti uses the verb 'remember' a lot at different points of the poem and this repetition helps to emphasize the fact that she has different things she wants her lover to remember about her. In the first half of the poem she says 'remember me' three times but then in the second half of the poem it changes to just 'remember' which is a different instruction.

An unnecessary sentence, and not correct as the poem does not rhyme in couplets.

This is correct but repeats the same point. It would be improved by suggesting a reason for saying this and linking that to a specific feeling.

Candidate shows they are aware of alternative meanings and interpretations of same word, but needs to give more detail.

Activity 5

a Read the student response with examiner's comments on page 124. Consider the following questions with a partner:

- Why is the second sentence unnecessary?

- How would you develop the point about the phrase 'do not grieve'?

- Why do you think the examiner feels the student is starting to analyse the structure of the poem towards the end of the extract?

- What would you go on to write about next?

b Following your discussion, write the next two paragraphs of the response. Consider the different areas you could include based on the work you have covered so far with 'Unseen poems'. Write a paragraph about the language and the imagery included in the poem.

c Swap your work with a partner. Read through their response and provide feedback by suggesting at least one thing that has been done well and one thing that you think could be improved.

d After the feedback, amend your response to improve it. Check your own work by re-reading it.

Support

Rossetti has used a number of different features in the poem:

- enjambment
- punctuation
- rhyme
- imagery
- language.

Choose two from the list and write about how Rossetti uses them. These will be the next two paragraphs of the student answer.

You could start by using one of these sentence openers:

> Rossetti's use of enjambment means that the reader has...

> The rhyme pattern of the poem is...

> 'Remember' is repeated several times, which has the effect of...

- To read, understand and respond to texts (AO1)

- Use textual references, including quotations, to support and illustrate interpretations (AO1)

- Analyse subject, form and structure, using relevant subject terminology (AO2)

4 How to compare poems

The first question of the unseen poetry section will ask you to comment on just one poem, but the second question will ask you to compare the second poem with the first. The question will focus on a common theme between the poems. The eight marks available for this response will be awarded only for points made that actually compare the two texts. There will be no points awarded for any comments on either poem that are not comparative.

There are 96 marks for the whole of Paper 2. The comparison question is the last question on the paper, and you should allow yourself about ten minutes to respond to it. You will need to think carefully about which aspects of the poems you are going to compare.

For example, you might want to:

- compare the use of imagery

- compare the language used to present the narrators (speakers)

- compare the language used to present aspects of the texts, for example, other characters, events referred to or feelings shown

- compare the structure and form.

In order to make a comparison that is valid, you will first need to ensure you read both texts carefully. Read *both poems* and *both questions* on the unseen section before you start to write about either of the texts. This will enable your subconscious brain to start working on the questions while you write!

When you tackle the comparison question, you will already have written at some length about the first poem so you should be familiar with that one. You will need to read the second poem again carefully and identify aspects of it that are similar to or that contrast with the first poem.

Read the two poems on page 127. The first is 'For My Niece' by Kate Tempest; the second is 'On Her Way to Recovery' by Grace Nichols. As you read, consider the following sample exam question.

> In both poems, the speakers describe their feelings as they think about someone they love growing up. What are the similarities/differences between the ways the poets present these feelings?

For My Niece

I hold you in my arms,
your age is told in months.

There's things I hope you'll learn
Things I'm sure that I learned once.

But there's nothing I can teach you.
You'll find all that you need.
No flower bends its head to offer
teaching to a seed.

The seed will grow and blossom
once the flower's ground to dust.

But even so, if nothing else, one thing I'll entrust:

Doing what you please
Is not the same

As doing what you must.

On Her Way to Recovery

My thirteen year-old daughter
is now taller than me.
Illness seems to have stretched her a bit.

She, who was on her back
for four days and four nights,
feverish, heavy limbed, uneating,

Got up this morning
pulled on her sneakers, my long red dressing gown,
and went out into the garden.

'Don't worry,' she says,
coming suddenly into the room
where I'm lying. 'I dressed warm.'

Startled. Pleased.
I glance up at the red-robed gazelle
on her way to recovery.

Activity 1

a Having read the poems, look again at the question. With a partner, discuss what the following parts of the question need you to do:

- What are the similarities and/or differences? (Consider why there is a slash between the words. What does that suggest you should do with the texts?)
- The ways the poets describe their feelings.

Look again at the poems with your partner and identify words and phrases that might be used to address these parts of the question.

b Copy and complete the table below to help you start the comparison process. You may wish to adapt it, adding other aspects that you want to compare.

Aspects to compare	For My Niece	On Her Way to Recovery
Use of imagery		Suggests being ill has stretched her – almost a good thing?
Language used by speaker	Lots of pronouns – 'I' and 'you', to show difference between them?	
Language used to present niece/daughter		
Language used to present feelings	Sounds affectionate – 'hold you in my arms'	
Use of form/structural features		Repeats 'four' – to emphasize how long she was ill.

c Share your ideas with a partner and discuss the similarities and differences that you have identified between the texts. Do you feel you have found enough evidence to address the question? If not, add some other aspects for comparison.

Stretch Consider how much influence each speaker feels they have over the children. What can we infer about their present and future relationships?

Once you have identified aspects of each text that can be compared, you need to start the written response by comparing features and maintain a focus on comparison throughout. Remember, you do not have long to answer this question, and the end of the exam time is approaching, so it is important to write down your ideas promptly.

Look at the student response below, and the examiner's annotations and comment. The student has addressed the same question, using the two poems you have looked at.

Opens with direct reference to the question – shows they are focused on it.

Clear example of difference between the topics of the poems. Refers to question, that is feelings (emotions) and shows awareness of why these are different.

Compares by linking through reference to same feature – imagery

Both poets clearly show the speaker has strong emotions linked with the growing up of their family members. Each one describes a particular stage in the life of the child they write about, and reflect on their own feelings about that. Tempest is writing about a baby, and Nichols about a teenager, so their emotions are different. Tempest describes her niece as a 'seed'. This metaphor shows the way that the speaker recognizes her niece's life is just beginning and implies that there are many years of growing ahead of her. Nichols also uses a metaphor to describe her daughter as a 'gazelle'. This has a different effect as it appears to recognize that her daughter is ready to move quickly away from the family.

Focuses immediately on similarity between texts.

Quote supported by explanation of imagery and its impact on reader's understanding.

Shows student can identify another effect from the use of the metaphor.

Overall – a strong opening paragraph as the student shows consistent focus on the task and texts, supported with textual references.

Activity 2

a Look again at the student response. Discuss with a partner which aspects of the poems you would write about next.

b Think about your discussion with your partner and use the student's response as a model to continue your answer. Allow yourself 5–7 minutes to write about the aspects you decided were important.

c Swap your response with your partner. Check that their response has:

- continued to focus on the feelings of the speakers
- continued to identify similarities/differences
- used textual references (for example, quotes).

Comment positively on one feature that your partner has done well and suggest one thing that could be improved.

d Amend your own response following the advice from your partner.

Support You might find the following words and phrases helpful when writing your comparison:

Whereas…   **Although…**

In contrast…   **Similarly…**

Unlike…   **As well as…**

The poets both…

The difference between…

In the exam, you won't have enough time to create a detailed plan as in the table you made in Activity 1. However, it may be useful to jot down a quick note of aspects to include before starting to write the full response. By practising doing this with different poems, you will become quicker at recognizing the features that can be included in the comparison.

The poems above were both written by contemporary poets. The next pair of poems that you are going to look at were written in the early 20th century. You must be prepared to tackle texts from any century.

Read the texts that follow. The first is 'The Way through the Woods' by Rudyard Kipling, and the second is 'Sea Fever' by John Masefield. As you read, consider the question:

> In both poems, the speakers describe their feelings about a particular place. What are the similarities/differences between the ways the poets present those feelings?

The Way through the Woods

They shut the road through the woods
Seventy years ago.
Weather and rain have undone it again,
And now you would never know
There was once a road through the woods
Before they planted the trees.
It is underneath the coppice and heath
And the thin anemones.
Only the keeper sees
That, where the ring-dove broods
And the badgers roll at ease,
There was once a road through the woods.
Yet, if you enter the woods
Of a summer evening late,
When the night-air cools on the trout-ringed pools
Where the otter whistles his mate,
(They fear not men in the woods
Because they see so few.)
You will hear the beat of a horse's feet,
And the swish of a skirt in the dew,
Steadily cantering through
The misty solitudes,
As though they perfectly knew
The old lost road through the woods…
But there is no road through the woods.

Sea Fever

I must go down to the seas again, to the lonely sea
and the sky,
And all I ask is a tall ship and a star to steer her by,
And the wheel's kick and the wind's song and the
white sail's shaking
And a grey mist on the sea's face and a grey dawn
breaking.

I must go down to the seas again, for the call of the
running tide
Is a wild call and a clear call that may not be
denied;
And all I ask is a windy day with the white clouds
flying,
And the flung spray and the blown spume*, and the
sea-gulls crying.

I must go down to the seas again, to the vagrant
gypsy life,
To the gull's way and the whale's way where the
wind's like a whetted knife;
And all I ask is a merry yarn from a laughing fellow
rover,
And a quiet sleep and a sweet dream when the
long trick's over.

*spume – white foam found on waves

Activity 3

a Spend a couple of minutes making notes about both poems that you might compare. You could do this in four bullet points with annotations, as in the example below:

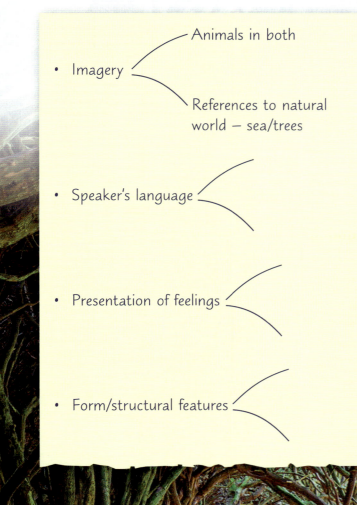

- Imagery — Animals in both

  References to natural world – sea/trees

- Speaker's language

- Presentation of feelings

- Form/structural features

b Use the notes you have made to write a response to the question. Ensure you monitor how much time you spend doing this. Remember you will only have about ten minutes to write this answer.

c Swap your response with a partner. Use the ideas from the examiner's annotations above to pick out aspects that have been done effectively. Offer advice about ways that your partner could improve their answer.

d Finalize your own response, taking into account your partner's comments.

5 Preparing for the exam

- To read, understand and respond to texts (AO1)

- To use textual references, including quotations, to support and illustrate interpretations (AO1)

- To analyse subject, form and structure, using relevant subject terminology (AO2)

It is a popular myth among students that you cannot revise for an English exam! In fact, like any other subject, you can improve your chances of getting a good result in your English Literature GCSE by preparing carefully for the exam. However, unlike most other subjects, because part of your exam is on unseen poems, you will not know exactly which texts you will be asked to write about.

What you *do* know is that the questions will ask about how something in the poem or poems is presented, which might be feelings or an idea. You know that the first question will just be about one poem, but the second question will ask you to compare two poems.

By reading a wide range of poetry, you will increase your understanding of different ways that language can be used to express emotions and ideas. You will also encounter vocabulary that you may be less familiar with, and exploring this will expand your own vocabulary and help you to understand the subtle differences between the meanings of words.

Activity 1

a Group the words below according to what you believe they mean. Decide on the most appropriate groupings and be ready to justify your choices. You may not use a dictionary to assist you! (Clue – there are probably three main groups.)

lamentation   felicitation   hopeful   blessing   mourning

distress   weeping   jovial   sorrow   grief   optimism

congratulate   positivity   compliment   woe   cheerful

b Share your groupings with a partner. Discuss the choices each of you has made and agree on a final grouping.

c Join with another pair and share your final grouping. Does their grouping match yours?

d Discuss the ways that the different words are similar in meaning but also convey something slightly different from the other words in that group.

e Rank the words in each group, with the strongest word at the top of your list and the weakest at the bottom. Do you all agree on the order these words appear in?

f What do you learn from carrying out an activity like this? How does this link with the study of poetry and your understanding of how poets choose and use words?

Part of the challenge of the English Literature exam will be remembering the material you need in order to answer the questions. In some ways, the unseen part of the exam is slightly more straightforward, as you will not need to memorize quotations since both poems will be printed on the paper. However, you should make sure you have learned the key literary terms that you have come across during your preparation work, as well as what they mean and how you should use them.

Activity 2

a Copy the table below and complete it with a meaning for each of the key terms and an example. You can make up your own example, or find a suitable one in the poems you have read. The first one is done for you.

b Identify another four key terms you need to know and add them to your table.

c Exchange your work with a partner and challenge them to provide the meaning of the four key terms you have written and give an example.

d Complete your partner's challenge and return the work. Check your partner's work and make sure it is correct. Identify any errors and discuss with your partner before amending.

Key term	Meaning	Example
rhyme	Words that sound the same, especially at the ends of lines.	Drank, bank, clank Trash, cash, smash
structure		
enjambment		
metaphor		
alliteration		
abstract		
theme		

Using textual references

In both questions on the unseen section of the exam, you will need to use **textual references** to support your points. The examiner will be looking to see if you understand the text, and one way to show you do is by providing the evidence in the form of extracts from the poems.

The points you make about the poems need to:

- relate closely to the question being asked
- refer precisely to appropriate sections of the text
- cover a range of aspects, including language, form and structure.

To make an important point, quoting directly from the text is necessary. However, you must comment on the quote – you should not use the text without explaining why it is significant.

It is also acceptable to **paraphrase** sections of the texts as this can also help to demonstrate your understanding of what the poet is saying. This would be done instead of using a quote.

Another way of showing you are focused on the text is to refer to specific parts of the poem, perhaps by indicating particular lines or parts of it. For example, you could say 'The second and fourth stanzas contain rhyming couplets…' or 'The verb in the third line…'

Activity 3

a Read the statements below and decide if you think they are true or false. Write a reason for your choice.

- You have to use a quote in every sentence.
- The examiner will award extra marks for all quotations.
- Any textual references need to link to the question.
- Quotations are only one method of referring to the text.
- Copying out long quotations (for example, five lines) is a good idea.
- It is fine to write short sections of text in your own words.

b Share your responses with a partner and discuss your reasoning about each statement.

The skill of incorporating different textual references can be developed through practice. Some of the student responses you have already read used different forms of supporting evidence for their points.

Read the poem 'Migrations' below by Ben Okri, considering the following sample exam question:

> How does the poet present the speaker's feelings about migration?

Read the extract from a student response to this question, on page 136. The examiner's comments in the annotations focus on the way that the student has used textual references.

Migrations

This world is a cauldron
In which we are mixed.
Time is an illusion.
No condition is fixed.

And so in our millions
We walk or swim or break
Across boundaries, fleeing
Wars, evils and hunger to make

A new home in what seems
A void, an empty space,
Without our histories,
Or tales of our race.

But about us scream the inhabitants
Who've never known barren
Lands, or tyranny, or such pain
That pushes us from the warren

Of cruel histories into lands
Whose earth may not receive
Us. But we're like pollen.
We're fertile, and we grieve.

Response opens with a clear indication that the student understands the main meaning of the text. A quote is not needed here as it is a summary of the overall message.

The quote here supports the earlier assertion about reasons, but also indicates the student can use text appropriately.

Student qualifies the comment by suggesting how a reader responds to the poem.

Okri shows that the speaker recognizes that people have to move from place to place in the world, through no fault of their own. In the opening stanza, Okri suggests everyone is from a mixed-race background and that things continuously change. He goes on in the next stanza to mention a number of reasons why people may migrate from one county to another – 'wars, evils and hunger'. This list of three problems indicates to the reader that such issues are ongoing in different countries. It also creates an emotional response as the reader starts to sympathize with the speaker. Okri also uses a list of three verbs to show the ways that people move and this also emphasizes how desperate they are to escape their country's problems.

This is a paraphrase of the opening two lines. The student shows that they recognize the significance of what is being said.

Reference to language feature shows the student can identify the methods used by the poet.

Repeating about technique for a different effect shows the student can adapt information and apply it in a different way. Identifying the type of word being used shows that the student can use technical terms and is aware of how language effects are crafted. The student also draws attention back to the question by starting to explore the feelings of the migrants.

Activity 4

a Continue the response above to answer the sample exam question on page 135.

- Identify what other language features, images and feelings you can include.
- Consider which words or phrases you need to quote, which ones can be paraphrased and which you might simply refer to – 'In each stanza…' or 'The final sentence…'
- Allow yourself about 15 minutes to write the next section.

b Exchange your response with a partner. Put yourself in the role of the examiner by identifying where your partner uses textual references effectively. Write annotations with your comments to help them improve their skills and return the work to them.

Exam practice

The poem below, 'As Luck Would Have It', is by Mark Robinson. The question set on this poem is:

> How does the poet present the different feelings about the birth of the speaker?

As Luck Would Have It

I was born in the back bedroom of a council house,
breech[1] and purple from bruising, not picked up
for three days except when absolutely necessary.
I was born in a room that looked out over
the playing fields of my primary school.
I imagine my mum and dad, and my nan,
gripping the window ledge as eager boys below
played football while I cried and cried and cried.

I was born weeping and bursting my lungs,
as unanswered calls swept through rooms
and through houses, until the whole terrace
was holding its breath, until the Beatle-cut[2] fathers
had to walk down the gardens in the rain
to smoke fag after slow musty fag in the dusk.

[1] Breech – when a baby is born either feet or bottom first, instead of head first, as would be usually expected
[2] Beatle-cut – a popular hairstyle in the 1960s that copied the hairstyle adopted by the pop group The Beatles

Activity 5

a Re-read the poem and pick out phrases and words that convey the feelings in the poem. These might be the feelings of the speaker or the other people mentioned.

b Compare your chosen words and phrases with those of a partner. Discuss how you identified feelings that you can write about to answer the question. What do you think is the main feeling the poet wants to convey?

c Look again at the poem and identify any language features that the poet has used. Think about the effect that these have on you as the reader.

d Write a complete response to the question, based on the words, phrases and language features you have identified and discussed. Try to do this as if in an exam, by working independently on the task for about 25 minutes. There are some sentence starters you can use in the support feature on page 138.

Support

You might find some of the following sentence starters useful to complete Activity 5 on page 137:

> Robinson shows how the birth of the speaker was quite an ordinary event in the 'back bedroom of a council house'...

> There are different feelings about the birth as the poet refers to three other members of the family – mum, dad and nan – as well as...

> The poet shows how the birth of the child was difficult, 'purple from bruising', which made the family...

> In the first stanza there is a suggestion that the baby was not wanted...

Read the second poem, 'Lamentations' by Siegfried Sassoon. This is the poem that you will have to compare with 'As Luck Would Have It' on page 137. The question is different:

> In both poems, the speakers describe someone being distressed. What are the similarities/differences between the ways the poets present those feelings?

Lamentations

I found him in the guard-room at the Base.
From the blind darkness I had heard his crying
And blundered in. With puzzled, patient face
A sergeant watched him; it was no good trying
To stop it; for he howled and beat his chest.
And, all because his brother had gone west[1],
Raved at the bleeding war; his rampant grief
Moaned, shouted, sobbed, and choked, while he was kneeling
Half-naked on the floor. In my belief
Such men have lost all patriotic feeling.

[1] Gone west – died

Activity 6

a Spend up to five minutes identifying features of the texts that you can compare. Remember you may have only about ten minutes to write this section of the exam.

You may need to consider aspects of:

- imagery
- speaker's language
- presentation of feelings
- form/structural features.

b Write your response to the comparison question. Do this in exam conditions again. Limit yourself to no more than 12 minutes of writing time.

c Share your repsonses to both questions with a partner. Read through their answers and provide feedback on what they have done effectively. Suggest ways that they could make improvements.

d Set yourself two learning targets that will help you improve your responses in this section and include these in your revision planning.

 Stretch Discuss how each poet shows the reader their attitude to the events in the poem.

- Are these attitudes the same as the speaker's?
- Identify a line or two of the poem that shows the poet's attitude to the events.
- Explain to a partner how these lines show the poet's attitude.

Progress check

a When you have completed the activities about unseen poems, look back over your work and assess how confident you are with the skills listed below.

Skills	I am confident that I can do this.	I think I can do this but need a bit more practice.	This is one of my weaker areas, so I need more practice.
I can identify the main expectation of the unseen poetry questions.			
I can identify key points about the subject and theme to discuss in a response.			
I can write about the language that the poet uses to create specific effects for the reader.			
I can discuss the use of imagery in the poetry and how it helps to convey the poet's ideas to the reader.			
I can explain how poets use form and structure to create effects for the reader.			
I can select appropriate quotations to support key points about the poetry.			
I can select relevant aspects of a poem for comparison with another poem.			
I read a range of unseen poetry in order to practise and develop my skills of analysis.			

b Pick out one skill that you would like to target for improvement. Plan how you will improve that skill and monitor your progress.

Developing your literature skills

Introduction

There are five sections that make up the Literature exam that you need to study. These are:

- Shakespeare
- the 19th-century novel
- modern prose or drama texts
- the poetry Anthology
- unseen poetry.

The marks for each section are added up to give you your final grade.

Although this may seem like a lot of work to cover, many of the same skills are tested in the different sections. This means that the examiner will be assessing how you apply your literary skills whether you are writing about one of Shakespeare's plays, a novel, modern prose or poetry.

What are these skills?

These skills are divided into groups known as Assessment Objectives, or AOs.

Here is a summary of which skills are tested in each section of the exam:

	AO1	AO2	AO3	AO4
Shakespeare	✓	✓	✓	✓
19th-century novel	✓	✓	✓	
Modern prose or drama	✓	✓	✓	✓
Poetry Anthology	✓	✓	✓	
Unseen poetry	✓	✓		

This part of the Student Book will help you to understand these objectives, or skills, while Part 4 will give you advice on how to apply these skills in the exam.

If you look at the Assessment Objectives fully written out in this chapter they might seem rather daunting, but we can simplify them like this:

- **AO1** is all about reading, understanding, responding to and referring to texts. Marks are also awarded for writing about texts in a suitably literary style.

- **AO2** is concerned with the writer's craft, which means the technical aspects of the texts you are studying (their language, form and structure) and about using the correct specialist terms to describe these.

- **AO3** requires you to think and write about the ideas in the text and their context. This means looking at the context of ideas and themes, the context in which the text was written, the context in which it is set (location, time, culture), the literary context, such as genre, and the context of different audiences.

- **AO4** covers spelling, punctuation, sentence structure and vocabulary in your written answers.

The chart opposite gives a breakdown of the percentage of marks allocated to each AO in your Literature exam.

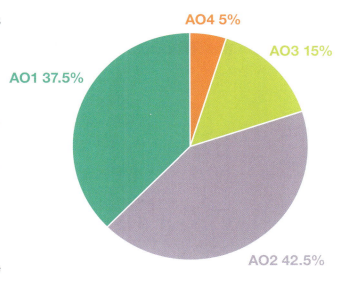

AO4 5%
AO3 15%
AO1 37.5%
AO2 42.5%

Activity 1

Read the following words and phrases and decide which AO they are most relevant to by completing the table below. You might find it easiest to note your answers in a table like the one below.

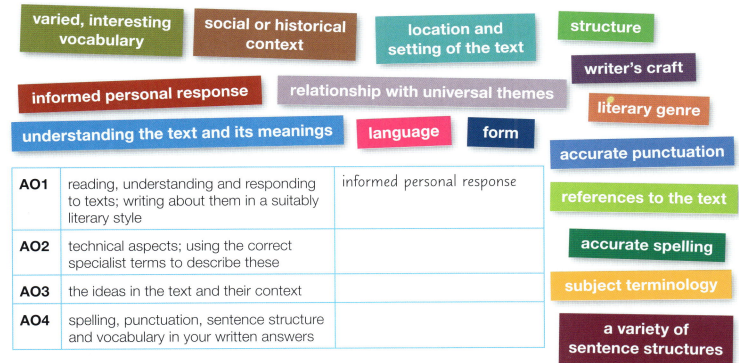

varied, interesting vocabulary

social or historical context

location and setting of the text

structure

writer's craft

informed personal response

relationship with universal themes

literary genre

understanding the text and its meanings

language

form

accurate punctuation

references to the text

accurate spelling

subject terminology

a variety of sentence structures

AO1	reading, understanding and responding to texts; writing about them in a suitably literary style	informed personal response
AO2	technical aspects; using the correct specialist terms to describe these	
AO3	the ideas in the text and their context	
AO4	spelling, punctuation, sentence structure and vocabulary in your written answers	

You now have a good overview of the Assessment Objectives. The next units will look at each AO in more detail.

The activities that follow assume that you have read a substantial part of your set texts for the Literature exam. You may find it helpful to revisit some activities at the end of your course, for revision.

A close look at AO1

In order to understand fully what AO1 is and what it requires you to do, we need to break it down into its component parts.

Here is the full AO, as presented by the exam board:

> AO1: Read, understand and respond to texts. Students should be able to:
> - maintain a critical style and develop an informed personal response
> - use textual references, including quotations, to support and illustrate interpretations.

There is a lot of information packed into this AO. Let's look at one part at a time.

'*Read, understand* and respond to texts.'

To 'read' your set texts is an obvious requirement. 'Understanding' seems fairly straightforward, but may be a little more complex than you first think.

Activity 1

a Take one of your set texts from Paper 1 (Shakespeare and the 19th-century novel). Write a summary of the text – for someone who has not yet read it – in exactly 50 words.

b Now consider what you have written (or swap with a partner and look at their summary) from the point of view of 'understanding'. Did you concentrate mostly on the plot – the story the text tells? Discuss with a partner whether there is more to understanding a text than simply being able to recall its plot.

To further our understanding, perhaps we should ask the question 'What is this text about?'

Activity 2

Choose a different text from the one you considered in Activity 1. You could take a play you have studied, or an individual poem from your Anthology cluster. Now answer the question 'What is this text about?' in exactly 50 words, but allow yourself no more than 20 words to describe the plot or story.

What are the differences between your two answers? What does this tell you about 'understanding'?

traditional markets of wear-resisting materials whilst others are already well-established in the electrical and electronic fields. The new high temperature ceramic superconductors could offer new opportunities for industrial innovation particularly in electronic devices.

The basic principles of the powder metallurgy process are given in the Introductory volume of the current series of three books. A further volume provides state-of-the-art reviews of the important advances which are being made in the science and practise of the technology. The Case Studies presented in the present volume have been submitted by authors who are recognised internationally as experts in their chosen field and illustrate the applications and shortcomings of basic knowledge to the production of technological artefacts. Whilst not intended to be exhaustive, the studies cover most of the processes involved in powder metallurgy. It is hoped that the volume will be of value equally to the student as to material and design engineers who may wish to consider it as an introduction to the more comprehensive coverage of the subject which is given in the overview volume.

Further Reading

1. W. D. Jones, Fundamental Principles of Powder Metallurgy. Edward Arnold (Publishers) Ltd, London, 1960.

2. R. M. German, Powder Metallurgy Science. Metal Powder Industries Federation, Princeton, N J, 1984.

3. H. H. Hauser and M. Kumar Mal, Handbook of Powder Metallurgy. 2nd Edn. Chemical Publishing Company INC., New York, 1982.

4. Powder Metallurgy. State of the art. Vol 2. eds W. J. Huppmann, W. A. Kaysser, and G. Petzow. Verlag Schmid GmBH, Freiburg, 1986.

5. F. V. Lenel, Powder Metallurgy: Principles and Applications. Metal Powder Industries Federation, Princeton, N J, 1980.

6. Powder Metallurgy: The process and its products. British Powder Metallurgy Federation, Wolverhampton.

7. K. J. A. Brookes. Cemented Carbides for Engineers and Tool users. International Carbide Data, East Barnet, Herts, 1983.

Case Study 1
Automotive Component:Anti-Locking Brake System Speed Sensor Ring

D. WHITTAKER

Department of Materials Engineering and Materials Design, University of Nottingham, UK

1. The Problem

To provide, at minimum cost, a component comprising:-

- a toothed rim with a tight tolerance requirement on circumferential tooth spacing

- a flat inner portion, with splined central hole. This portion of the component was to act as the primary washer/spacer in a wheel/axle assembly and therefore had a high compressive strength requirement.

2. Introduction

Anti-lock braking systems were first introduced to the passenger car market during the 1980s. By the end of the decade, these systems were specified as standard on the larger and "top-of-the-range" models by most automotive manufacturers, but could be obtained as optional extras across a somewhat wider range of models. There was good reason to suppose that the longer term trend would be toward the specification of these systems as standard across the whole-range of car models.

Various systems were developed and introduced in the late 1980s. The particular system considered by this case study was the one preferred by Ford Motor Co. in Europe. In line with the normal industry approach of specifying these systems for the larger, more expensive models, they were fitted to the Granada and Sierra models. This involved an approximate annual usage, at two per vehicle, of 250,000 sensors on the Granada. On the Sierra, the part by 1989 was an optional extra, with a usage of approximately 100,000 p.a. However, if the part became standard on top Sierra models, this quantity could considerably increase.

The system adopted by Ford involved using the inner portion of the component as the primary washer/ spacer in the wheel axle assembly. This introduced a compressive strength requirement, which was the subject of a specific component proof test, to be discussed in greater detail in section 7 of this case study.

The outer portion of the component was a ring with circumferential teeth on the outside diameter. There was a tight dimensional tolerance on circumferential tooth spacing and outside diameter.

In one aspect of design, the sensors for the two models were different. As shown in Figs. 1 and 2, the outer ring was common to the two types, but the axial disposition of the washer component in relation to the ring varied.

This component was initially introduced as one machined from wrought steel bar stock and case-hardened. Ford Motor Co. already had significant experience in the use of PM components for a range of applications, however, and were therefore receptive to the suggestion that a PM alternative could be developed.

This development process will be discussed in more detail in the next sections.

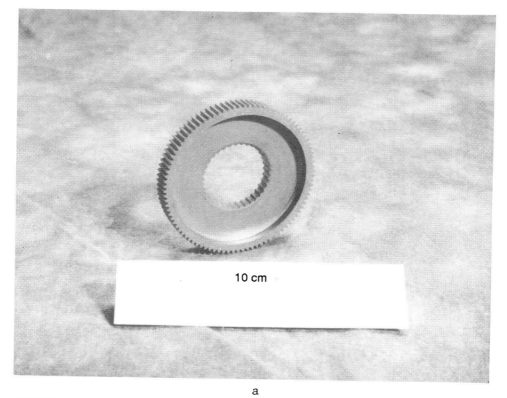

a

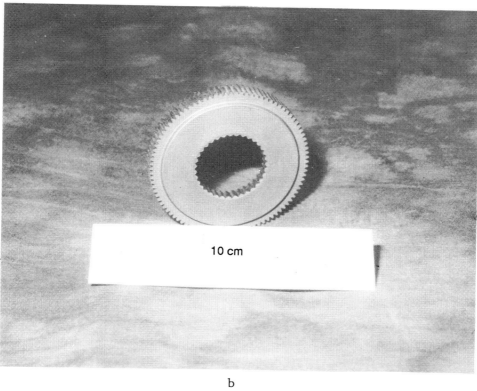

b

Figure 1. ABS Sensor Ring for Ford Granada.

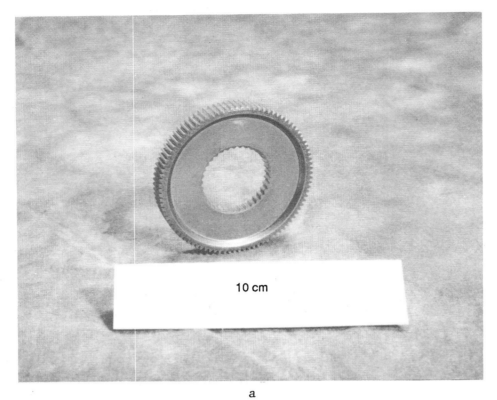

a

b

Figure 2. ABS Sensor Ring for Ford Sierra.

3. The Development of the PM Component

Initially, the compressive strength requirement in the washer portion of the component seemed to preclude the use of a PM material at conventional pressed-sintered density level.

As a first development, therefore, the idea was pursued of attaching an outer-ring made by the P.M. route, to an inner washer portion (with splined central hole) made by fine blanking and subsequent heat treatment. The assembly of these two parts was done by press-fitting. As the outer ring had no particular load carrying requirement, a relatively low strength P.M. material i.e. Fe-P at 7.0 g/cm density, was employed. An example of the P.M. outer ring is shown in Fig.3 and the assembled component (the Sierra variant) in Fig.4.

The production of the component by this assembly route gave much higher material utilisation and therefore significant finished component cost saving than earlier machining routes.

However, around 1985 - 1986, a PM material development occurred which led to the belief that the component could be made in one piece by the conventional press-sinter PM route. This material development, Hoganas' Distaloy G, will be described in some detail in the next section, as it was a very important contributor to the overall development of this component as a production item by the PM route. The switch to a one-piece component, as opposed to an assembly, more than compensated for the higher cost associated with the use of Distaloy G. The cost saving offered by the fully PM component, compared with the original machined part, was estimated as being around 40%. One contributor to the cost-effectiveness of this single-piece PM route was the ability to eliminate the requirement for a case hardening operation.

4. The Development of the Material (Distaloy AG)

In developing high strength ferrous PM materials, use can be made of a number of important mechanisms. In common with fully dense wrought steels, the use of alloying additions to enhance hardenability, either during cooling after sintering or in a subsequent heat treatment, is an important contributor. However, unlike fully dense material there is a further factor which exerts a considerable influence on mechanical properties - the density level. Figure 5 shows an example of the influence that density can exert [1].

There have essentially been two approaches to high strength PM material development - fully pre-alloyed and partially pre-alloyed materials.

In *full pre-alloyed* materials, each individual powder particle is a true alloy. This approach maximises the hardenability effect of the alloying additions but, unfortunately, sacrifices compressibility (and eventually sintered density level). With conventional single press/sinter PM processing, these materials are unlikely to offer density levels higher than 7.0 g/cm ^{3}.

The so-called 'partial pre-alloying' approach attempts to achieve a closer approach to the optimum combination of compressibility and hardenability. These materials are in fact not really alloys at all. They are based on a high compressibility iron powder, with the alloying additions in elemental powder form attached by a low temperature, diffusion alloying process [2] and can achieve density levels up to 7.2 g/cm³ after a single press/sinter treatment. The advantage of this approach over conventional blended mixtures of elemental powders lies in the fact that the alloying additions are held in place, thus ensuring hardenability on a macro-scale. There is of course, residual compositional (and microstructural) inhomogeneity on a microscopic scale after sintering. Because of this microscopic inhomogeneity, alloying additions are not utilised as effectively as with fully pre-alloyed materials. In other words, high compressibility is retained at the expense of some sacrifice in the effectiveness of the hardenability additions.

The partially pre-alloyed materials were developed largely during the 1970s with the Hoganas Distaloy grades being leading examples of this material type. These materials have a dominant position in their usage in higher strength conventional PM Products. Fully pre-alloyed grades tend to find more use in powder forged products where their low compressibility at the green stage is not significant.

Figure 3. Outer ring as PM component.

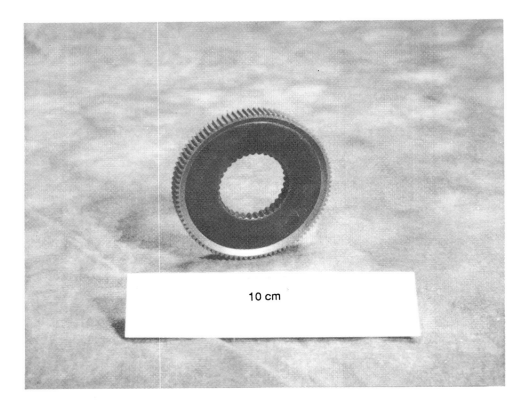

Figure 4. Assembled ABS Sensor ring with PM Outer ring and fine blanked steel washer.

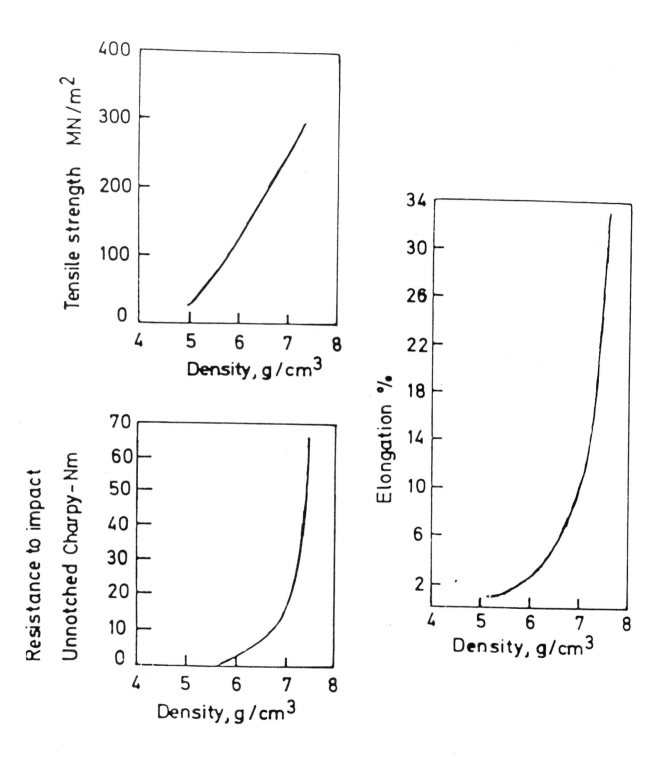

Figure 5. Relationship between mechanical properties and density of powder based samples [1].

In the mid-1980s, GKN Powder Metallurgy Division identified a requirement for an enhancement of properties beyond those currently offered by the highest strength partially pre-alloyed grades available. A collaborative development was therefore pursued with Hoganas, with the following as-sintered property targets as guidelines:-

Tensile strength > $950N/mm^2$

Elongation   ~ 4%

Density   > 7.30 g/cm^3

In order to maintain economic competitiveness, there were further stipulations that processing should be limited to the single press/sinter route with a maximum compaction pressure of 618 N/mm^2 (40 tons/in.^{2}) and a maximum sintering temperature of 1150°C.

Also it was mandatory that any material developed must be capable of achieving dimensional tolerance control equivalent to existing high strength materials.

A new material, Distaloy AG, was developed by Hoganas to satisfy these target requirements. The approach adopted was to remain with the partial pre-alloying concept, but, in addition, to stimulate shrinkage in sintering using fine powders.

It is well established [3] that the reduction in surface energy is a major driving force for sintering shrinkage and that fine powders provide high surface energy per unit volume. Sintering shrinkage can be stimulated by the use of fine powders either as the base material or, as in the case of this material, as an alloy addition.

At this time all high strength PM materials were designed to give low levels of size change during sintering, in order to guarantee the ability to hold close dimensional tolerances. The danger in adopting a material giving significant shrinkage during sintering, was that this ability would be lost, particularly with a very hard material for which sizing would not be possible. In order to avoid this problem, alloying additions were bonded to the iron particles using two different methods, diffusion alloying and bonding with organic binders [4], in order to ensure compositional homogeneity and therefore closely controlled shrinkage during sintering.

Distaloy AG was developed to have a nominal composition of 8% nickel, 1% molybdenum, balance iron with a 0.5% graphite addition and a lubricant content of 0.6%.

On compaction at 600N/mm^2 and sintering for 40 min at 1150°C in a 95%N$_2$/5H$_2$ atmosphere, the as-sintered properties were typically as given in Table 1.

Although a linear shrinkage of 0.8% was obtained with this material, production trials at GKN Firth Cleveland Limited confirmed that tolerances could be controlled to a similar level to those obtained with an established powder grade, Distaloy AE (Fe 4% Ni, 1.5% Cu, 0.5% Mo). The results of these trials are shown in Table 2.

Further detail on the development of Distaloy AG can be found in Refs. 4 and 5.

5. The Production Process

Distaloy AG is delivered to the PM component manufacturer with all alloying additions, including graphite and lubricant, fully mixed and bonded.

The production route employed for this speed sensor ring was then as follows:

Table 1 Distaloy AG - As-sintered properties

Dimensional change, %	− 0.8
Sintered density, g/cm^3	7.35
Hardness, HV_{20}	270
Tensile strength, N/mm^2	1000
Elongation	3

Table 2 Dimensional changes during sintering at 1150 °C in N_2/H_2 atmosphere

MATERIAL	DIMENSIONAL CHANGE, %	
	External spline	Internal spline
Distaloy AG + C	−0.67 ± 0.03	−0.68 ± 0.04
Distaloy AE + C	−0.29 ± 0.04	−0.24 ± 0.03

- Compaction
  - pressure = 618N/mm² (40 tons/in.²)
  - Green density ~ 7.1 g/cm³

- Sintering
  - Temperature = 1150°C
  - Time at temperature = 40 mins
  - Atmosphere = 95% N_2/5% H_2
  - Sintered density ~ 7.35 g/cm³

- Finishing Operations
  - Grinding of outside diameter of teeth

6. Quality and Process Control Requirements

The quality system, in operation for the production of these components, complies with the requirements of the Ford Q-101 standard.

This standard is based on Ford's operating policy of continuous improvement in quality, which has resulted in a change of emphasis from defect detection to defect prevention through the application of Statistical Process Control (SPC), employee involvement and training.

It is necessary for suppliers to maintain an effective system for quality control, utilising advanced quality planning techniques and statistical process control on significant characteristics. The system provides for the control of incoming material quality, for the prevention of in-process discrepancies, for positive corrective action when required and for the prevention of shipment of non-conforming products to Ford.

The use of Failure Modes and Effects Analysis (FMEA) is an important contributor to advanced quality planning. An FMEA is a powerful tool which assists in the elimination of risk by a disciplined analysis of possible failure modes ranked on grounds of seriousness, probability and likelihood of detection. In the context of production of PM components FMEAs are more commonly applied to the manufacturing process than to component design.

Performances of the process is monitored, using SPC methods, not only in terms of inspection of products but through the measurements of intermediate "outputs". In PM production, inspection of products would involve measurements such as weight and length at the compaction stage or diametral tolerances after sintering. Examples of intermediate outputs to be monitored would be temperatures, cycle times, etc.

Where action on the process is required, this might consist of changes in the operations (e.g. operator training, changes to the incoming materials, etc.) or the more basic elements of the process itself (e.g. the capability of the equipment, etc.).

The effect of actions need to be monitored and further analysis and action taken when necessary.

7. Performance Evaluations on the Product

A special test-rig was devised by Ford in order to carry out a test for compressive strength of the central washer portion of this component. The test-rig configuration was as shown in Fig. 6.

The test method was to increase applied load and to carry out a visual inspection of consequent damage to the component. The test was run as a comparative one between the PM component, in hardened and tempered Distaloy AG, and the previous "standard" machined steel part in case hardened BSS 230 M07.

Ford's criterion for acceptance of the original machined steel part in this test was that the washer must withstand a load of at least 150kN without cracking or exhibiting permanent deformation above 0.25mm. To

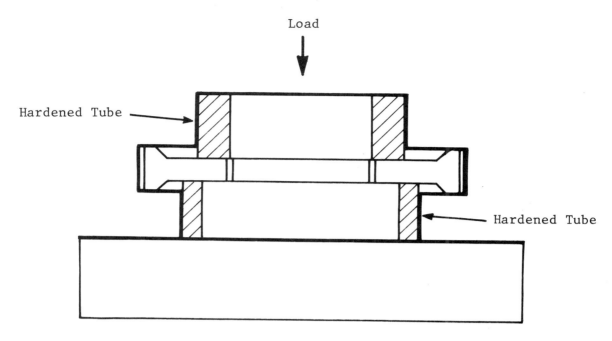

Load

Hardened Tube

Hardened Tube

Washer must withstand a load of 180 kN min without
cracking when tested as shown and checked to
BS6072 1981 max permanent deformation 0.25

Figure 6. Ford test rig configuration for assessment of compressive strength of ABS sensor ring.

Table 3 ABS sensor ring proof test

LOAD kN	CRACKING AND PERMANENT DEFORMATION	
	Machined steel part BSS230M07 Case hardened	P.M. part Distaloy AG
120	None	None
150	None	None
180	Slight	None
200	Extensive	None
250	Virtual breakdown	Slight

maximise their confidence on switching to a PM part, Ford in fact increased this minimum load requirement to 180kN. As results in Table 3 show, the PM part passed this increased test criterion without difficulty and, indeed, performed considerably better than the previous standard machined part.

8. Future Market Potential

The projected growth in total usage of anti-locking brake systems is seen as being very strong, in that ABS seems likely, in the longer term, to become standard on most vehicles. As some systems incorporate four sensors per vehicle whilst others use two, this would suggest a potential market of over 30 million sensors p.a. in the European market alone.

However, it is difficult at this stage to predict whether future systems will incorporate the current type of sensors or whether they may be superceded by an entirely different technology.

Even if current systems prevail, it is unlikely that the particular system discussed here would find usage with motor manufacturers other than Ford. Whilst other ABS systems often incorporate a PM sensor ring, they do not have an integral primary washer/spacer. Lower strength PM materials are therefore used for these applications.

It is difficult, at this stage, to predict the future market potential of the material utilised in this application, Distaloy AG. Previous high strength grades, such as Distaloy AB (Fe-1.75 Ni-1.5 Cu-0.5 Mo) and Distaloy AE (Fe-4.0Ni-1.5 Cu-0.5 Mo), were initially slow to penetrate the market, but, after a decade or so, their use represented perhaps 10% of all PM structural parts. However, Distaloy AG's potential market penetration could be more questionable, as it presents problems in terms of sizing (which may eliminate it from some applications on tolerance control grounds) and of finish machining.

9. Conclusion

The decade of the 1980s has seen a major growth in the use of anti-lock brake systems. At the beginning of the decade they were virtually unknown; at the end of the decade their usage was already well-established in top-of-the-range models with a significant promise that they would become standard across a wide range of models.

The usage of speed sensor rings had therefore grown to a respectable level in the second half of the decade with the prospect of a much higher usage during the 1990s.

Many of these speed sensor rings utilised PM Products.

The particular variant, on which this case study was based, was slightly unusual in that a portion of the sensor ring itself acted as the primary washer/spacer and therefore had a high compressive strength requirement.

At the beginning of the 1980s, the conclusion would have been drawn that although the shape and tolerance requirements were suitable for cost-effective manufacture by PM, there was no existing material with sufficient strength capability for the part to be made in one piece, by conventional single press/sinter PM. A material development (of Distaloy AG) which was proceeding in parallel with the growth of ABS systems in the mid-1980s was in fact the key to this part being produced as a one-piece PM component.

This case study is therefore of interest for two reasons: it represents one of the first excursions by the PM industry into a brand new area of automotive systems and was also the very first production application of the new high strength material, Distaloy AG.

10. References

1. H.F. Fischmeister, L. Olsson and K.E. Easterling, Powder Metallurgy International, <u>6</u> (1),1974.

2. G. Wastenson, Powder Metallurgy, <u>18</u> (35), p.124,1975.

3. A.R. Poster and H.H. Hausner, Modern Developments in PM, <u>2</u>, p.26,1966.

4. J. Tengzelius, Metal Powder Report, p.757, November 1988.

5. U. Engstrom and S. Allroth, "Horizons of Powder Metallurgy, Part II" Proceedings of International Powder Met. Conference, Dusseldorf, p.1039, July 1986.

Case Study 2
PM High Speed Steels

P.BREWIN

Powdrex Ltd, Munday Works, Morley Rd, Tonbridge U.K.

1. Description of the part

The part chosen for this case study is a high speed steel trimming die, shown in Fig.1. This component is used in high speed heading presses to cut or trim the hexagonal heads on bolts. The feedstock to the trimming machine is a cold or hot headed bolt blank of the form shown in Fig. 2. This blank is held on the shank by the top punch of the heading machine, and the head forced into the die. The bolt head hexagon form is cut by the die internal form.

The sintered blank consists of a relatively simple cylindrical outside form, with a complex tapered hexagonal internal profile. The base of the part is flat, while the top surface is convex.

High speed steel trim dies are typically produced in M2, M3/2, M35 compositions (Fig. 3) and are used at hardness levels of 60-65 Rockwell C. High Speed Steel Trim Dies are often PVD coated.

2 . Reasons for Choosing PM

The manufacture of high speed steel trim dies from bar is a difficult and expensive process. The most widely used methods are:

Method 1
1. Load fully annealed M2 high speed steel bright bar into capstan lathe. 2. Face to give convex top surface. 3. Cut bar to length. 4. Drill pilot hole. 5. Broach internal hexagon. 6. Hob internal form to give 2.5 degree taper. 7. Harden 8. Grind top surface to give cutting angle 8. Grind outside diameter to tolerance.

Method 2
1. Load fully annealed M2 high speed steel bright bar into capstan lathe. 2. Face to give convex profile 3. Cut bar to length 4. Drill pilot hole 5. Punch hexagon form using mandrel 6. Harden 7. Grind top surface to give cutting angle 8. Grind outside diameter to tolerance.

In both methods the main problem is the production of the internal hexagon form, which has to be tapered in order to provide chip clearance during the heading operation.

In method 1 this is achieved in a two-stage machining operation, In the first stage the basic hexagon profile is provided by a relatively crude broaching operation; in the second stage the internal taper is provided by an accurate hobbing operation.

In method 2 the internal profile is achieved in a single step. However, due to the low ductility of annealed high speed steels, cold forming is limited to those compositions which can be annealed to below 180 VPN, This means that method 2 can only be carried out on the lower carbon nil cobalt high speed steels. In turn, cold formed trim dies can only be hardened up to 63 HRC, higher hardnesses requiring carbon contents which cannot be cold formed.

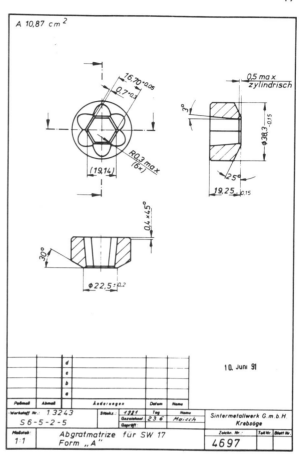

Figure 1 (a)   Sintered blank for 17mm hexagon trim die. (Courtesy of Sintermetallwerk Krebsoge)

Figure 1 (b)   Section drawing for sintered blank for 17mm hex trim die. (Courtesy of Sintermetallwerk Krebsoge)

Figure 2 17mm hexagon trim die showing bolt before and after head trimmimg.

Alloy (AISI) Equivalent	M2 S5-5-2	M3 Class 2 S6-5-3	M35 S6-5-2-5
Carbon	0.9	1.2	0.9
Chromium	4.0	4.0	4.0
Cobalt	<1.0	<1.0	5.0
Molybdenum	5.0	5.0	5.0
Tungsten	6.5	6.0	6.5
Vanadium	2.0	3.0	2.0
Iron	balance	balance	balance

Figure 3 High Speed Steel trim dies: Typical chemical compositions used (figures are wt.%)

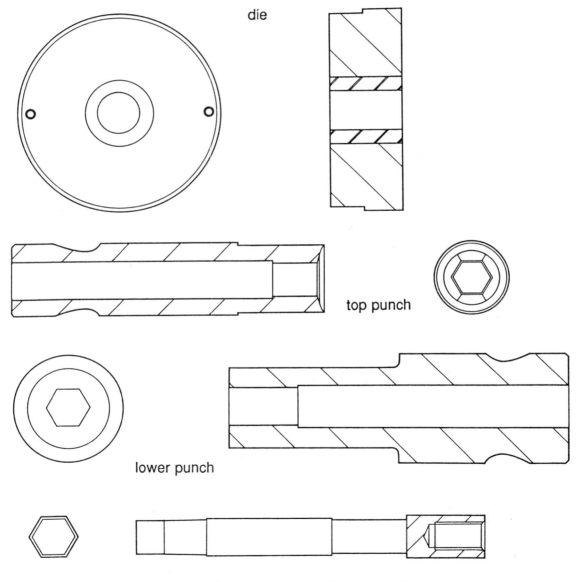

Figure 4 High Speed Steel hexagon trim die: Compaction tooling

Manufacture of trim dies by PM involves tooling of the type shown in Fig.4. It will be seen that the tapered internal hexagon form is provided by a core rod, The alloy composition used is M35 high speed steel, the composition and properties of which are shown in Fig.5.

3. Design Criteria

Figure 6 is a fully toleranced drawing of a commercial trim die blank.

In the production of this part there are several key criteria:

Tooling Design   - Tolerance levels on core rod and outside diameter;
                     Powder fill;
                     Uniformity of pressed density.

Sintering aspects - Sinter temperature range for satisfactory density and microstructure;
                     Control of hexagon inside diameter

Hardening   - Refinement of as sintered grain size.

3.1 Tooling Design

Some aspects of tool design for sintered high speed steels are identical to those that are well known in the sintering of low alloy powders. Others are different, and are particular to a material which, following compaction, is to be sintered to full density. The main difference stems from the fact that in the sintering of low alloy powders one of the chief objectives is to PREVENT size change through sintering, as the parts are to be sold chiefly on the basis of dimensional accuracy. In contrast, in sintered high speed steels the objective is always to PROMOTE size changes through sintering, so that the target material properties may be obtained.

The chief implication of this difference is that on sintered high speed steels control of pressed density is more important than in conventional powder metallurgy.

In arriving at the correct tooling design it is necessary first to consider the compaction cycle.

Figure 7 is a schematic of the powder compaction step for this part:

Stage 1 Bottom punch level with top of die from previous compaction stroke; filling shoe over die.

Stage 2 Withdraw bottom punch to give required powder fill volume.

Stage 3 Top punch starts compaction stroke.

Stage 4 Bottom punch starts compaction stroke as soon as top punch enters die.

Stage 5 Top punch compacts until within 0.2mm of start of core rod taper; bottom punch to required position (approx 0.5-1.0 mm from start of core rod taper).

Stage 6 Top punch withdraws from die.

Stage 7 Bottom punch moves upward until level with top of die, thus ejecting part.

The compaction step includes several key operations which must be correctly controlled if a satisfactory sintered part is to be produced. The first aspect of this is close control of the size of the hexagon where this intersects with the top convex surface of the die. In sintering, the part will 'move' from approximately 75% of full theoretical density ("FTD") to over 99% FTD. This volume change of 24% corresponds to a change

Grade:	AISI M35

Chemical analysis:

Carbon:	0.82/0.88
Chromium:	3.75/4.50
Molybdenum:	4.75/5.25
Tungsten:	6.0/6.75
Vanadium:	1.75/2.05

Usual condition as supplied: Annealed 269 HB max

Recommended heat treatment:

Hardness range (HV)	Preheat temp.(°C)	Hardening Temp. (°C)	Time (s)	Section thickness(m)	Tempering temp. (°C)	Time (h)
800-815	850	1160	50	6	570	1 x 3
830-855	850	1180	50	6	560	1 x 3
845-870	850	1200	50	6	550	1 x 3
868-895	850	1220	50	6	550	1 x 3

Figure 5 M35 High Speed Steel trim die: Material specification.

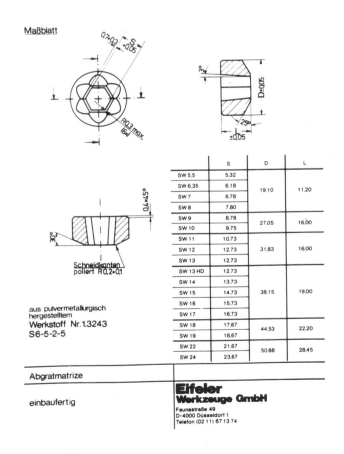

	S	D	L
SW 5.5	5.32		
SW 6.35	6.18	19.10	11.20
SW 7	6.78		
SW 8	7.80		
SW 9	8.78	27.05	16.00
SW 10	9.75		
SW 11	10.73		
SW 12	12.73	31.83	16.00
SW 13	12.73		
SW 13 HD	12.73		
SW 14	13.73		
SW 15	14.73	38.15	19.00
SW 16	15.73		
SW 17	16.73		
SW 18	17.67	44.53	22.20
SW 19	18.67		
SW 22	21.67	50.88	28.45
SW 24	23.67		

Maßblatt

aus pulvermetallurgisch hergestelltem
Werkstoff Nr.1.3243
S6-5-2-5

Abgratmatrize

einbaufertig

**Eifeler
Werkzeuge GmbH**
Faunastraße 49
D-4000 Düsseldorf 1
Telefon (02 11) 67 13 74

Figure 6 Hexagon trim dies: Finished part drawings after hardening and grinding.
(Courtesy of Sintermetallwerk Krebsoge)

in linear dimension of 8%. Therefore any process variable which affects the volume change will result in changed linear dimensions. In this respect the major variable is pressed density, which must be controlled during compaction to correspond to a small fraction of the linear size change on the most critical dimension. On the sintered trim die this is the hexagon, as this is the most difficult feature to rectify by post sinter machining.

Since the core rod is tapered, the punch movements on this tool must be controlled by position and not by load. Part bulk pressed density is equal to powder weight divided by pressed volume. As modern automatic powder presses can control punch position to a high degree of accuracy, the main variable in the equation is therefore powder weight. For the powder weight filled during the compaction stroke to be consistent from stroke to stroke it is necessary to have free flowing powder. Figure 8 shows a typical powder used for this part.

The second aspect in compaction of this part is the need to achieve a true cylinder on the outside diameter. Because the sintering of these materials involves relatively large size changes, achieving a true cylinder requires the same pressed density on part top and part bottom. Failure to achieve the same density at the top and bottom can lead to a tapered part. During compaction of a part of this type, this is achieved by compacting simultaneously from top and bottom. To effect this, the bottom punch should start to rise immediately the top punch starts to enter the die. Thereafter the top and bottom punches should move at the same speed until the required density has been reached.

Pressed density is related to superficial hardness (Fig.9). The setting up operation may be monitored by carrying out hardness checks on the pressed part top and bottom using a Rockwell 30T indenter. Top and bottom densities may be judged equal when the two readings are equal within 2 points.

In arriving at tooling dimensions the main considerations are:

1. The top internal hexagon dimension may be enlarged by grinding the top die surface.
2. An undersize internal hexagon dimension (which may be corrected by surface grinding) corresponds to an undersize external die dimension (which cannot be corrected by surface grinding).
3. All dimensions may be increased or decreased by increasing or decreasing compacted density.

Calculation of the corresponding tooling dimensions must therefore take into account grinding allowances on the sintered and hardened part as well as manufacturing variations which may be expected to occur during pressing and sintering. These considerations may be summarised as follows:

Core rod outside diameter =   mean finish ground size MINUS grinding allowance MINUS anticipated sintering size variation

Tool die inside diameter =   mean finish ground size PLUS grinding allowance PLUS anticipated sintering size variation.

3.2 Sintering Aspects

Sintering of high speed steels takes place in batch type vacuum furnaces at rotary pump vacuum levels (0.1-0.001mm Hg). Successful sintering involves considerations of the factors most affected by sintering temperature: density and microstructure. The relationship between these is sometimes expressed in terms of the 'sinter gate' (Fig.10). The lower temperature of the gate is the lowest temperature at which the material achieves the required density; the higher temperature of the gate is that at which the material structure becomes unacceptably coarse.

As sintered density increases upwards from 97% of FTD, residual porosity in sintered high speed steels is fine and uniformly distributed, and has less effect on mechanical properties than grain size and carbide distribution. The minimum density for adequate cutting performance depends to a large extent on the cutting operation. In the case of the trim die it is set at 99% of Full Theoretical Density ("FTD"). In the case of M35 FTD is 8.23 gm/cc and therefore the minimum acceptable density is 8.15 gm/cc.

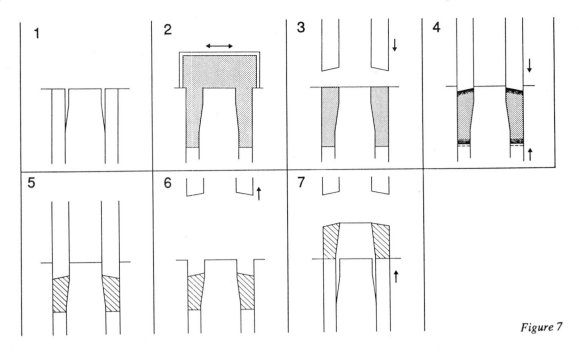

Figure 7

Element	Range	Notes	
C	0.90/0.96		
Cr	3.75/4.50		
Co	4.50/5.50		
Cu	no spec.		
Mn	<0.40		
Mo	4.70/5.20		
N	no spec.		
Ni	no spec.		
O	<1000ppm		
P	<0.04		
S	<0.04		
Si	<0.45		
V	1.75/2.05		
W	6.00/6.75		
AD(U)	2.25/2.45	gm/cc	
AD(L)	no spec.		
TD(U)	no spec.		
TD(L)	no spec.		
FL(U)	<45	s/50gm	Hall flow φ 2.54mm
FL(L)	no spec.		

(U) = figure for unlubricated powder
(L) = figure for powder with admixed 0.5w/w stearate type lubricant

COMP	>6.0	gm/cc at 600 MPa unlub'd; aspect ratio h/d 1.0
GSTR	>15.0	MPa; measured at 600 MPa unlub'd; MPA bar; support span 50mm
SIEVE	<2%	% over 150 microns
	>20%	% below 45 microns

Figure 8 M35 High Speed Steel trim die: Powder specification

As the sintering temperature is raised so the carbide and grain structures coarsen. Detailed microstructural work has shown there are several different carbide types in the as sintered high speed steel. The quantity and type of each carbide depends on the composition of the high speed steel and the details of the sinter cycle used. Additional heat treatments such as annealing, austenitising and tempering further modify the microstructure. The heat treated structure of liquid phase sintered material differs from conventional structures due to the fact that the starting condition is different.

The carbides that have been identified in sintered material are as follows:(In the following the designation M refers to a metallic element which forms a carbide. In general the carbides are complex, For example the M_6C carbide found in an M2 type high speed steel has been reported to consist of 35 wt% W, 20 wt% Mo, 36 wt% Fe, 4 wt% Cr, 3wt% V and 2 wt% C.)

Carbide type	Description
MC	This exists in two forms. The first forms are blocky carbides formed during atomisation, and in the second form thin grain boundary film type carbide formed during the solidification of the liquid phase during sintering.
M_2C	This carbide may form in a limited number of alloys during both atomisation and sintering. It is particularly deleterious as it exists in the form of colonies of thin plates, which form either as grain boundary networks or lie even within grains, thus catastrophically reducing impact strength.
M_6C	This carbide forms during cooling after sintering. This is due to the fact that it is almost completely dissolved at the sintering temperature either in solid solution or in the liquid phase. The carbide tends to be blocky and coarsens rapidly if the sintering temperature is too high. As it is not continuous it is not deleterious to impact strength in the same way as M_2C carbides.

Carbide modifiers may be added to the powder at the atomising stage in order to allow a degree of control over the carbide types and amounts that are formed. This technique is particularly effective in controlling the M_2C type carbides. Additions of silicon, usually of the order of 1 wt%, can be used to suppress the formation of this carbide in effect replacing it with the less harmful M_6C.

The disadvantage of high silicon content is that it significantly affects the surface tension of the alloy in the molten state, and high silicon powders have a more spherical shape than low silicon. Silicon also reacts with dissolved oxygen which is the most potent element in reducing the surface tension of steel. M35 type high speed steel of the composition in Fig. 5 does not contain sufficient silicon to prevent the formation of M_2C carbides. Therefore the allowable sinter temperature range is narrow approximately +/-2°C.

Quality control of sinter charges is carried out in 2 stages. In the first stage between 6 and 24 samples are taken from positions in the sinter charge known to represent the extremes of temperature. These samples are then checked for density and microstructure. In general the 'coolest' part of the charge will tend to have the lowest sintered density, and the 'hottest' part have the coarsest microstructure. Diameter (or die dimension) and density are correlated, and the relationship plotted graphically. From this graph the minimum and maximum acceptable sizes are deduced.

Providing both extremes on the samples selected are acceptable on both density and microstructure, the charge is now unloaded, and all parts are checked for diameter and accepted or rejected on this basis.

3.3 Hardening

On completion of the sinter soak the charge is normally cooled to room temperature by nitrogen gas circulation. Since the charge is closely stacked, parts on the outside are in the gas path and therefore subject to higher cooling rates than parts on the inside. In the faster cooled parts the material microstructure is highly

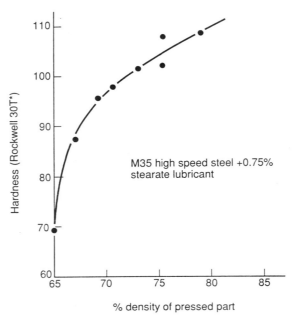

M35 high speed steel +0.75% stearate lubricant

% density of pressed part

Figure 9 Superficial hardness vs pressed part density.

*Rockwell 30T = Rockwell superficial method 30kg 1/16" ball

Figure 10
The "sinter gate".

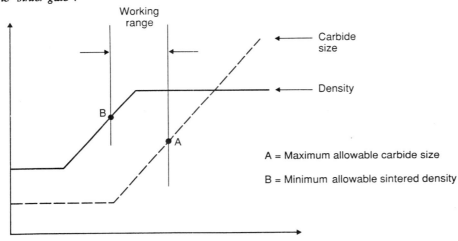

A = Maximum allowable carbide size

B = Minimum allowable sintered density

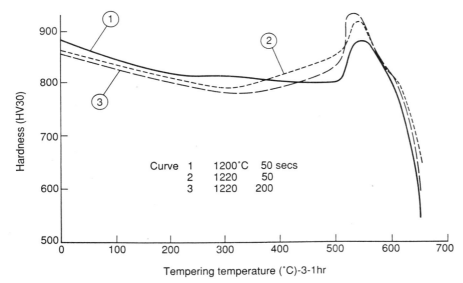

Curve	1	1200°C	50 secs
	2	1220	50
	3	1220	200

Tempering temperature (°C)-3-1hr

Figure 11 M35 high speed steel hardening response.

non-uniform, containing a mixture of untempered martensite at the one extreme and retained austenite at the other: in the slower cooled parts the material consists of intermediate bainite structures. At this stage, irrespective of cooling rate, the grain size is relatively coarse (in the region ASTM 5-8 intercept), a reflection of the fact that the material has been at a sintering temperature in excess of 1240°C for 1-2 h.

It is essential that this structure be homogenised before the steel is re-austenitised for hardening, This homogenisation is achieved by heating to a temperature of 850-900°C, at which the entire material matrix reverts to austenite. The material is then cooled to room temperature sufficiently slowly to allow this austenite to transform to pearlite and cementite, and to allow grains to re-nucleate,

On completion of this annealing treatment the material may now be hardened and tempered in the same manner as conventional cast and forged steels. Examination of austenite grain boundaries will show intercept values about 50% of the as sintered condition, confirming that true re-nucleation has occurred as a result of the annealing.

The most important factor in high speed steel high treatment is always the resultant material hardness. The usual objective of heat treatment is to obtain the best compromise between wear resistance and toughness; wear resistance incressing with increasing hardness but toughness reducing. As will be seen from Fig.11 given hardness level can often be achieved more than one way:

either (1) by austenitising at low temperature and tempering to near the hardness peak,

or (2) by austenitising at high temperature and also tempering at high temperature.

While the heat treatment of liquid phase sintered high speed steels is similar to conventionally produced material of the same composition, it is not identical. In the characterisation of a new material, therefore, it is important to establish the secondary hardening peak corresponding to any one austenitising temperature. In general:

For tools subject to impact - austenitise at the lowest possible temperature to achieve the finest possible grain size and therefore highest toughness.

For tools requiring maximum hot hardness - temper above the tempering temperature at which peak hardness occurs, so as to achieve the highest degree of hardness retention at high temperature.

The hardening temperature used in the case of trim dies is shown in Fig.12.

4. Manufacturing Route

4.1 Powder Production
The process route for the manufacture of the powder is shown in the schematic diagram (Fig.13).
   The finish annealed powder must conform to the specification shown in Fig.8.

4.2 Powder Preparation
   • Check incoming powder, especially carbon, oxygen, fill density and powder flowrate.

   • Admix 0.75% stearate type lubricant to the powder and blend to homogenise.

4.3 Compaction
   • Set up press tool. Ensure top punch compacts to 0.1/0.2mm of start of core rod taper. Ensure bottom punch compacts to within 0.5/1.0 mm of start of core rod taper. Set bottom punch to powder fill position.

Heat treatment recommendations for sintered trim dies made from M35

- **austenitizing :** 1100°C in vacuum
- **quenching :** nitrogen
- **tempering :** 3 times 560°C for 90 minutes
- **final hardness :** 60-62 HRC

Figure 12

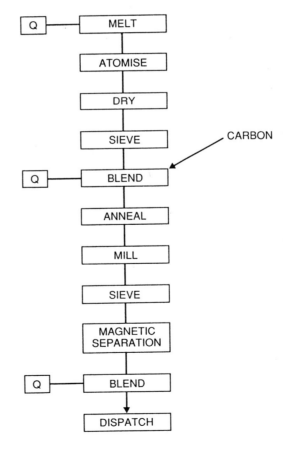

Q= KEY QUALITY CHECK

Figure 13 Powder production schematic

- Production test run of 6 parts, Check:
  (a) position of core rod taper on top and bottom of pressed part (b) superficial hardness of pressed part top and bottom.
- Calculate pressing tolerances as follows:
  Pressed weight +/- 0.2% of mean weight
  Pressed depth +/- 0.05 mm of mean depth
- Start production run. Continuously monitor:
  (1) Pressed part weight and depth. (2) position of hexagon taper.

Fine control of pressed part weight may be achieved during a compaction run by varying speed of operation of press (number of compaction cycles per minute; faster press speed increases energy of vibration during fill and therefore increases fill weight; however too fast press operation can lead to starvation as press operation speed exceeds powder flowrate).

Fine control of pressed part depth and position of hexagon taper is achieved by punch movement.

4.4 Sintering

- Place load parts onto ceramic plates and place onto graphite load trays, Remove press lubricant by low temperature gas or vacuum furnace treatment.

- Place load trays into sinter furnace and heat to sintering temperature using programmed cycle as in Fig.12.

- Cool to room temperature using fast nitrogen gas circulation.

- Carry out quality control checks on selected parts from charge (see section 3.2).

- Unload charge and carry out 100% size checks.

4.5 Heat Treatment and Finishing

- Load parts into annealing furnaces and carry out transformation anneal to cycle as per Fig.15.

- Harden parts using cycle as per Fig.12.

- Place parts on mandrel to centralise. Grind parts on outside diameter.

- Check hexagon dimension and grind die top surface to size.

Cycle stage	1	2	3	4	5
Slope (°C / hour)	500	400	350	300	fast cool
Level (°C)	800	1000	$T_{sinter}-30$	T_{sinter}	ambient
Soak time (hours)	0.1	1.0	1.5	2.0	-
Note: depending on thermocouple location T_{sinter} = 1240/1248/°C					

Figure 14 M35 High Speed Steel trim die: Sintering cycle.

Cycle stage	1	2	3	4	5
Slope (°C / hour)	300	100	100	50	fast cool
Level (°C)	600	800	850	500	ambient
Soak time (hours)	0.1	1.0	4.0	0.1	-

Figure 15 M35 High Speed Steel trim die: Annealing cycle.

CASE STUDY 3
Seat Tilting Mechanism
G. GREETHAM

Manganese Bronze, Elton Park Works, Ipswich, Suffolk, U.K.

1. Introduction

This case study is concerned with the design and development of a tilting mechanism for an office chair, and illustrates not only the wear resistant properties of the components finally developed, but also the very effective way in which the powder metallurgy process and the design process were integrated to make a cost effective product.

The market for office furniture is highly competitive and success depends upon many factors, some of which are:
1. *Aesthetic appeal*. Clearly the furniture has to be acceptable visually.
2. *Functionality*. The external controls used to actuated the internal tilting mechanism must be easy to use and work reliably.
3. *Cost*. To compete, the chair has to be competitively prices for the target market.

2. Objective

As success has to be a combination of good mechanical design and aesthetics, the objective was to design a tilting mechanism that would be cost effective, reliable, and be small enough to be enclosed within the accepted general profile of the chair. It was essential that there were no handles, or knobs protruding to mar the shape of the chair, and, to provide a compact mechanism the titling mechanism had to be designed as close to the axis of tilt as possible so as to be encased within the other structural parts of the chair.

3. Initial Design

The first design consisted of three co-axial cylindrical components, and enabled two of these, which were mutually rotatable, to be locked together in a number of different positions by means of a ball. Figure 1 shows an exploded view of the mechanism. The essential features are the helical slot in the central cylinder, the width of which will accommodate a ball; a longitudinal slot in the outer cylinder, the width of which is smaller than the ball diameter; a raised internal, longitudinal surface in the outer cylinder adjacent to the longitudinal groove; and a series of depressions in the inner cylinder to accommodate the ball during the operation of the mechanism.

By rotation of the outer cylinder with respect to the central cylinder, the logitudinal slot is brought in line with the ball which then falls back into the slot and is able to move. Rotation of the central cylinder with respect to the outer cylinder now causes the ball to travel along the helical slot in the central cylinder. The raised internal surface contacts the ball and pushes it into whichever indentation is closest in alignment in the inner cylinder. When the ball has been located in a particular seat the reverse movement of the outer cylinder with respect to the central cylinder locates the ball positively in the inner cylinder seat and central cylinder slot. The part of the outer cylinder now in contact with the ball is the smooth internal surface of the cylinder.

When used in a chair, the base and the back are connected mechanically to the inner and central cylinders respectively, and the outer cylinder is connected to a suitably designed hand operated control.

4. Initial Production Consideration

During the design of the tilting mechanism consideration was given to possible methods of manufacture. Initial reactions to the manufacture of the cylindrical components were not encouraging. Due to their inherent circular cross-section, and the fact that two had to have slots in them, machining was the only process which could provide the accuracy required for reliable operation. It was clear that the mechanism had to be redesigned to allow a cheaper, more cost effective process to be used. It was at this stage that powder metallurgy was suggested as a possible manufacturing route.

Powder metallurgy was not a possible production route for the cylindrical design, as the slots would have to be machined in after production of the cylinders.

5. Second Design

It was clear from the earlier design that the cylindrical mechanism, although functionally correct, would be too expensive to manufacture and consideration was then given to translating the cylindrical movement into linear motion. The mechanism was redesigned to provide such motion and is shown in Fig. 2. The three cylinders have now been replaced by three plates. The central plate has a hole which houses the ball; the RHS plate has a hole smaller than the diameter of the ball and a small recess; the LHS plate has a series of indentations into which the ball will locate. Moving the RHS plate relative to the central plate allows the ball to move into the hole in RHS plate releasing it. The LHS plate, can then rotate about the same axis as the RHS plate. When the ball is located in the required indentation the LHS plate is moved in the opposite direction, and this then traps the ball in the hole in the central plate and an indentation in LHS plate. Schematically the plates are shown in position in the chair in Fig. 3, with the central plate attached to the base, the LHS attached to the back of the chair, and the RHS plate connected to a hand operated mechanism.

When the plates were considered for manufacture three processes were considered, namely investment casting, machining and powder metallurgy.

6. Material Considerations

Before deciding on the process of manufacture the necessary mechanical and dimensional requirements for the three plates were considered. To function reliably the three plates had to have the following properties:-

1. The plates had to be flat on the faces that rubbed together to ensure that the ball would locate properly in the indentations in the two outer plates.

2. Dimensions had to be sufficiently accurate to ensure that the indentations would hold the ball in place during operation of the mechanism, and allow free movement of the ball in the adjustment mode of operation.

3. The flat surfaces had to have sufficient wear resistance to ensure that they did not scuff and bind during operation.

4. The indentations had to be sufficiently wear resistant to avoid wear of the edges of the indentations. Wear of these indentations would result in imprecise location of the ball in the indentation with a subsequent unacceptable small movement of the chair back about its mean position. Such wear would no doubt lead eventually to the failure of the raised areas between spherical indentations, resulting in a groove. This would lead to failure of the chair to be positioned in any one position precisely.

7. Manufacturing Process

The manufacturing processes designated for examination, machining, investment casting, and powder metallurgy were considered in turn for these three components.

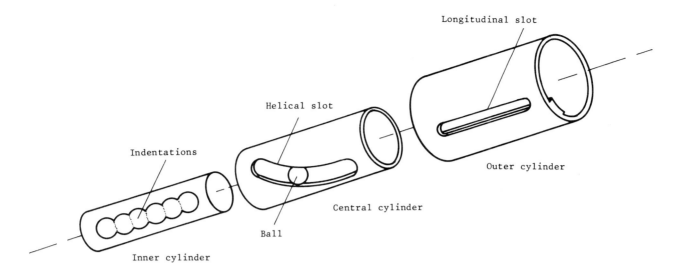

Longitudinal slot

Helical slot

Indentations

Outer cylinder

Central cylinder

Ball

Inner cylinder

Figure 1

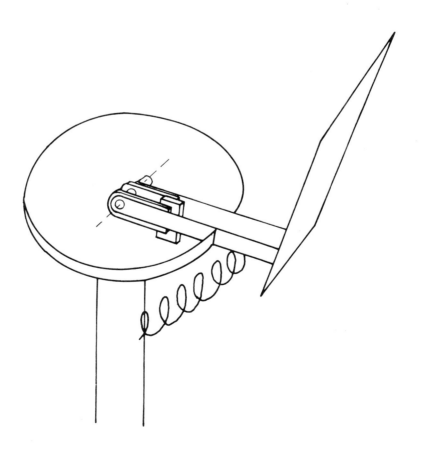

Figure 3

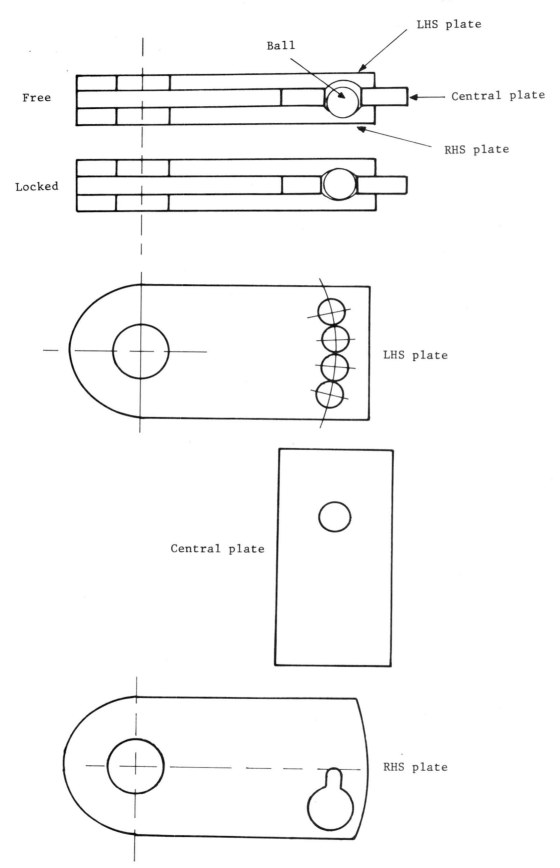

Figure 2

Machining was ruled out initially on cost, and eventually investment casting was eliminated on the ground of cost and also on the dimensional tolerances that could be attained for the components. The powder metallurgy route was considered as the only one capable of producing the shape economically. An examination of the three components showed that they could be produced by pressing with the thickness in the direction of pressing. Indentations and holes were possible as-pressed, and the only operation to provide dimensional accuracy was to grind the central plate on both sides and the two side plates on their inward facing surfaces only.

8. Materials

In order to prove the mechanism three stages were carried out:-

Stage 1. The first plates were machined from mild steel plate and carbonitrided to give a surface hardness of about Rockwell C 25.

Stage 2. Following the successful completion of Stage 1, powder metallurgy plates were made, machined to size and carbonitrided to give a surface hardness of about Rockwell C 25. The material chosen was a relatively simple iron based alloy containing nominally 0.3-0.6%C, 3-6% Ni, 1-3% Ni, 0.3-0.7% Mo.

Stage 3. Tools were designed and manufactured to produce the three plates to the correct dimensions. These components were again carbonitrided to give a surface hardness of about Rockwell C 25.

9. Testing

The testing of office chairs and stools is covered by British Standard. There are several levels of performance acceptable depending on intended use as below:

Test Level	Description.
1	Delicate and fine chairs and stools intended only for careful functional use.
2	Chairs and stools for careful domestic use.
3	Chairs and stools for general domestic and careful contract use.
4	Chairs and stools for general contract use, where rough treatment and careless handling occur.
5	Chairs and stools for severe contract use.

The mechanism design had to perform to level 5, the roughest contract use. In particular, the tilting mechanism was tested by anchoring the chair to the ground and applying a force at right angle to the back of the chair as in Test 4a in Table 1. Note that for successful operation the chair had to withstand 200,000 loadings.

Early simplified trials were carried out by Imperial College before full scale testing was undertaken at the Furniture Institute Research Association. The results of these tests are given in Table 2.

10. Development of the Final Manufacturing Route

The general manufacturing route was initially established as:

• briquette to form green compact sinter to final density of 6.8g/cc
• carbonitride to produce a hard case of at least Rockwell C 25 grind surface (or surfaces) as required.

Although the earlier components that had been produced by machining had been satisfactory it became apparent that the carbonitriding treatment, which involved heat treatment in a cyanide salt bath at about 875C for at least 0.75h, was causing unacceptable distortion of the plates. This then lead to excessive grinding to give the required surface flatness.

Table 1

Test No.	Test	Description	Test Level 1	Test Level 2	Test Level 3	Test Level 4	Test Level 5
1a	Seat static load test	Seat force (N)	–	1100	1300	1600	2000
1b	Back static load test	Back force (N)	–	410	560	760	760
		Balancing seat force (N)	–	1100	1300	1600	2000
2	Arm sideways static load test	Force applied (N)	–	300	400	600	900
2	Wing sideways static load test	Force applied (N)	–	200	300	400	500
3	Arm downwards static load test	Force applied (N)	–	700	800	900	1000
4a	Seat fatigue test	No. of cycles – 950 N seat force	12500	25000	50000	100000	200000
4b	Back fatigue test	No. of cycles – 330 N seat force	12500	25000	50000	100000	200000
5a	Leg forwards static load test	Maximum forward force (N)	300	375	500	620	760
		Balancing seat force (N)	760	780	1000	1250	1800
5b	Leg sideways static load test	Maximum sideways force (N)	250	300	390	490	760
		Balancing seat force (N)	760	780	1000	1250	1800
5c	Diagonal base force test	Force applied (N)	125	250	375	500	620
6	Seat impact test	Drop height (mm)	–	140	180	240	300
7a	Back impact test	Drop height (mm)	–	120	210	330	620
		Angle (degrees)	–	28	38	48	68
7a	Wing impact test	Drop height (mm)	–	120	210	330	620
		Angle (degrees)	–	28	38	48	68
7b	Arm impact test	Drop height (mm)	–	120	210	330	620
		Angle (degrees)	–	28	38	48	68
8	Drop test	Drop height (mm)					
		(a) stacking chairs and stools	150	300	450	600	900
		(b) non-stacking and pedestal chairs	–	150	200	300	450
		(c) low chairs or easy chairs	–	75	100	150	250
9	Swivel test	No. of cycles	–	25000	50000	100000	200000
10	Seat height adjustment and wear test	No. of cycles	–	–	10000	15000	25000

A final modification of the route was made as follows, after again carrying out the necessary proving trials at FIRA:

briquette to from green compact
sinter to a final density of 6.8g/cc (careful handling was also introduced to avoid damage to the parts when leaving the end of the sintering belt)
(drill and tap holes where necessary in one plate)
grind surfaces
steam treat
bead blast
 pack

The modifications made were for the following reasons.Treatment in steam at a few pounds/in² pressure for 0.5h at 400C, followed by 1 h at 550C produced a component with a sufficiently wear resistant surface for the application. As this treatment is a metallurgically gentler process than the carbonitriding treatment used initially, the components could be ground before this treatment. The steam treatment did not introduce any distortion, and it is generally accepted that such a treatment will give good wear resistant properties to sintered components, the oxide produced during this process keying into the surface and producing a relatively hard, adherent coating.

Bead blasting was introduced for aesthetic purposes. When carried out, components invariably look better, having a smooth metallic sheen to them.

The three finished components are shown in their relative positions, in Fig. 4. Note that they have slightly more complex outlines than is shown in Fig. 2. Other functions were required of these plates necessitating the fixing of other components to them. As the complexity increased, the cost effectiveness of the powder metallurgy process also increased.

11. Conclusions

The case study presented shows that effective collaboration between the designer and the powder metallurgy producer can lead to a cost effective product. The powder metallurgy components in this case were finally given a wear resistant coating of iron oxide using a technology developed specifically PM parts. By a step-by-step approach to the final production technique the cost of the components was steadily reduced to provide the chair manufacturer with a cost competitive, and technically acceptable solution to the original problem.

12. Acknowledgements

Acknowledgements for permission to present this case study are to Adrian Stokes and Associates, who designed the ingenious tilting mechanism; to Manganese Bronze Ltd., who produced the final schedule for the components and provided a cost effective set of components; and to Gordon Russell Plc, who take the components and assemble them with other components (into a highly competitive tilt and swivel office chair).

CASE STUDY 4
Hardmetal Component - The Indexable Insert

R.EDWARDS

Plansee Tooling Ltd, Cliff Lane, Grappenhall, Warrington, U.K.

1. Introduction

Before discussing a specific case it would be wise to point out that <u>all</u> hardmetals are made using the powder metallurgy route. They cannot be produced by conventional melting and casting techniques. Their structure and therefore their properties depends on keeping the sintering temperature below that where WC decomposes into W_2C and C[1].

When the powders have been mixed and blended into the required compositions they are compacted. At this point two possible methods of production may be used. The first is the classical one whereby the powders are pressed in a die to the final shape of the product. They are then placed in a furnace where the binder used to assist pressing is removed and then the temperature is raised to that where satisfactory sintering will take place. All this is carried out in one continuous operation usually in a vacuum furnace.

The second method is used either where it is not possible to manufacture the shape by direct pressing because of its complexity or where the quantities ordered do not justify the cost of producing a die. In these circumstances the powder is compacted into a block which is then placed in a furnace where the pressing binder is removed and the temperature is raised to about 800°C. This is known as "dewaxing and presintering". When the blocks are removed from the furnace they have a consistency similar to a stick of chalk and are strong enough to be machined into the required shape. This is usually done on special purpose machines using diamond tooling. When the required shape has been machined the 'formed' piece is sintered. The component retains its shape during sintering but is subject to a very high volume shrinkage.

The shrinkage which takes place when sintering hardmetals is appreciable. A piece which is 25 mm long in the 'green' state will shrink to about 20 mm during sintering. A volumetric shrinkage of at least 45% occurs. This high shrinkage is an important factor when attempting to achieve close dimensional accuracy with hardmetals and has relevance to points which are discussed later in this section of the book.

2. Historical Background

Until the mid 1950s almost all metal machining where hardmetal was used was carried out with tools which had hardmetal tips brazed onto them. When the cutting edge became worn the tool was removed from the machine and taken away to have the cutting edge reground. This meant that the machine was stopped whilst the tool was removed and replaced by a reground one from the tool crib. It also meant that the position of the new tool had to be set so that cutting could recommence in the same position as the tool which had just been taken out.

Regrinding is not a cheap operation and often includes the grinding in of chipbreakers as well as reforming the cutting edge profile.

In the USA in the late 1940s toolholders were being produced which had pieces of hardmetal clamped into pockets at the nose of the tool. The pieces were either square, triangular or round. Their dimensions were referenced by:

1. The measurement of the inscribed circle which could be drawn within their profile; 2. Their thickness; 3. The radius of the cutting corner (not relevant to round pieces).

At this time they were designated according to a USA Industry Standard. The designation system was a combination of letters and numbers. The letters indicated the shape, the basic cutting geometry and the accuracy of the insert. The numbers referred to the size of the inscribed circle, the thickness of the insert and the size of the cutting corner radius.

EXAMPLE: SNU 432

S = Square

N = Negative (The insert has negative top rake when mounted in the toolholder)

U = Utility (Apart from lapping the top and bottom faces to make the insert flat, the insert is as sintered with appropriate dimensional tolerances)

4 = 4 x 1/8" i.e. 1/2" inscribed circle

3 = 3 x 1/16" i.e. 3/16" thick

2 = 2 x 1/64" i.e. 1/32" corner radius

These inserts were known as "Throwaway Tips" which was an unfortunate choice because once the piece had been used it still had quite a high scrap value. Since the late 1960s they have been known as "Indexable Inserts" and are still known as such to the present day.

3. The Market

The situation today is very different from that in the late 1950s. At that time industry in Europe was very reluctant to accept the advantages of the indexable insert. Its introduction would mean the removal of the need for regrinding brazed tools and also less involvement in setting time. The then climate of labour relations did not make it easy for management to introduce new ideas like this into the plants.

Credit for the eventual change over to clamped tooling as it is today must go to the Swedish company Sandvik who put tremendous effort into the marketing of this product and now international standards exist for the whole range of inserts and tools used for almost every type of machining operation.

There have probably been three major contributions to the machining of metals in this century. They are:

1. The invention of hardmetal in 1926;
2. The exploitation of indexable inserts from 1950;
3. The introduction of coatings in 1969.

Each follows on from the other for without the existence of the indexable insert, coating would not have been a viable proposition.

The market for indexable inserts is huge. About 60% of the total hardmetal produced is used for machining. At least three quarters of this is made up of the various types of indexable insert.

4. The Development Progression

The original indexable inserts were not especially complicated. They had simple shapes:- squares, triangles and rounds. There were two types of insert. Negative inserts, "N" in the second letter position, which were pressed in parallel sided dies with plain top and bottom punches. Positive inserts, "P" in the second letter position, which had an 11° angle on their sides which was incorporated in the die. Dimensions were measured in imperial units (inches). The Utility inserts, "U" in the third letter position had a comparatively wide tolerance band which was readily achievable by direct pressing followed by sintering. It was only necessary to lap the top and bottom faces to ensure flatness. Good flatness is essential to ensure that the insert is properly supported by the seating provided in the toolholder and that it does not vibrate during cutting, otherwise chipping of the cutting edge is likely to occur. "U" tolerances meant +/- 0.005" (0.13 mm) on the plan dimensions and also on the thickness.

If the utility tolerance was not accurate enough for indexing purposes the insert could be ground to the "G" tolerances which are +/- 0.001" (0.025 mm) on both plan dimensions and thickness, and examples of these early inserts are still in existence today.

One vital feature in metal cutting is that the chip which is formed during cutting must break into small pieces which fall into the well of the machine and can then be removed either by chip conveyors or by cleaning out at a later stage when the machine is stopped. This ensures the safety of the operator and also prevents snarl up which can do damage to both tool and workpiece.

When brazed tools are used they usually have a groove ground into the rake face just behind the cutting edge. This groove acts as a chipbreaker and is optimised by adjusting its width and depth until acceptable chips are produced. The toolholders which carried the early indexable inserts had overhead clamps which pressed down onto the top face of the insert and held it securely. Between the insert and the clamp was a piece of hardmetal with an angled leading edge which deflected the chip during cutting and caused it to turn over on itself and break.

This "obstruction" method of chipbreaking is somewhat crude. The chips do not flow freely and with heavier cutting they can damage the insert and also give rise to higher cutting temperatures than would be experienced with a chipgroove. The overhead clamp itself is a disadvantage. It can suffer damage from the cutting swarf and is an encumbrance in boring operations. These factors led to the next stage of development. A clamping system avoiding the overhead principle and at the same time the incorporation of a chipgroove in the insert itself.

The indexable inserts for this system have a cylindrical shaped hole in the centre and a chipgroove all round the cutting face. Clamping was effected by causing a pin to move towards the abutment faces of the toolholder pocket and firmly clamp the insert against them.

The development had now reached a stage where powder metallurgy technology came into its own. The chipgrooves could only be produced in one of two ways; either by directly pressing them in or by spark machining the profile into the face of the insert. With the quantities involved it is totally uneconomical to consider the spark machining method thus the grooves were profiled into the punch and reproduced during the pressing operation.

Once this stage had been reached the way was open to design and develop even more complicated profiles in the rake face of the insert. Most of these profiles could never be conventionally ground into a basic shape of insert. They could only be produced in volume by the powder metallurgy route.

In the last ten years the cutting geometry of indexable inserts has developed at a rapid rate. For instance there now exists a range with extremely high top rake and positive inclination. Such inserts are designed to cut aluminium and its alloys, refractory metals, non-ferrous metals and plastics.

In parallel with these developments the range of shapes was extended to cater for more machining operations such as profiling, turning and facing, drilling etc. The new shapes included an 80° rhomboid designated "C". A 55° diamond designated "D". A 35° diamond designated "V". A trigon shaped insert designated "W" together with several other styles. The whole range is covered in the ISO Standard 1832 dated 1977 entitled "Designation of Indexable Inserts for Cutting Tools"[2]. At the present day almost every machining operation can be carried out with indexable inserts.

5. Main Process Steps Involved

The whole basis of the use of these inserts is that they are indexable. This means that any insert which is released, turned and reclamped must relocate such that the new cutting corner is positioned in virtually the same place as the one which has just been changed. The accuracy of the location depends partly on the engineering built into the toolholder but primarily on the dimensional accuracy of the hardmetal indexable insert. The accuracy which can now be repeatedly attained with as sintered hardmetal inserts is good enough for most turning operations. However, this accuracy requires special attention to those parts of the process which influence the dimensions of the finished product. If greater accuracy is required, for example with inserts used in milling cutters, then the periphery of the insert is ground to the required tolerance.

A simple outline of the manufacturing process for hardmetal has already been covered. The part of the process which has particular interest to the production of indexable inserts centres around the pressing operation [3] and the rest of this section will concentrate on that one aspect.

In the case of these inserts indexability requires consistency of dimension and form. Punches and dies are produced to such precision that the inserts as pressed in the game die are virtually identical to one another. However, they then have to be sintered and during this process they will reach full theoretical density. If one part of the pressed insert differs in pressed density from another then because they will reach the same final density they will shrink differently. In this case some distortion from the pressed form will occur which will give rise to a dimensional deviation from the ideal final product.

There are two main reasons why pressed density (usually known as green density) may vary within a pressing. The first is the distribution of the powder when the die is being filled and the second is the effect of die wall friction during the actual compaction of the powder.

The majority of the presses used for compacting indexable inserts are the mechanical type. In one crank of the press the die is filled, the top punch enters the die, compaction takes place, the top punch retracts, the bottom punch moves up in relation to the die thus ejecting the pressing, this latter movement is then reversed leaving the cavity ready to be filled again. Typical average pressing rates are at least 10 per minute.

The powder is normally contained in a hopper above the die set and is delivered to the fill shoe via a tube. The intention in the filling operation is that the same weight of powder will be uniformly delivered into the die cavity at each cycle of the press. The flow characteristics of the powder are therefore critical.

In order to assist compaction, hardmetal powders have a pressing lubricant or "binder" added to them. Various waxes are used and a typical amount is 2% by weight. Waxed and sieved powder is very floury in consistency and has poor flow characteristics. In this condition it is totally unsuitable for producing indexable inserts. Some form of granulation is necessary to improve the flowability of the powder.

The granules must have a narrow particle size range. Fines mixed with coarse uniform particles adversely affect the flowability. Currently, spray drying is the best state of the art. It produces granules having a spherical form. Selective sieving separates out the fines and the excessively coarse particles.

The hardness of the granules is also very important for they must crush during the pressing process otherwise they cause a characteristic type of porosity in the finished product.

Having obtained a satisfactory flowable powder attention then has to be paid to the "placing" of the powder in the die. If the lower punch is already in the fill position when the fill shoe comes over the die then the powder tends to be thrown to the back of the cavity. Corners are danger areas in filling.

The ideal method is to bring the fill shoe over the die cavity before the lower punch descends, then, whilst the fill shoe gently oscillates, the punch retracts to a lower position than the final fill depth allowing an excess of powder to fill the die cavity. The punch then lifts to the actual fill position pushing out the excess powder into the fill shoe which is still sitting over the cavity. The fill shoe then retracts taking away the excess powder within its body and compaction takes place.

The problems of die wall friction are classical. Indexable inserts have a favourable Punch Area: Thickness ratio. Very little hollowing of the sides occurs during sintering and that which does take place falls within the allowable tolerance levels. Providing the press movements are set correctly so that top and bottom punches both move relative to the die itself the effect of friction of the die wall is not important.

The profiles of the rake faces of indexable inserts are pressed in by the punches. The chipgroove profiles of modern inserts are too intricate to be put into the punch faces by grinding. Additionally, the punches are tipped with hardmetal so that good wear life will be achieved. The punches are spark machined using copper tungsten electrodes (another powder metallurgy product).

The shrinkage of the powders depends on their chemical composition and also on the grain size of the tungsten carbide powder used. It is possible to adjust for the very slight variations that occur in any one composition from batch to batch by slight adjustments in pressing pressure. However, it is not possible to cater for the shrinkage range that occurs between the so called steel cutting grades of hardmetal and the cast iron grades. Most hardmetal producers will use up to three different sizes of the same style of die to cater for the shrinkage of their powders. Unless they do this they will not be able to achieve the tolerance limits required for the indexable inserts they are making.

The use of CAD/CAM linked to computer controlled machines for forming the electrodes is a modern trend. It helps to ensure repeatability when recutting is necessary and also reduces the design and manufacturing time. The accuracy of the dies and punches is absolutely critical for this product. The great majority of turning inserts are used without any further machining of the periphery. All dimensional control depends on the efforts put in at the pressing stage.

6. Quality Control Procedures

With quality control there are two main objectives in mind:

1. To ensure that the metallurgical quality is within the required specification;
2. To ensure that the product conforms to the dimensional criteria which are laid down in the standard.

The raw materials must be checked to see that they meet the purchasing specification. This will involve chemical analysis and particle size range.

After the powders have been blended and granulated they will be checked to ensure they will give the correct metallurgical, [4, 5] physical and mechanical properties and also that their pressing characteristics are what is required.

It is general practice to set up the die rig away from the press. When this has been done it will be fitted into a press and test samples run off. These are then sintered and used to make any final adjustments to the getting of the die rig.

Once production commences samples are taken at regular intervals during pressing and checked for weight and thickness. The results are continuously monitored and used to carry out any necessary adjustments to the press settings during the production run.

After sintering, samples are taken from selected positions in the furnace and checked to ensure that the properties of the indexable inserts are to specification.

These tests include density, [6] coercive force, [7] hardness [8] and magnetic saturation. Some inserts will also be deliberately broken and a visual examination of the fracture will be made. Additionally some manufacturers carry out machining tests to ensure that the inserts will perform correctly when put into the field.

Each manufacturer will adopt his chosen method of statistical sampling and will make whatever dimensional checks are required to ensure that the inserts conform to the standard.

As many of the inserts will be used without subsequent grinding the quality of the cutting edges is critical. A small chip or snip on one of the corners will render that cutting edge useless. Great care is taken in handling the inserts at all stages after compaction and checks are made at the final inspection stage to ensure that edges have not suffered damage.

In some cases further processing is required. Inserts which need more precision have to be ground e.g. for milling. Some of the as sintered inserts are lapped on the top and bottom faces to ensure that they seat correctly in the toolholders. Additionally many of the inserts in use today will be coated. Final checks are done to ensure that these finishing processes have been carried out correctly.

7. Coating

It is almost certainly true to-say that without the existence of the indexable insert the remarkable development of coatings for hardmetals would not have taken place. The fact that the inserts are only used once on each available cutting edge and are then discarded for salvage makes them the perfect vehicle for coating. They are not reground and so the problem of recoating after the first layer has become worn does not exist.

The first coatings on indexable inserts were introduced to the market in 1969. They were thin layers of Titanium Carbide (TiC) about 10 microns thick. They were deposited by the CVD process (Chemical Vapour Deposition).

In 1973 the so called "Goldmaster" coatings were developed by Metallwerk, Plansee, Austria, which were transitional layer coatings starting with TiC changing to TiCN and finishing with an outer layer of TiN which is gold in colour - hence the name [9].

In the mid 1970s ceramic coatings based on alumina came onto the market. Since then multilayer coatings up to 10 layers in a total thickness of less than 10 μm have resulted in cutting life which would not have been thought possible twenty years ago.

8. Chip Control Grooves

One of the most important requirements in machining metals is to control the flow of swarf which emanates from the machining operation. When cast iron is turned on a lathe the swarf breaks up into small chips which fall away into the bed of the machine where they can be carried on conveyer systems to a collecting point. However, if steel is used as the workpiece material the swarf will come away in long unbroken spirals unless some deliberate attempt is made to break it up. This type of swarf is extremely dangerous to the operator and it quickly becomes a problem in the machine by fouling up the movements of the tools, also in the changing of the workpiece when the operation is finished and by causing possible damage to the tool cutting edge and to the surface of the machined component [10].

The technique of "chipbreaking" causes the swarf to turn over on itself when ideally it breaks into small curls. Specially developed profiles in the rake face of the indexable inserts will direct the swarf in the manner required. The simplest form is a shallow groove located just behind the cutting edge. Wider grooves will handle heavier cuts (thicker chip sections) whilst very light cuts will have better swarf control if narrower grooves are used.

There is no simple groove solution. The variety of materials to be machined, depths of cut and feed could result in designing an ideal groove for each individual case. Each manufacturer offers a selection of grooves which he has designed to be suitable for a quoted range of machining conditions.

The introduction of CAD/CAM techniques has allowed the designers to come up with chipgrooves having forms which could never have been conceived if grinding was the only production method available. The designer can now generate a form in the computer and transfer it to the programming of three dimensional milling machines which can produce the spark machining electrodes which then cut the punches needed to press the designed profile of the indexable insert.

9. Competitive Processes

Since hardmetal is made by the powder metallurgy process there are really no alternative methods of manufacture.

10. Future Developments

The future development of the indexable insert will be closely linked to the development of machines and machining systems. Already there are "packages" in existence which are completely automated and which will pick out a forging from a mixed lot, scan it and recognise it. Having done so the follow on stages are set up to accept it, machine it, inspect it and place it into a storage system for transmission to the next place of its journey through the factory. Such packages are known as Flexible Machining Systems.

The FMS is designed to run completely unattended. It is essential that no swarf is created which can tangle up in the tools, in the holding and clamping systems and on the component itself. If this happens then the sensing devices will detect the problem and the machine will stop. These machines are very expensive and down time is extremely costly. The chip control grooves in the cutting insert have to produce the correct type of swarf and they must be capable of machining different components which may also involve different workpiece materials. Thus future development is geared to more intricate chipgroove forms which will require good pressing technology to produce them.

Automated insert changing is always under consideration. The method of holding the insert in position on the toolholder plays a vital part in determining the possibilities for automatic indexing and changing of worn inserts. It would be logical to assume that any new tooling designs for automatic indexing will involve inserts which have a specially shaped hole through their centre.

11. Conclusion

The indexable insert is a classic example of the art of producing forms by compressing powders in shaped dies with profiled punches. Many of these forms can only be produced by a moulding technique as opposed to some form of machining.

The indexable insert slashed machining costs when it became the accepted way of cutting. It then became the catalyst and the vehicle in the development of hard material coatings. Today this combination gives three- to five- fold improvements in cutting edge life from those twenty years ago. Of even greater importance is the ability of the coated inserts to cut at speeds at least double those of uncoated inserts.

The indexable insert has also played a large part in influencing the design of CNC machines, machining centres and flexible machining systems. As a result, productivity of machined parts has increased well beyond what would have been thought possible when the early developments were taking place.

12. References

1. W. Schedler, Hartmetall fuer den praktiker, 1988, 1.2.1, p.4.

2. ISO 1832-1977, Indexable inserts for cutting tools.

3. W. Schedler, Hartmetall fuer den praktiker, 1988, 3.4.1, p.92-95.

4. ISO 4499, Determination of Microstructure.

5. ISO 4505, Determination of Porosity and Free Carbon.

6. ISO 3369, Measurement of Density.

7. ISO 3326, Measurement of Coercive Force.

8. ISO 3878, Measurement of Vickers Hardness.

9. W. Schintlmeister, O. Pacher and T. Raine, Wear 48, 1978, p.251-266.

10. W. Schedler, Hartmetall fuer den praktiker, 1988, 8.1.3.4, p.319-324

Case Study 5
The Production of Molybdenum Rods for use as Electrodes in Electric Glass-Melting Furnaces

R.G.R. SELLORS AND J.G. HEYES

Plansee Metals Ltd, Unit 1, Herschel Ind, Centre, 20 Church St, Slough Bucks SL1 1PT, U.K.

1. The Requirement

The bulk melting of glass, using furnaces with rod electrodes to pass electric current through the molten charge, is now a standard technique.

While electric melting has many economic and technical advantages, severe operating conditions are imposed upon the rod electrodes which should be manufactured from a material having low reactivity with molten glass to avoid unwanted erosion of the electrode or coloration of the glass. Other essential properties are a high melting point, high electrical and thermal conductivities, resistance to thermal shock, a high hot strength and resistance to creep to avoid breakage or distortion in service.

The refractory metal molybdenum, produced by either powder metallurgy or by arc-melting possesses this unique combination of properties and is the most commonly-used electrode material for the electric melting of most types of glass; the important exception being crystal glass.

2. Properties of Molybdenum and its Application as an Electrode in Electric Glass—Melting Furnaces

If so-called refractory metals are arbitrarily classed as those transition group metals melting above 2000°C, there are only four with major commercial applications in the elemental form, i.e. molybdenum, tungsten, tantalum and niobium. Of these, owing to its combination of favourable properties and relatively lower cost, molybdenum is the most widely used. The other naturally-occurring refractory metals hafnium, rhenium, osmium, iridium, and ruthenium are rare and have only limited commercial applications.

2.1 Physical and Mechanical Properties of Molybdenum

Molybdenum is a light grey metal with a body-centred cubic crystal lattice and an interesting combination of physical and mechanical properties, the most significant of which are summarized in Tables 1 and 2 respectively.

The relatively high density of 10.2 gm/cm³ means that handling large glass-melting electrodes during installation or replacement in a furnace can be strenuous. For other applications, eg in the aerospace industry, care is required in component design to keep weight to a minimum.

The high melting point of 2617°C allows molybdenum to be used not only for key components in glass-melting furnaces but also for heating elements, heat radiation shields and charge trays in high-temperature vacuum or hydrogen furnaces.

Mechanically-worked, pure molybdenum begins to recrystallise at about 900°C while above 1500°C spontaneous grain-growth occurs. This results in a marked reduction in strength and hardness.

Table 1 Physical properties of molybdenum

Property	Unit	Test	Value for Mo
Density	g/cm^3	20°C	10.2
Melting point	K °C	– –	2890 2617
Temperature of oxidation onset in air	K °C	– –	573 300
Vapour pressure	Pa	1500°C 1750°C 2000°C 2400°C	2.5×10^{-7} 5.5×10^{-5} 3.2×10^{-3} 5.0×10^{-1}
Evaporation rate	mg/cm^{2}h	1300°C 1500°C 2000°C 2300°C	2.5×10^{-7} 8.0×10^{-5} 1.0 40.0
Ductile-brittle transition temperature	K °C	– –	293–423 20–150
Linear thermal expansion coefficient	10^{-6}/K	20°C 20–1000°C 20–1500°C	5.3 5.8 6.7
Specific heat	J/gK	20°C 1000°C 1500°C 2000°C	0.25 0.31 0.35 0.44
Thermal conductivity	W/cmK	20°C 1000°C 1500°C	1.42 1.05 0.88
Electrical resistivity	μΩcm	20°C 1000°C 1500°C 2000°C	5.2 27 43 60
Surface load capacity	W/cm^2	below 1800°C 10–20 above 1800°C 20–40	
Recrystallisation temperature	K	start/end: Annealing time = 1 hour	1173/1473 900/1200

Moreover, because the ductile - brittle transition temperature is sharply reduced, recrystallised and coarse-grained molybdenum is brittle at ambient temperature. This can present handling problems in process applications, e.g. furnace charge trays, in which molybdenum is operated at high temperatures but is regularly reduced to room temperature to unload and reload. Great care is required to avoid breaking the recrystallised molybdenum component. However, recrystallisation is not a problem where molybdenum is maintained at a high temperature in a continuous process application such as a glass-melting electrode or a quartz-melting crucible. In such applications, the molybdenum components are only allowed to cool at the end of a melting campaign and are normally destroyed as the melt solidifies.

Even at high temperatures molybdenum has a low rate of evaporation and an outstanding resistance to corrosion and erosion by a wide range of aggressive materials, including molten-glass. However, it has the disadvantage of oxidising in air at temperatures above 300°C. In practice, to avoid heavy oxidation, molybdenum should never be exposed to air or other oxidising atmospheres at temperatures above 400°C. At temperatures up to 600°C layers of molybdenum dioxide (MoO_2) are formed but, above that temperature, volatile molybdenum trioxide (MoO_3) is stable. At 800°C catastrophic oxidation occurs with the formation of clouds of molybdenum trioxide smoke. Nevertheless, molybdenum electrodes can be used to melt glass for long periods by locating the hot forward section below the surface of the protective molten glass within the furnace while the rear section, exposed to air outside the furnace, is water-cooled.

In other high-temperature applications molybdenum must always be used under a vacuum or be protected with hydrogen, nitrogen, inert gases or mixtures of these gases.

Some molybdenum components used for glass-fibre production or for stirring molten glass require expensive platinum cladding to give complete protection from oxidation. Although no oxidation-resistant alloy of molybdenum has yet been developed, successful protection has been achieved for relatively short periods by applying coatings of iron/chromium/aluminium alloys or molybdenum disilicide ($MoSi_2$) to molybdenum.

The high electrical and thermal conductivities of molybdenum are important in the glass-melting electrode application. In other applications, in which molybdenum is suddenly exposed to high temperature or thermally cycled, the combination of high thermal conductivity and low coefficient of thermal expansion gives exceptional resistance to thermal shock and thermal fatigue. The low coefficient of thermal expansion, compatible with that of alumina (Al_2O_3) also makes molybdenum an ideal heat-sink material for a range of high-power electronic devices.

Molybdenum has a tensile strength of 440-590 N/mm² at room temperature but this diminishes to about 100 N/mm² at 1200°C and to only about 20 N/mm² at 1800°C. Furthermore, as a glass-melting electrode, molybdenum is exposed to high temperatures for many months so that resistance to creep becomes a key factor. Although data are limited, it is clear that the creep resistance of molybdenum is highly sensitive to grain size and reduces significantly at higher temperatures. Results of tests at 1750°C by Eck [1], with small, horizontal molybdenum rods clamped at one end, show that rapid deflection by creep occurs with a small grain size (2000 grains/mm²) at a stress as low as 3.25 N/mm² and with a larger grain size (100 grains/mm²) at a stress of 14.80 N/mm².

However, although glass-melting electrodes may be expected to operate at 1200-1800°C, the most common temperature range for molten glass is 1400-1500°C at which the hot strength and creep resistance of molybdenum are acceptable in service. In more extreme applications such as quartz-melting crucibles operating at 2000°C or above, hot strength and creep can become important factors determining service life.

In the form of rod, molybdenum is not a difficult metal to machine (Section 3.6), while as sheet it has sufficient ductility above the ductile-brittle transition temperature to allow fabrication by guillotining, bending and deep-drawing.

Provided its readiness to oxidise is countered by appropriate furnace design and operating technique, molybdenum has an ideal combination of physical and mechanical properties for use, in rod form, as a glass-melting electrode. This application represents one of the most important markets for molybdenum (Section 2.4); currently accounting for approximately 10% of the world consumption of the pure metal.

Molybdenum rods also have other applications in the glass and the related quartz and ceramic industries, e.g:

1. Electrodes in ceramic-melting furnaces.

2. Thermocouple sheaths, stirrers and gas bubblers in glass-melting furnaces.

3. Mandrels for quartz tube production.

There are also applications in these industries for molybdenum produced in forms other than rod e.g:

- glass-melting or ceramic-melting electrodes in the form of heavy plates.

- quartz-melting crucibles either fabricated from sheet or isostatically pressed and sintered.

- glassware moulds machined from forged blanks.

- nozzle and die assemblies machined from heavy plate or forged blanks for glass or quartz tube production.

- glass delivery channels fabricated from sheet.

In glass-melting applications it is normal to use pure molybdenum for components in contact with the molten glass. Although the dispersion-hardened molybdenum alloy TZM (Mo, 0.5 Ti, 0.08 Zr, 0.01-0.04 C) exhibits even greater hot strength and resistance to recrystallisation, the carbon unfortunately reduces certain glass constituents and causes undesirable bubble formation. The HD grade of molybdenum, doped with small amounts of potassium silicate and intensely worked, is highly creep-resistant but has only limited applications in the glass industry because the required heavy mechanical working can only be imparted to sheet, rod or wire up to 3 mm thickness or diameter.

While the use of molybdenum in the glass industry is important, especially as a glass-melting electrode, the properties and manufacturing steps described in this chapter are also generally applicable to molybdenum used in the production of a wide range of components for other industries. In particular, key applications for molybdenum rod, sheet, wire or fabricated parts occur in the lighting, electronics, special furnace, aerospace, defence, nuclear, automotive and chemical engineering industries.

2.2 Capabilities and Limitations of Molybdenum as a Glass-melting Electrode

Although glass-melting furnaces using iron or graphite electrodes to pass electric current through the charge date from the 1930s, molybdenum electrodes were first used about forty years ago.

With its outstanding combination of physical and mechanical properties (Section 2.1, Tables 1 and 2), chemical resistance to most constituents of molten glass, relatively low cost and ease of machining (Section 3.6) molybdenum has proved to be ideally suitable for use as an electrode when melting a wide range of glasses including soda lime, borosilicate, opal and neutral glasses. Only lead oxide (PbO) and the refining agents arsenic oxide (As_2O_3) and antimony oxide (Sb_2O_3) attack molybdenum strongly. Molten "crystal" glasses which contain lead oxide therefore attack molybdenum electrodes resulting in unnacceptable colouration of the glass by molybdenum trioxide (MoO_3). When such crystal glasses are melted electrically, tin oxide (SnO_2) is, despite higher cost, preferred as the electrode material owing to its high resistance to oxidation by the melt. This is especially important when producing high-quality decorative ware. However, unlike molybdenum

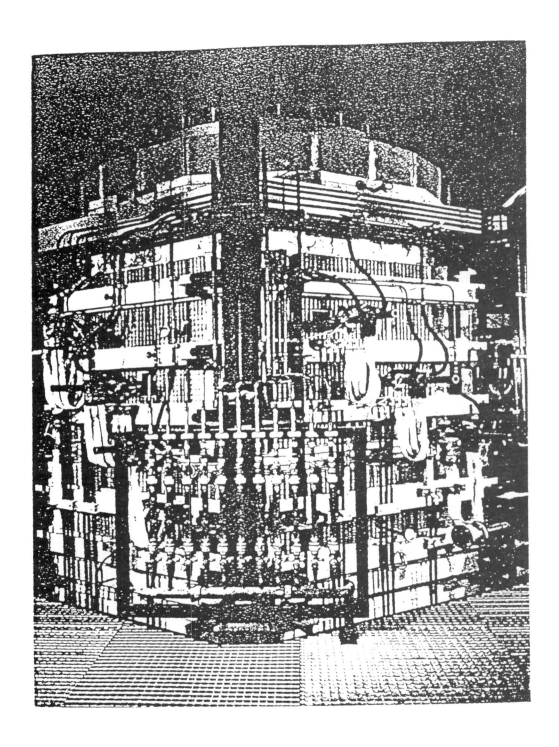

Figure 1. All-electric glass-melting furnace with molybdenum electrodes. (By courtesy Nikolaus Sorg GmbH and Co., KG.)

electrodes which are resistant to thermal shock, tin oxide electrodes must be installed cold and warmed up slowly with the refractory structure of the furnace.

While most molybdenum glass-melting electrodes are produced from rod, heavy plates can also be used. However, the latter can only be installed in a cold furnace and cannot be replaced or supplemented during a glass-melting campaign. Design considerations also limit plate electrodes to smaller furnaces.

A typical modern all-electric glass-melting furnace with molybdenum electrodes is illustrated in Fig. 1. Details of the installation of molybdenum rod electrodes through the furnace wall are shown in Figs. 2 and 3.

Molybdenum electrodes are normally installed in a furnace once the glass is molten and are used either as the sole source of heating in so-called "cold top" in all-electric furnaces or as "boosters" in fossil fuel furnaces. In the latter application, electrical power is used to replace some oil or gas heating, to improve the quality of the glass or to increase the output of an existing furnace. As illustrated in Figs. 2 and 3, the molybdenum electrodes are usually installed through water-cooled stainless steel holders either horizontally through the refractory walls (sidewall entry) or vertically through the bottom of a furnace (bottom entry). Some designs even use a mixture of both horizontal and vertical electrodes. Another common application is the electric heating of a furnace forehearth from which molten glass is extracted for moulding into final products. So far, the application of a surface coating to molybdenum (Section 2.1) has only been used successfully on electrodes used in forehearths.

Such a coating allows initial heating in air at temperatures up to 1200°C so that electrodes can be fully installed before a new forehearth begins operation. Although the coating is lost early in the glass-melting campaign, the slight colouring of the glass as the coating deteriorates can normally be tolerated.

Molten glass in holding furnaces may also be maintained at constant temperature electrically. The various electric melting techniques are becoming increasingly common in countries where the electricity supply is both reliable and favourably priced, or where the reduction of pollution is a major consideration (Section 2.3).

2.2.1 Standard Forms of Molybdenum Glass-melting Electrodes

The dimensions, tolerances, threads and weights of typical molybdenum glass-melting electrodes are summarised in Fig. 4. Electrode "burn off" may be reduced by using electrodes of larger diameter which allow lower current densities to be employed. However, electrodes with the standard smaller diameters of 31.75mm and 50.8mm are the most commonly used because molybdenum has a density of 10.2 gm/cm^3 and electrodes of larger diameter are heavy and unwieldy to instal or replace, especially in mid-campaign. The weakest part of an electrode is the screwed joint, especially when mounted horizontally, owing to stresses from the flow of glass and the density difference between molybdenum and glass.

2.3 Advantages of Melting Glass in an Electric Furnace

The main advantages claimed [3] for electric glass-melting furnaces compared with furnaces fired by gas or oil are as follows:

1. Ease of control.

2. Greater refining capability and homogeneity leading to improved glass quality.

3. More uniform temperature distribution within the molten glass.

4. Increased glass output from a more efficient release of energy directly into the body of molten glass, rather than to the surrounding furnace.

5. Cheaper, smaller furnace using less refractory brick for a given glass output and requiring less maintenance.

Table 2 Typical mechanical properties of forged molybdenum glass-melting electrodes

Forged Mo electrode diameter (mm)		20–32	32–50	50–102
UTS (N/mm²)	20°C	590 min	490 min	440 min
	1200°C 1500°C 1800°C	Approx. 100 Approx. 60 Approx. 20		
Elongation (%)	20°C	20 min	15 min	10 min
Vickers hardness No (HV10)	20°C	215–250	210 min	210 min
Modulus of elasticity (kN/mm²)	20°C 1000°C 1400°C 1500°C	320 270 250 240		

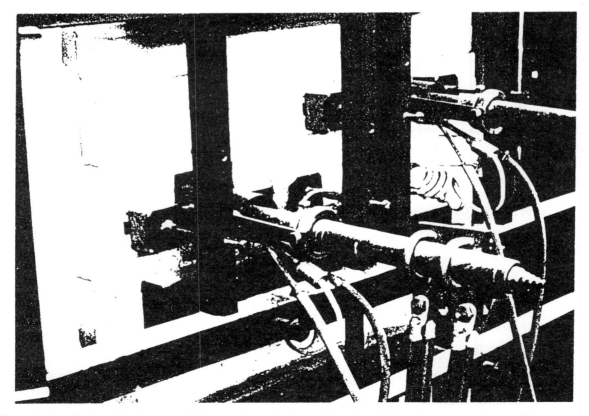

Figure 2. Installation of horizontal molybdenum electrodes through the sidewall of a glass-melting furnace.(By courtesy King, Taudevin and Gregson Ltd.)

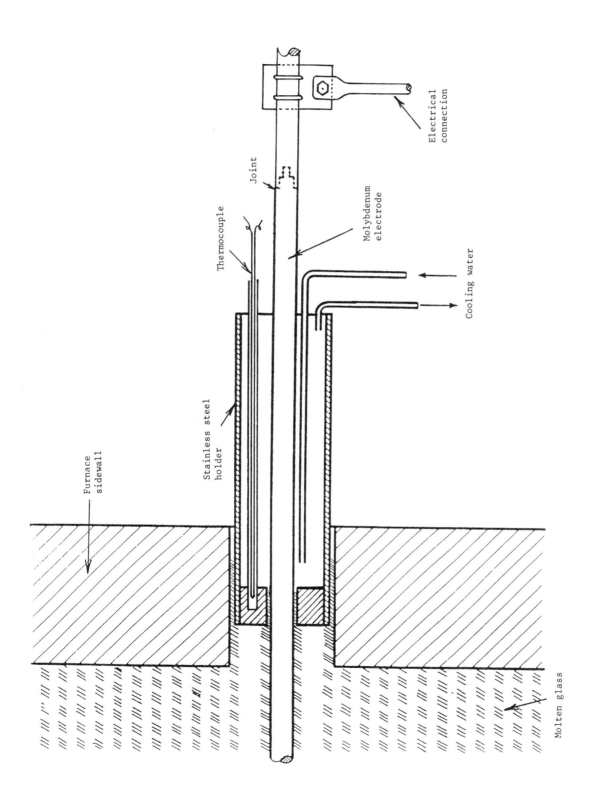

Figure 3. Schematic diagram showing design details of a horizontally-mounted molybdenum glass-melting electrode.

Lower atmospheric pollution. Particulate emissions are reduced because "carry over" is avoided owing to the absence of flames. Gaseous emissions are reduced because combustion products are reduced in "boosted" furnaces or even eliminated in all-electric "cold-top" furnaces. From both electric and fossil-fuel furnaces about equal quantities of non-toxic gases such as carbon dioxide, oxygen and water vapour are driven off from the "batch" of unmelted raw materials.

However, emissions of toxic, volatile components such as boron, lead, selenium and arsenic are reduced. Such volatiles are trapped in the cool "batch" and are safely refluxed down into the molten glass; resulting also in reduced "batch" costs.

2.4 Size of the World-wide Market for Molybdenum and for Molybdenum Glass-melting Electrodes

Small quantities of molybdenum, in the form of various compounds, are used as lubricants, catalysts, pigments or analytical reagents. However, most of the molybdenum mined is ultimately consumed, as ferro-molybdenum, in the manufacture of steel and other alloys to improve their mechanical properties or corrosion produced world-wide per year in recent years, only about 4% has been used as pure molybdenum or in molybdenum-based alloy [3]. Nevertheless, the applications of molybdenum in the latter forms are strategically important and arise from the outstanding combination of physical and mechanical properties summarised in Tables 1 and 2 respectively.

The current annual world-wide demand from glass manufacturers for molybdenum rod electrodes is approximately 360 tonnes and increasing. This represents about 10% of world output of elemental molybdenum or its alloys. Prior to coating or machining threads on the ends of the electrodes the current delivered price is approximately £18 000 - £25 000 per tonne (1990 prices).

3. Manufacture of Molybdenum Glass-melting Electrodes by the Powder Metallurgy Route

Figure 5 illustrates, in the form of a flow-diagram, the principle stages in the manufacture of molybdenum rods from powder and also the extensive in-process quality controls that must be applied in a modern plant.

The manufacture of molybdenum and the other refractory metals includes several energy-intensive operations. In particular, electrical power is required for the production of large volumes of hydrogen for use as a reducing and protective atmosphere for the furnaces employed in the reduction, sintering, reheating and annealing operations.

Manufacturing plant is, therefore, ideally sited where cheap and reliable electric power is available.

The progressive increase in density of molybdenum as manufacture proceeds from loose powder through the stages of pressing, sintering and forging to the fully-worked product is illustrated in Fig. 6.

3.1 Occurrence and Recovery of Molybdenum

Elemental molybdenum does not occur freely in nature and the most important source is the mineral molybdenite (MoS_2). The largest deposits of molybdenum ore are located in Alaska, Arizona, Colorado, and New Mexico in the USA and in the Canadian province of British Columbia. Molybdenite also arises as a by-product from copper ores mined in Chile.

The ores are readily available but contain only about 0.5% molybdenite which is recovered by crushing, grinding and flotation techniques. The resulting concentrate is roasted in excess air at about 600°C to oxidise the molybdenite to the so-called technical grade of molybdenum trioxide.

For the production of molybdenum metal an even purer grade of molybdenum trioxide is required as a raw material and this is achieved by sublimation of the technical oxide or via the thermal decomposition of ammonium molybdate. The purity of the final product has improved markedly in recent years and contains above 99.5% molybdenum trioxide.

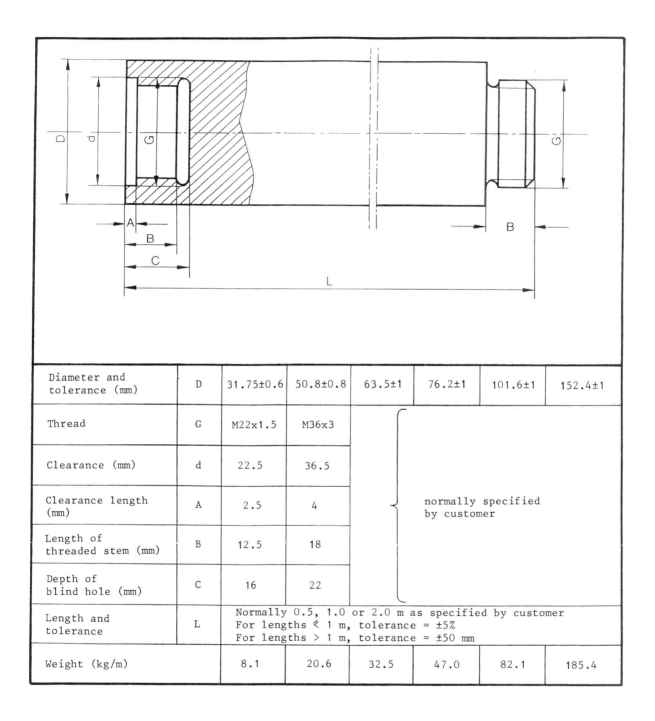

Diameter and tolerance (mm)	D	31.75±0.6	50.8±0.8	63.5±1	76.2±1	101.6±1	152.4±1
Thread	G	M22x1.5	M36x3				
Clearance (mm)	d	22.5	36.5				
Clearance length (mm)	A	2.5	4		normally specified by customer		
Length of threaded stem (mm)	B	12.5	18				
Depth of blind hole (mm)	C	16	22				
Length and tolerance	L	Normally 0.5, 1.0 or 2.0 m as specified by customer For lengths ⩽ 1 m, tolerance = ±5% For lengths > 1 m, tolerance = ±50 mm					
Weight (kg/m)		8.1	20.6	32.5	47.0	82.1	185.4

Figure 4. Dimensions, tolerances threads and weights of typical molybdenum glass-melting electrodes.

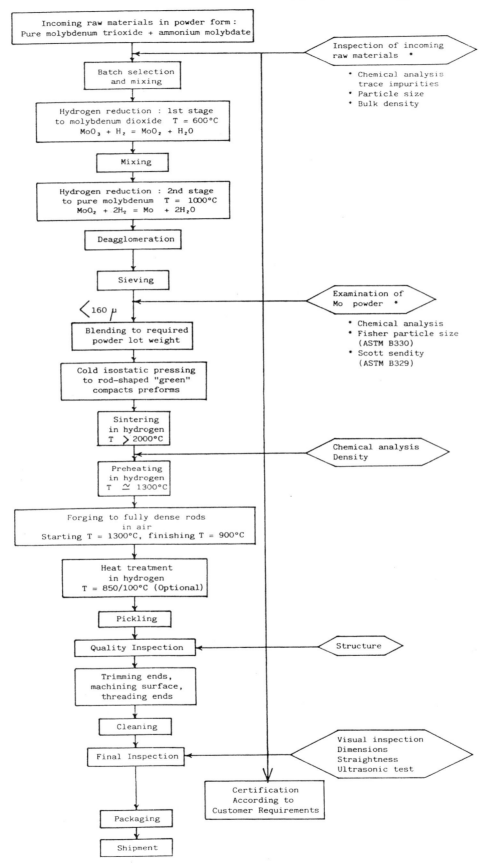

Figure 5. Flow-diagram of the production of molybdenum rods by the powder metallurgy route.

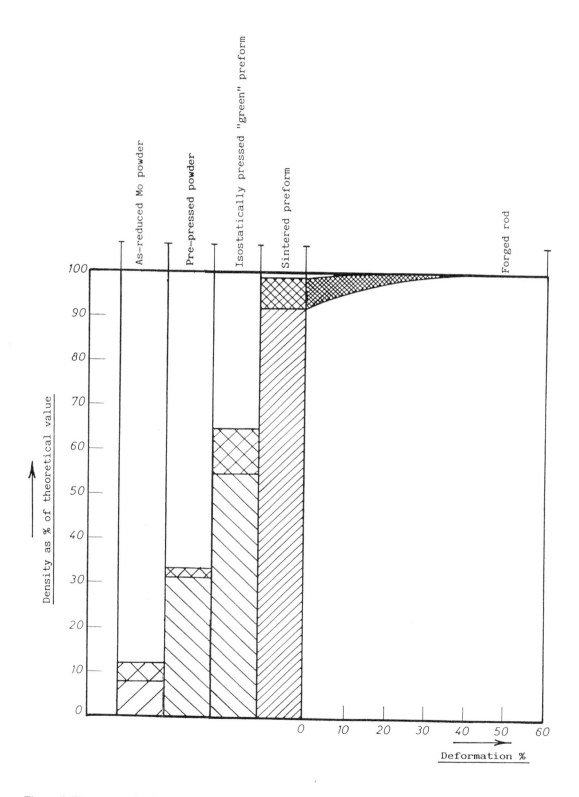

Figure 6. The progressive increase in density of molybdenum through the stages of manufacture from powder to rod. (After Eck[7].)

3.2 Competitive Processes for the Production of Molybdenum

Although molybdenum can be manufactured by the vacuum arc melting of semi-sintered bars into water-cooled moulds, powder metallurgy remains the preferred route. It has been estimated [1] that the powder metallurgy route is used to manufacture more than two thirds of the annual world requirement of molybdenum, either as semi-finished or fabricated products. This is because the powder route has a greater yield of usable products and a reduced inclination to preferred orientation. Also the finer grain size in the powder product facilitates subsequent hot working by extrusion, forging, rolling, swaging or drawing.

The powder metallurgy route is also more suitable for the preparation of molybdenum alloys with a uniform distribution of alloy additions or dopants and for the production of very large parts; possibly weighing up to 5000 kg.

3.3 Production of Molybdenum Powder

Owing to its high melting-point, molybdenum cannot be atomised to powder and, although other methods of manufacturing molybdenum powder have been reported [6], the most common method remains the reduction of molybdenum trioxide by hydrogen.

In the reduction plant the starting materials for the production of molybdenum powder are, typically, high-purity molybdenum trioxide and ammonium molybdate powder from various sources (Fig. 5). In a modern plant the raw materials are blended from incoming batches which have been selected by computer according to their analyses. Hydrogen reduction follows in two stages. Firstly, molybdenum trioxide is reduced to dioxide at about 600°C. The second stage, at about 1000°C reduces the dioxide to pure molybdenum powder. The hydrogen-reduction stages are carried out, in scrupulously clean conditions, in tube furnaces through which TZM boats containing the oxides are pushed sufficiently slowly to ensure complete reduction. The reduced powder is then delagglomerated and mechanically sieved. The oxygen level of the powder is below 0.05% but, to minimise the risk of airborne contamination, the powder should be transported throughout the reduction process within a virtually closed system. In a typical molybdenum powder (Fig. 7) a final guaranteed purity of at least 99.5% molybdenum should be achieved with very low values of trace elements. Table 3 shows both the guaranteed and typical composition of a molybdenum powder produced in a modern hydrogenreduction plant.

3.4 Pressing and Sintering Molybdenum Preforms

To guarantee consistent quality of the final products, molybdenum powder lots of about 3 tonnes should be blended and analysed for trace impurities and particle size distribution before cold compaction. At this stage the loose powder density is between 8 and 12% of the theoretical value for molybdenum (Fig. 6). The most common technique for consolidating powder into a "green" compact or preform is by linear pressing in a rigid metal die, using a hydraulic or mechanical press. However, this technique is unsuitable for pressing long, rod-shaped preforms of circular cross-section and cold isostatic pressing is used instead. The molybdenum powder is loaded into cylindrical moulds in the form of rubber or polyurethane bags supported by a perforated sheet metal former as shown in Fig. 8. Often vibration or tamping is used to increase the density of the powder to 31-33% of the theoretical value for molybdenum (Fig. 6). The moulds are sealed and placed in a large pressure vessel which is then pressurised by means of water containing a corrosion inhibitor. The mould is subjected to a three-dimensional pressure of up to 3000 bars and the contained powder is consolidated to give a "green" preform similar in shape to that of the original mould but smaller in size. When the vessel is de-pressurised, the flexible mould returns to its original dimensions and releases itself from the compact which is then readily removed after the pressure vessel has been opened. A modern, large cold isostatic press is illustrated in Fig. 9.

The weight and size of an isostatically-pressed compact are only limited by the internal dimensions of the pressure vessel and the room occupied by moulds, supports and handling equipment. An isostatic press may be used to form large, single compacts which, in the case of molybdenum, could weigh up to 5000 kg at present.

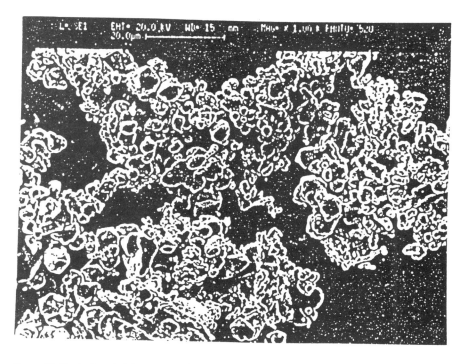

Figure 7. Typical molybdenum powder used in the manufacture of glass-melting electrodes.

Figure 9. Typical "wet-bag" isostatic press for compacting several "green" rod preforms per cycle from molybdenum powder.

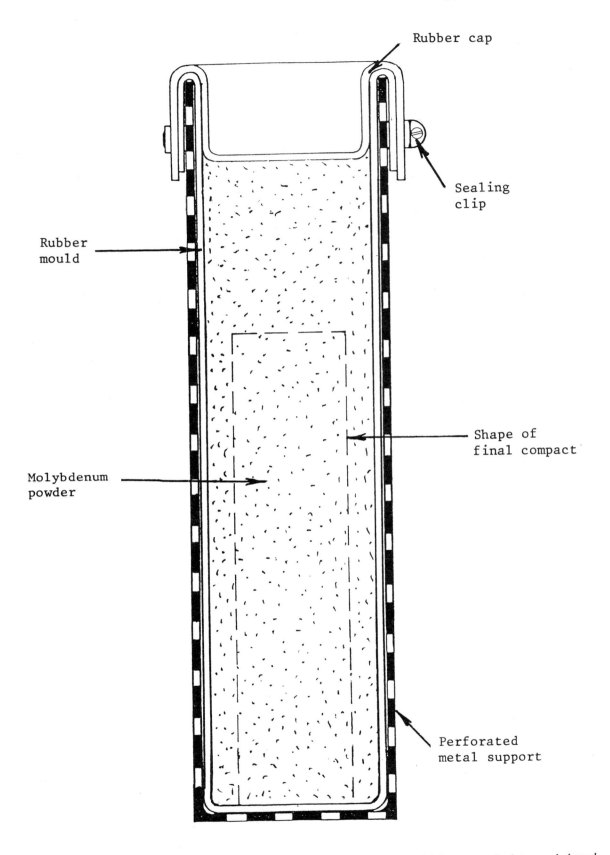

Rubber cap

Sealing
clip

Rubber
mould

Shape of
final compact

Molybdenum
powder

Perforated
metal support

Figure 8. Schematic diagram of a mould and support for the cold isostatic pressing of molybdenum powder into a rod-shaped
"green" preform.

Table 3 *Chemical analysis of a representative molybdenum rod produced by the Powder Metallurgy route*

Element	Guaranteed analysis	Typical analysis
Mo	min 99.95%	99.97%
	max (µg/g)	(µg/g)
Ag	5	less than 5
Al	20	less than 10
As	5	less than 1
Ba	10	less than 2
C	30	15
Ca	20	5
Cd	5	less than 1
Co	30	5
Cr	20	less than 10
Cu	20	5
Fe	100	50
H	5	less than 1
K	10	less than 5
Mg	10	less than 5
Mn	5	less than 5
N	10	less than 5
Na	10	less than 5
Nb	5	less than 5
Ni	10	less than 5
O	50	20
P	20	less than 5
Pb	10	less than 5
S	20	less than 5
Si	30	5
Ta	10	less than 5
Ti	10	less than 5
W	300	100
Zn	10	less than 5
Zr	5	less than 5

Alternatively, acceptable production rates and costs may be achieved for smaller compacts, such as preforms for molybdenum glass-melting electrodes, by pressing several moulds in a single cycle.

Apart from overcoming the shape limitations of linear pressing, cold isostatic pressing has the added advantage of producing compacts of highly-uniform density while requiring no binder or die lubricant. The "green" compact density of molybdenum is typically 60-65% of the theoretical full density (Fig. 6) and the "green" strength is adequate for normal handling, despite the lack of binder. Even machining and cutting may be undertaken without the need for pre-sintering. The absence of binder and lubricant also avoids complications with "burn off" in the subsequent sintering process.

To impart the higher strength and density necessary for subsequent forging, the rod preforms are next sintered in hydrogen at a temperature of 2000-2200°C within a 12 hour cycle. The sintering operation is the most critical for controlling the quality and service performance of the final molybdenum product. The levels of impurities, the grain size and the pore size are controlled to give an optimum sinter density between 93 and 98% of the theoretical value (Fig. 6).

"Green" compacts, including isostatically-pressed glass electrode preforms, are shown awaiting processing in a large sintering furnace in Fig. 10.

3.5 Forging Molybdenum Rods

Owing to its high-temperature strength, molybdenum requires robust presses and handling equipment for forging. Standard molybdenum glass-melting electrodes measuring up to 101.6mm final diameter (Fig. 4), are forged in air from sintered preforms, as illustrated in Fig. 11. Beginning at 1300°C forging progresses and the working temperature reduces until full density is reached (Fig. 6) after a deformation of 60-70%. Programmed forging and reheating steps ensure a high level of uniformity and optimum mechanical properties throughout the entire length of each molybdenum electrode. In service the optimised properties give a low rate of "burn off" and a high resistance to bending or fracture.

Standard electrodes of 152.4mm diameter and above cannot be sufficiently worked by forging and are usually extruded instead.

During forging or extrusion in air, molybdenum gives off dense clouds of molybdenum trioxide which must be collected in an efficient extraction system.

3.6 Finishing Forged Molybdenum Glass-melting Electrodes

Heavily oxidised molybdenum electrodes can be cleaned by the standard method of immersion in molten caustic soda containing a small amount of sodium nitrite at a temperature of 400-450°C. Parts to be cleaned must always be dry to avoid dangerous sputtering. After pickling, the parts should be cooled and any adhering melt residues removed by rinsing in hot water, dipping in dilute hydrochloric acid and finally in hot water.

Molybdenum is not a difficult metal to machine and Table 4 summarises the recommended conditions for drilling, turning, parting, threading, milling and grinding.

Invariably the ends of heavily-forged rod must be parted off. Although smaller molybdenum electrodes (e.g. 31.75mm diameter) may be supplied with a smooth, as-forged and cleaned surface, electrodes of larger diameters usually require a turned surface to achieve acceptable tolerances and surface finish.

For ease of subsequent replacement (Section 4), molybdenum electrodes are usually supplied with a male thread machined at one end and a female thread at the other (Fig. 4). Heavy thermocouple sheaths or bubbler tubes for glass furnaces can also be machined from molybdenum rods by deep gun-drilling.

With suitable ventilation, components are usually ultrasonically cleaned in trichlorethylene or similar solvent.

Figure 10. Isostatically-pressed molybdenum "green" rod preforms awaiting sintering.

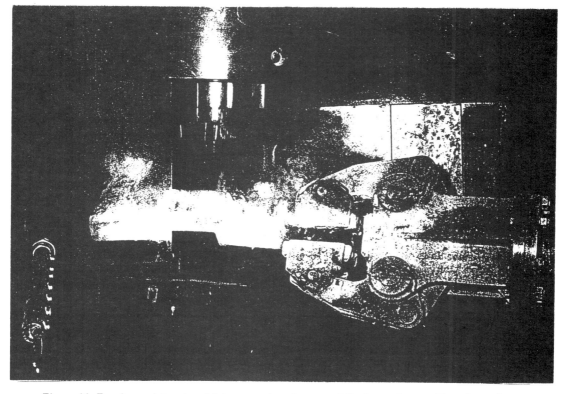

Figure 11. Forging a sintered molybdenum rod preform to a fully dense glass-melting electrode.

Table 4 Recommended conditions for machining molybdenum

DRILLING	THREADING

(a) <u>For diameter of drill up to 18mm</u>
    <u>High speed steel</u> (if possible with
    internal coolant channel)
    Feed: 0.05-0.1mm/rev
    Cutting speed: 10-15m/min
 	
(b) <u>For diameter of drill above 18mm</u>
(b) <u>Cemented carbide</u>
    Feed:
    for 18-29mm dia: 0.03mm/rev
    for 30-44mm dia: 0.05mm/rev
    for 45-53mm dia: 0.08mm/rev
    Cutting speed: 150m/min
 	
<u>Coolant/lubricant</u>
(a) Water-soluble emulsions
(b) Water-soluble emulsions or
    highly-chlorinated hydrocarbon*
Coolant pressure: 1.5 bar
	<u>Cemented carbide</u> (K20)
	    Depth of cut: 0.02-0.05mm/pass
	    Cutting speed: 30m/min
	    (300m/min possible with water-
	    soluble emulsions. A special
	    coolant supply from above and
	    below essential. Pressure
	    approx. 1.5 bar, flow rate
	    15 litres/min.)
	
	<u>Coolant/lubricant</u>
	    Highly-chlorinated hydrocarbon*
	    — continuous flood
	    Water-soluble emulsions —
	    special supply

TURNING	MILLING

<u>Cemented carbide</u> (High rake geometry K10)
    Feed: 0.1-0.3mm/rev for roughing
        or 0.03-0.1mm/rev for finishing
    Cutting speed: 100-140m/min
 	
<u>Coolant/lubricant</u>
    Water-soluble emulsions
	(a) <u>High speed steel</u>
	    Feed per tooth: 0.02-0.05mm
	    Cutting speed: 20-25m/min
	(b) <u>Cemented carbide</u> (K10)
	    Feed per tooth: 0.02-0.05mm
	    Cutting speed: 60-80m/min
	<u>Coolant/lubricant</u>
	(a) Water-soluble emulsions or
	    highly-chlorinated hydrocarbon*
	(b) Water-soluble emulsions. (If
	    coolant flow not possible, at
	    least use mist cooling)

PARTING	GRINDING

<u>Cemented carbide</u> (High rake geometry K10)
    Feed: 0.03mm/rev
    Cutting speed: 50m/min constant
 	
<u>Coolant/lubricant</u>
    Water-soluble emulsions —
    jet directly into groove
	Abrasive silicon carbide, hardness
	hardness H, I, J and K,
	particle size 60-120, with average
	structure and ceramic binder
	    Infeed: max 0.02mm
	    Grinding speed: 1500-1800m/min
	<u>Coolant/lubricant</u>
	    Water-soluble emulsions

Standards: Cemented carbide ISO K10 (K20 for threading); High speed steel
          Nr 1.3207: DIN 17007, AISI: TI, B.S.: BT 42

* When using highly-chlorinated hydrocarbons such as trichlorethylene or
  carbon tetrachloride, safety regulations must be observed!

3.7 Quality Control

To ensure consistency, rigorous quality controls are applied at all key stages of the manufacture of molybdenum electrodes as indicated in Fig.5. These controls include chemical analyses of the incoming raw materials, the reduced powder and the sintered preforms. The microstructures of forged electrodes are examined and, if specified by the end-user, physical or mechanical properties are measured and certified. At final inspection, prior to despatch, the electrodes are visually examined and dimensions and straightness inspected while the absence of cracking is verified by ultrasonic tests (Fig. 12). Apart from its use as a glass-melting electrode, molybdenum has many other critical applications in high-technology industries. Therefore, it is essential that any plant manufacturing molybdenum should have quality control procedures that at least meet the British Standard BS 5750 or its equivalent.

4. Performance of Molybdenum Glass-melting Electrodes in Service

While the temperature of a typical glass melt is maintained at about 1400-1500°C, the surface temperature of molybdenum electrodes under power will be considerably higher. Nevertheless, with its unique combination of physical and mechanical properties (Section 2.1, Tables 1 and 2) molybdenum performs economically as a glass-melting electrode. In particular, it has adequate hot strength and resistance to creep with a low rate of wear which varies from 20-70 mm/month per electrode depending upon the operating temperature, the glass composition, the refining agents used and the degree of erosion by the flow of glass through the furnace. Initially, rod-shaped electrodes wear to a point followed by a progressive decrease in length.

However, the only maintenance required is (a) advancing or replacing the electrodes to compensate for wear and (b) servicing the water-cooling system for the electrode holders (Fig. 3).

The installation or replacement of molybdenum electrodes part-way through a glass-melting campaign is skilled work, often undertaken by companies specialising in the design and construction of glass furnaces. Because electrodes are usually provided with a female thread at one end and a male thread at the other, (Fig. 4) a worn electrode may be extended into the glass furnace by screwing a new one on to the rear end and pushing through the water-cooled holder.

Molybdenum has sufficient thermal shock resistance to withstand such treatment. This procedure requires care but it allows a glass-melting campaign to continue uninterrupted for a period of two or three years.

5. Future Market and Technological Developments

As demands for higher quality glass and reduced environmental pollution increase, it is anticipated that the market for molybdenum electrodes will continue to increase; particularly in countries where the supply of electrical power is reliable and cheap.

Improvements in forging equipment and practice should eventually permit longer molybdenum electrodes to be produced while maintaining acceptable straightness, tolerances and surface finish. In some furnace designs longer electrodes would require fewer screwed joints and hence would reduce the risk of breakage in service, especially when mounted horizontally.

Molybdenum is likely to find other applications in glass melting as higher temperature processes are developed. For example, metal-lined furnaces and delivery tubes are being introduced in place of ceramic units. The main drawback of molybdenum remains its lack of resistance to oxidation, especially above 600°C. Attempts to develop a protective coating with long-term, reliable adhesion or an oxidation-resistant alloy of molybdenum have met with only limited success. So far, only short-term benefits in the forehearth application have been achieved with molybdenum disilicide or iron/chromium/aluminium coatings. However, if reliable, oxidation-resistant coatings or molybdenum alloys could be developed, the versatility of molybdenum glass-melting electrodes would be improved and there would also be important applications outside the glass industry, e.g. in gas turbines.

Figure 12. Ultrasonically testing finished molybdenum glass-melting electrodes.

In advanced glass-melting furnaces where corrosion resistance and hot strength are required at temperatures of 2000°C and above, molybdenum can be replaced, although at far higher cost, by tungsten or molybdenum-tungsten alloys [3]. However, great care must then be taken to select furnace refractories that can themselves withstand such temperatures.

6. Conclusions

The electric melting of glass has many economic and technical advantages although its use is dependent upon a reliable and cheap source of electrical power.

The refractory metal molybdenum is readily available and, owing to its favourable combination of properties, particularly at high temperatures, is increasingly used as an electrode in electric glass-melting furnaces. Molybdenum electrodes, usually manufactured by the powder metallurgy route, are suitable for melting most types of glass, the important exception being crystal glass containing lead oxide.

Molybdenum would have even wider applications in glass manufacture and other high-temperature applications if its tendency to oxidise in air at higher temperatures could be overcome by the development of an effective long-term coating or oxidation-resistant alloy.

The design and construction of even higher temperature plant for melting, homogenising, transporting and forming glass, quartz and ceramics should increase the market for molybdenum, tungsten and the alloys of these two metals.

7. Acknowledgements

The authors gratefully acknowledge the assistance given by Dr R. Eck, Dr S. Schider, Mr J. Sommer and Dr H. Wurzinger of Metallwerk Plansee GmbH, Reutte, Austria and by Mr E. Booth of King, Taudevin and Gregson Limited of Leigh-on-Sea, UK in the preparation of this chapter.

8. References

1. R. Eck, The State of the Art of Molybdenum Fabrication", Ceramic Engineering and Science Proceedings 6 (3-4), 154-166, 1985.

2. S. Schider, "Hochschmelzende Metalle in der Glastechnologie", Sprechsaal 121 (5), 349-353, 1988.

3. S. Schider, "Refractory Metals : Applications in the Glass and Ceramics Industries", Glass 65 (5), 185-187, 1988.

4. King, Taudevin and Gregson Ltd, "Cold Top Electric Furnaces", Glass 65 (5), 180, 1988.

5. Niklolaus Sorg GmbH and Co. KG, "Electric Boosting A to Z" Glass 65 (5), 183-185, 1988.

6. A.J. Aller, "PM Refractory Metals and Alloys : Part 1- Manufacture", Refractory and Hard Metals, March 1984, p. 21-29.

7. R. Eck, "Die Technolgie der hochschmelzenden Metalle", in Pulvermetallurgie und Sinterwerkstoffe, ed. F. Benesovsky, Metallwerk Plansee GmbH, 1982, Ch VI, p 76-103.

CASE STUDY 6
Elevated Temperature Alumininium Alloys

A. LAWLEY

Dept. of Materials Engineering, Drexel University, Philadephia PA 19104, U.S.A.

Abstract

Aluminium is an important material in the aerospace industry because of its fabricability, high strength-to-weight ratio and relatively low cost. In many intermediate temperature applications, however, it has been necessary to utilize titanium to achieve required elevated temperature mechanical properties, but at the expense of a penalty in weight and cost. Since future aircraft designs call for still higher exposure temperatures, there is a clear need to develop aluminium alloys capable of long-time service with mechanical property retention at temperatures up to ~500°C; this would provide acceptable design and cost factors for these aircraft. Such alloys could also find application in the automotive industry. Commercial ingot metallurgy age-hardening alloys have a ceiling temperature below 200°C. Established tenets of physical metallurgy dictate that to achieve this goal of 500°C, ultrafine and stable dispersoids must exist, uniformly distributed in the aluminium matrix. It is demonstrated that this form of microstructure can be achieved by powder processing, in particular a combination of rapid solidification and mechanical alloying.

1. Introduction

For many years, high strength aluminium alloys have served as the primary structural material in advanced aircraft. These alloys are easy to fabricate, relatively inexpensive, and exhibit a high strength to weight ratio. Conventional ingot metallurgy aluminium alloys do, however, undergo significant decreases in strength and stiffness with increasing temperature, and this has acted as a major design constraint in limiting aircraft speeds to the Mach 2 Level. Based on existing materials technology, aircraft operation at higher speeds mandates the use of titanium alloys for many structural components with an accompanying penalty in terms of cost and weight. Thus, the need exists for the development of a new series of high performance aluminium alloys, with improved properties and elevated temperature stability [1].

There are several inherent limitations to achieving property and performance goals via ingot metallurgy (IM). In particular, microstructures are relatively coarse and the macroscopic segregation of alloying elements is unavoidable. Such limitations have stimulated research into powder metallurgy (PM) as a processing alternative [2,3]. Of particular interest is the technology of rapid solidification processing of aluminium alloys, since it has been demonstrated that this approach provides enhanced alloying flexibility, and results in refined fine-scale homogeneous microstructures with minimal attendant solute segregation, compared to IM alloys [4-7].

To date several binary and ternary aluminium alloys have been investigated [4,6,14]. The selection of the second and third alloying elements has been based primarily on the following criteria: high liquid solubility in aluminium, a low solid solubility in aluminium, and a low rate of solid state diffusion in aluminium. The first criterion permits large alloying additions to be made to the melt, while the second criterion ensures almost complete precipitation on cooling to form a high volume fraction of second phase particles (e.g. intermetallics). If the particles are strong and non-deformable, dislocations will be forced to bow between them during deformation. For a given particle size, an increase in the volume fraction of the second phase particles decreases inter-particle spacing, which in turn increases strength. Further, if the intermetallic particles have high elastic moduli, then a material containing a high volume fraction of such particles will have a high Young's modulus.

The upper temperature limit is set by the stability or resistance to coarsening of the dispersed particles. Hence, it is necessary that the alloying elements selected have low rates of diffusion in solid aluminium. This third criterion minimizes the rate of coarsening of the dispersed particles at elevated temperatures.

On the basis of these criteria, the alloying elements selected in the development of a new class of high temperature aluminium alloys are the transition elements Cr, Mn, Fe, Ni and Co, and the rare earth element Ce. Alloy systems that show distinct promise in achieving property and performance goals at elevated temperature are Al-Fe-Ni, Al-Fe-Ce and Al-Fe-Mo [4,6,7,12]. The fine-scale intermetallic dispersoid, uniformly distributed throughout the aluminium matrix, is achieved by atomization of the molten alloy with its intrinsic component of rapid solidification. Subsequently the powder is hot consolidated to full density. Microstructures produced in this way are significantly more stable than the conventional age-hardened microstructures above ambient temperature. The scale of the dispersoids (~0.2μm) is, however, too coarse to promote long-time microstructural stability in the 300 to 500°C regime.

A fine-scale uniform distribution of dispersoids can also be introduced into a PM alloy by mechanical alloying (MA). In this process, a controlled mixture of the powder constituents is charged into a high-energy ball mill. The action of the mill causes the powder mixture to gradually, but consistently, weld together and brake apart until a uniformly alloyed composition is produced [15-18]. A schematic showing the stages involved in MA is shown in Fig. 1.

In the context of rapidly solidified (atomized) aluminium alloys containing intermetallic dispersoids, MA results in a fine-scale dispersion of Al_2O_3 since the process breaks up oxide films present on powder particle surfaces. It also introduces small dispersoids of Al_4C. The source of carbon is the process-control agent added to prevent excessive welding during MA. Unlike the larger intermetallic dispersoids (~0.2μm) that form during solidification of the atomized droplets, MA results in fine-scale oxides and carbides ~30 nm in size.

2. Product

The effect of dual rapid solidification-mechanical alloying on the elevated temperature stability and mechanical properties of PM Al-Fe-Ni [19,20] and Al-Fe-Ce alloys [21] is cited in this article.

Al-Fe-Ni powder of nominal composition Al-4.9 w/o Fe-4.8 w/o Ni was air atomized by Alcoa; this composition falls within the two-phase Al + $FeNiAl_9$ region of the ternary phase diagram at ambient temperature. At this composition, the powder contains a 0.25 volume fraction of $FeNiAl_9$ intermetallic dispersoid. After blending with pure aluminium powder to reduce the volume fraction of dispersoid to 0.19 and addition of the process control agent (~1.5 w/o stearic acid), the powder mix was mechanically alloyed. The MA powder was cold isostatically pressed in aluminium cans, outgassed, sealed and hot extruded to full density (extrusion ratio 16:1) at a temperature below 490°C.

Similarly, Al-Fe-Ce powder of nominal composition Al-8.07 w/o Fe-3.95 w/o Ce was gas atomized by Alcoa. The dispersoid in the atomized particles is a mix of $Al_{13}Fe_4$ and $Al_{10}Fe_2Ce$ with a combined volume fraction of 0.23. Procedures for mechanical alloying, cold compaction, canning, outgassing and extrusion were similar to those described for the Al-Fe-Ni PM alloy. However, a lower extrusion temperature (425°C) was used.

2.1 Al-Fe-Ni

Representative microstructures of the extruded non-MA and MA Al-Fe-Ni alloy, as revealed by transmission electron microscopy, are shown in Fig. 2. In each condition, the volume fraction of $FeNiAl_9$ dispersoid is 0.19. Compared to the non-MA condition, the MA alloy contains fine oxides/carbide dispersions (~30 μm) uniformly distributed in the aluminium matrix, and at the interfaces between the matrix and the intermetallic

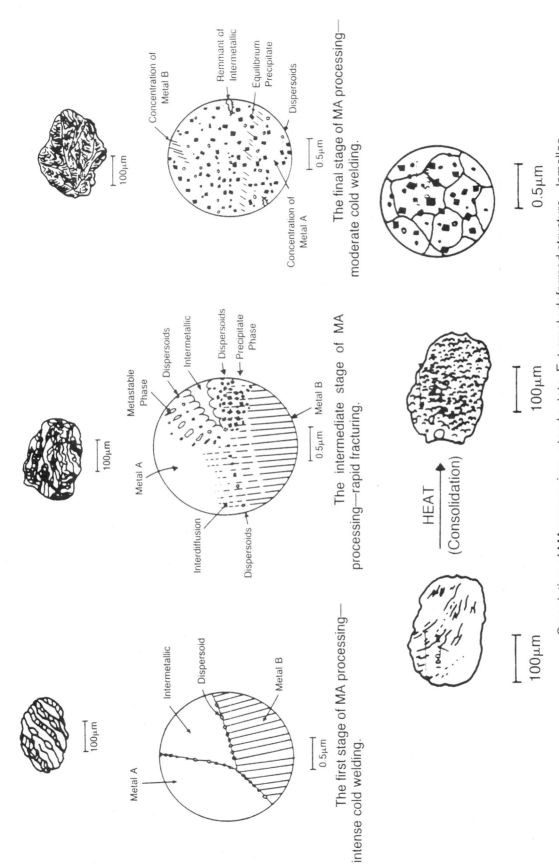

Figure 1. Schematic of stages occuring in mechanical alloying [18].

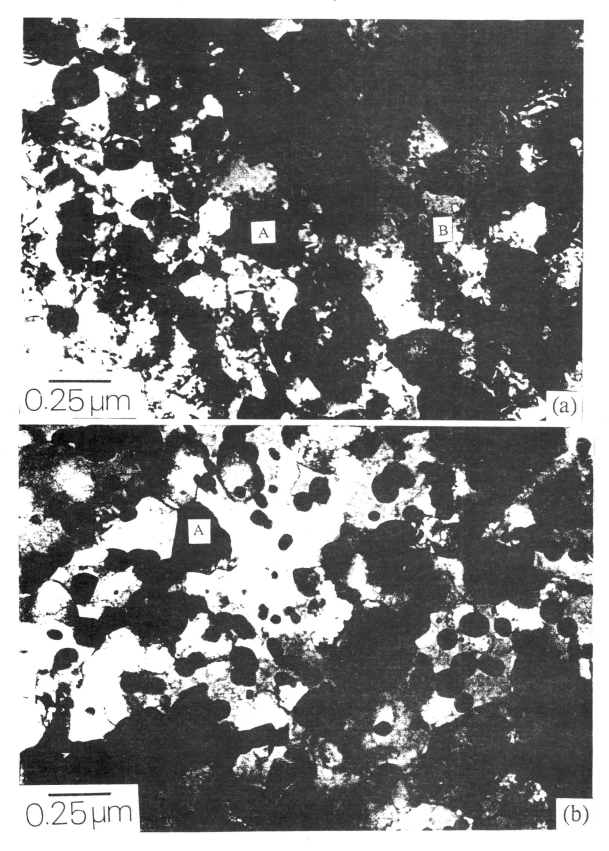

Figure 2. Microstructure of Al-Fe-Ni alloy (a) Mechanically alloyed (b) Without mechanical alloying A = FeNiAl₉ B = oxides and carbides.

particles. The average size of the FeNiAl$_9$ dispersoids (~0. 18μm) is slightly larger than those in the non-MA condition (~0.11μm). Matrix subgrain sizes are comparable in both the MA and the non-MA Al-Fe-Ni. A schematic of the microstructure of the MA and non-MA conditions of the alloy is shown in Fig.3.

A measure of the stability of the microstructure in the MA condition is gained from Fig.4. The two transmission electron micrographs show the microstructure after exposure times of 18 x 10^4 s (50 h) and 10.4 x 10^5 s (288 h) at 450°C. Only limited coarsening of the microstructure has occurred, cf. Fig.2 and Fig.4. Hardness response, measured at ambient temperature following isothermal exposure at 150°C, is also included in Fig.4. This confirms the microstructural stability of the alloy in the MA condition; after 2.2 x 10^{6}s (624 h) at 450°C, the decrease in hardness is ~10% of the original level, whereas in the non-MA condition, the corresponding decrease is ~70%. Observation of the microstructure in the non-MA condition revealed considerable coarsening of the FeNiAl$_9$ dispersoids, accompanied by grain growth.

A comparison of mechanical properties in the MA and non-MA conditions confirms the microstructural stability of the former at elevated temperature. Strength is only slightly impaired after 2.16 x 106 s (600 h) at 450°C. Similarly, creep resistance over the temperature range 250-350°C is improved by several orders of magnitude as a result of MA processing.

2.2 Al-Fe-Ce

The behavior of the Al-Fe-Ce alloy is similar to that of the Al-Fe-Ni alloy with respect to microstructural stability and strength retention, as a result of mechanical alloying [21]. Thus, MA introduces fine-scale dispersoids of oxides and carbides in the nanometre size range. In general, the microstructure is more homogeneous in the MA material. A range of dispersoid sizes and morphologies exists. Microstructures were also examined close to the fracture surface after tensile testing at ambient and elevated temperatures. The dispersoid structure appears to be insensitive to plastic deformation. After 60 seconds at 610°C, the dispersoids in the MA material are still relatively fine.

Room temperature hardness for both non-MA and MA material after isothermal exposure at 450°C for times up to 10.4 x 10^5 s (288 h) is shown in Fig. 5. In the as-extruded condition the MA material is harder than the non-MA material by about 18R$_b$ points. These data confirm the superiority of the MA material compared to the non-MA material with respect to hardness retention, and hence elevated temperature microstructural stability. After 10.4 x 10^5 seconds (288 h) at 450°C, the hardness decreases in the MA and non-MA materials are about 8% and 68%, respectively.

Hardness response, measured at room temperature, following isochronal (60 s) elevated temperature exposure is shown in Fig. 6. In the non-MA material hardness decreases slowly when the exposure temperature is below ~400°C; above this temperature there is a sharp drop in hardness. In comparison, the MA material retains its hardness at exposure temperatures up to 500°C, beyond which hardness drops significantly.

Comparison of the creep response of non-MA and MA materials at the same conditions of stress and temperature is made in Fig. 7. The corresponding steady state (minimum) creep rates are summarized in Table 1; these data demonstrate the significant enhancement in creep resistance as a result of MA.

Table 1. Steady state creep rate

Temperature	Stress	Not Mechanically Alloyed	Mechanically Alloyed
350°C	103 MPa	4.1 x 10^{-7} s^{-1}	8.3 x 10^{-10} s^{-1}
380°C	83 MPa	2.6 x 10^{-7} s^{-1}	1.6 x 10^{-9} s^{-1}
380°C	103 MPa	4.9 x 10^{-5} s^{-1}	1.4 x 10^{-9} s^{-1}

3. Future technological development

This case study highlighting the dual PM approach of rapid solidification (via atomization) and mechanical

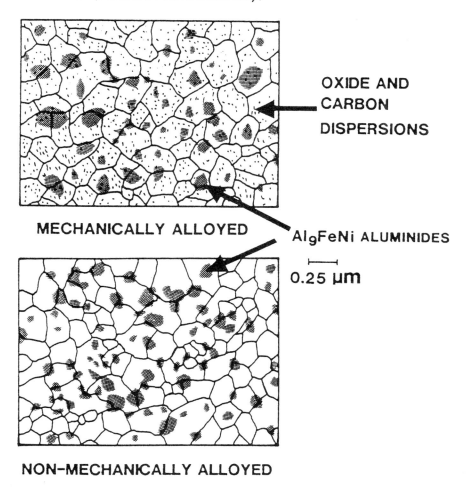

Figure 3. Schematic of mechanically alloyed and non-mechanically alloyed Al-Fe-Ni.

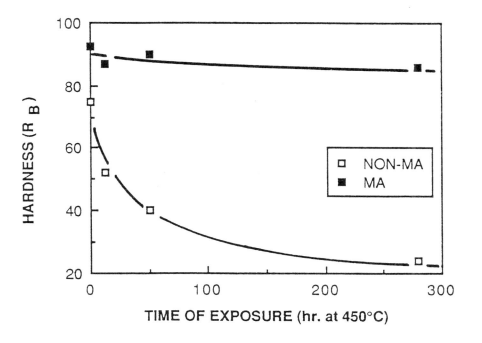

Figure 5. Room temperature hardness following elevated temperature exposure (isothermal); Al-Fe-Ce.

HARDNESS (B)

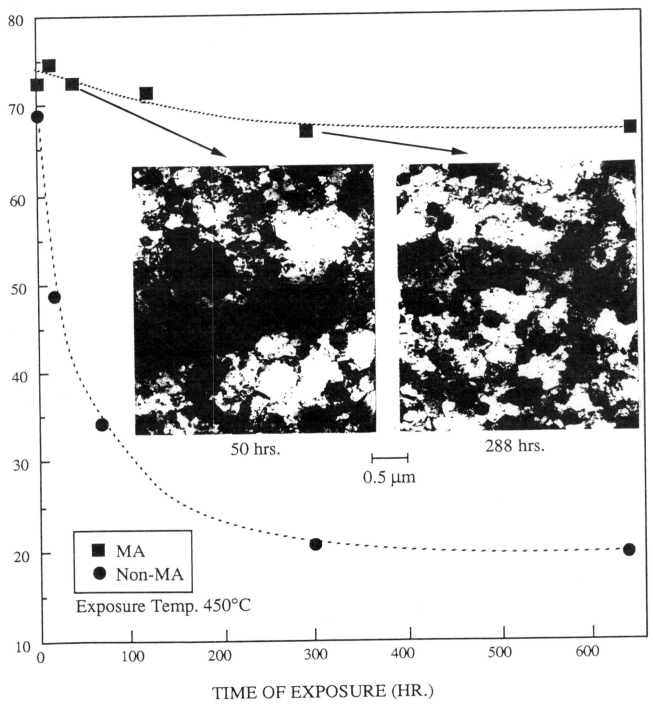

Figure 4. Microstructures and ambient temperature hardness after isothermal exposure at 450°C; Al-Fe-Ni.

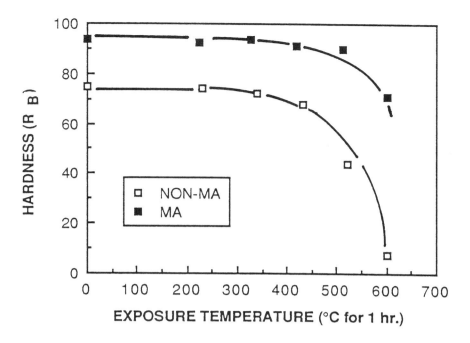

Figure 6. Room temperature hardness following elevated temperature exposure (isochronal); Al-Fe-Ce.

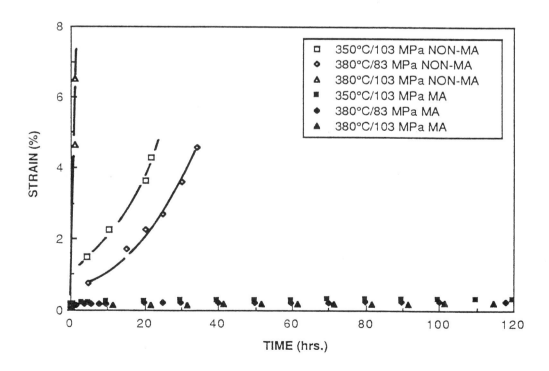

Figure 7. Comparison of creep curves for non-MA and MA Al-Fe-Ce.

alloying is far from complete. The presence of the nanoscale oxides/carbides in the Al-Fe-Ni and Al-Fe-Ce PM alloy clearly promotes a significant increase in the resistance to coarsening of the intermetallic dispersoids at elevated temperature. In turn this translates into improvements in strength retention and creep resistance, with a realistic expectation of application at service temperatures above 300°C but still short of the 500°C temperature goal. To optimize microstructural stability, a basic understanding of the interaction of the nanoscale oxides/carbides with the intermetallic dispersoids and the aluminium matrix, and of the associated coarsening mechanisms, is essential.

There is also a need to optimize processing and alloy compositions. The gain in microstructural stability and strength as a result of mechanical alloying is achieved at the expense of ductility. It is necessary to trade (in part) strength for ductility, while retaining microstructural stability at elevated temperature. Use of a smaller volume fraction of the intermetallic(s) brought about by compositional adjustment, and/or less extensive mechanical alloying are obvious future approaches in the quest for improving formability and ductility.

By virtue of their microstructure, these PM alloys are members of a growing generic breed of materials called hierarchical material structures. Such materials comprise different structural scales, ranging from the macroscopic to the nanoscale. Hierarchical material structures may perform several different functions, and may even encompass varying levels of architectural organization.

4. Conclusion

The principles of physical metallurgy dictate that for strength and strength retention at elevated temperatures, a stable, fine-scale dispersions must be present, uniformly distributed in the alloy matrix. This form of microstructure can be developed by powder metallurgy processing. It has been demonstrated that a combination of rapid solidification processing (via atomization) and mechanical alloying produces microstructures in Al-Fe-Ni and Al-Fe-Ce alloys that are stable at temperature above 300°C. The key to this stability is the presence of nanometer-scale oxides and carbides, and intermetallics in the aluminium matrix. To further improve elevated temperature stability, and to achieve a balance between strength and ductility, process and compositional optimization is needed.

References

1. W.D. Pollock, T.D. Bayha, F.E. Wawner, H.H. An and T.S. Luhman, Advances in Powder Metallurgy, Compiled by T.G. Gasbarre, Jr. and W.F. Jandeska, Jr., Metal Powder Industries Federation, Princeton, N.J., Vol. 3, 1989, p. 449.

2. S.J. Savage and F.H. Froes, J. Metals, 36, [4], 1984, 20.

3. A. Lawley, J. Metals, 38, [8], 1986, 15.

4. W.M. Griffith, R.E. Sanders, Jr. and G.J. Hildeman, in High Strength Powder Metallurgy Aluminium Alloys, edited by M.J. Koczak and G.J. Hildeman, The Metallurgical Society of AIME, Warrendale, PA.,1982, 209.

5. N.J. Grant, ibid., p. 3.

6. Rapidly Solidified Powder Aluminium Alloys, edited by M.E. Fine and E.A. Starke, Jr., ASTM STP 890, Am. Soc. for Testing and Materials, Philadelphia, PA, 1986.

7 . High Strength Powder Metallurgy Aluminium Alloys-II, edited by G.J. Hildeman and M.J. Koczak, The Metallurgical Society, Warrendale, PA, 1986.

8. D.L. Yaney, J.C. Gibeling and W.D. Nix, in Strength of Metals and Alloys, edited by H.J. McQueen, J.P. Bailon, J.I. Dickson, J.J. Jonas and M.G. Akben, Pergamon Press, Oxford, 1986, 887.

9. Y-W. Kim and W.M. Griffith, ibid., p. 485.

10. D.L. Yaney and W.D. Nix, Met. Trans., 18A, 1987, 893.

11. L. Angers, M.E. Fine and J.R. Weertman, Met. Trans., 18A, 1987, 555.

12. Aluminum Alloys: Their Physical and Mechanical Properties, edited by E.A. Starke, Jr. and T.H. Sanders, Jr., The Chameleon Press, London, 1986.

13. Y-W. Kim, W.M. Griffith and F.H. Froes, J. Metals, 32, [8], 1985, 27.

14. D. Legzdina and T.A. Parthasarathy, Met. Trans., 18A, 1987, 1713.

15. J.S. Benjamin, Met. Trans., 1A, 1970, 2943.

16. J.S. Benjamin, Sci. Amer., 234, 5, 1976, 40.

17. D.R. Maurice and T.H. Courtney, Met. Trans., 21A, 1990, 289.

18. R. Sundaresan and F.H. Froes, J. of Met., 39, [8], 1987, 22.

19. S. Ezz, M.J. Koczak, A. Lawley and M.K. Premkumar, ibid., Ref. No. 7, p. 287.

20. S. Ezz, A. Lawley and M.J. Koczak, ibid., Ref. No. 12., Vol. II, p. 1013.

21. S. Ezz, A. Lawley and M.J. Koczak, Dispersion Strengthened Aluminium Alloys, edited by Y.W. Kim and W.M. Griffith, The Metallurgical Society, Warrendale, PA, 1988, 243.

CASE STUDY 7
Porous Metal Filters

G. WILSON

M.S.E. Dept., University of Surrey, Guildford, Surrey , U.K.

1. Summary

Porous materials are extensively used in filtration products for separating solid particles from liquids or gases. When the operational requirements become severe, for example with respect to temperature, pressure, or corrosive environments, then the relatively high cost of porous metal filters can be justified, even for large industrial applications. Powder metallurgy processing, using powdered or fibrous starting materials, can be employed to produce porous metals with a very wide range of specific properties, just as it can with dense structural materials. The additional requirement to produce a controlled level of interconnected porosity together with a specific pore size - both within a shaped component - offers a substantial challenge to the powder metallurgist, whose continuing efforts are resulting in a wider range of porous metal products which offer new cost-effective solutions in separation technology to the chemical and process engineer.

2. Introduction to filtration

Most industrial operations and scientific processes, and virtually all biomedical procedures, require at some stage the separation of solid particles from liquids or gases. The particles may be the desired products or they may be the waste which is removed from the fluid end product. Filtration is a particular separation process which involves passing the fluid through a porous material or "medium". In principle the fluid is able to flow continuously through the medium, but particles which are larger than the "pore size" of the material are held back. The effectiveness of a filter is dependent both upon how efficiently it separates particles of a particular size and how the flow rate of the transmitted fluid varies over the course of time. Thus the filter must continue to perform for an adequate length of time before it becomes blocked. As will be apparent to anyone who has filtered coffee grounds or strained tea leaves, the success of filtration depends upon matching the properties of the porous filter medium to those of both the fluid and the suspended particles.

This simple concept of separation on the basis of size can be applied over a remarkably wide range of particle sizes, for example, from gravel or sand of several millimeters diameter, down to bacteria or protein molecules having dimensions measured in nanometres. In practice, there are three different modes of filtration, shown schematically in Fig. 1, in which the desired interaction between the filter medium and the suspension is indicated by the notional tape on the pores in the medium. In conventional "depth" filtration, the longest filter life is obtained when the trapped particles are distributed uniformly throughout the thickness of the medium. The filter may finally be discarded - or, if economically attractive - it may be mechanically or chemically cleaned for re-use. In conventional "surface" filtration, penetration of the medium is prevented so that the particles build up to form a layer or "cake" at the surface, which may be mechanically removed when the fluid flow becomes too low. If this is achieved *in situ* by a reverse flow or jet, then the filter can continue to perform indefinitely. In the final "cross-flow" approach, the fluid is passed at high velocity across the surface of the medium; this fluid motion keeps the surface essentially free of deposit and the particles are retained in the recirculating fluid until an optimum concentration is achieved. This latter approach is standard for continuously separating very fine (sub-micron) particles from liquids; the principle can even be extended to the removal of ions from water by reverse osmosis, where the "pore size" relates to diffusion paths within a nominally dense membrane. Although in principle a cross-flow filter can operate for an indefinite period, in practice some form of periodic cleaning is required to maintain adequate fluxes.

The detailed analysis of fluid flow through porous media can be highly complex, but there are some important observations which can be made from simple equations of fluid flow. For the usual case of viscous flow of a fluid through a porous medium, illustrated in Fig. 2, Darcy's law states that the pressure drop Δp across a sample of thickness l is given by

$$\frac{\Delta p}{l} = q \left(\frac{\mu}{k} \right) \tag{1}$$

where q is the volumetric flow rate/unit area (i.e. face approach velocity), m is the dynamic viscosity of the fluid and k, the viscous permeability coefficient, is a material constant (with units of m^2) which depends only upon the form and scale of the interconnected porosity. An important argument developed by Kozeny and Carman relates the value of k to the specific surface area of a porous material by means of a numerical constant. For porous metal filters, which have a fairly uniform pore size distribution and a fractional porosity, e, always less than about 0.8, the Kozeny Carman analysis gives the relation:

$$k = \frac{e \, d^2_r}{80} \tag{2}$$

where d_r is a measure of pore diameter. Combining equations (1) and (2) gives:

$$\frac{\Delta p}{l} = \frac{80\mu}{e \, d^2_r} \cdot q \tag{3}$$

This informative equation indicates that, to achieve a given fluid velocity, q, through a porous medium, the pressure differential which must be applied is

- directly proportional to the thickness of the medium, l (and the fluid viscosity, m)

- inversely proportional to the fractional porosity, e

- inversely proportional to the square of the pore diameter, d_r

Thus a fine pore-size filter material must be very thin if the pressure drop is not to become too great - which leads to the concept of a microporous membrane material for very fine separations. However, for coarser separations in the depth mode of filtration, the thickness of the medium must be deep enough to provide a significant capacity for holding particles from the suspension.

In a practical filter, another important variable is the surface area of the filter medium. Thus an increased surface area has a two-fold effect: it both provides a higher area for holding particles and it reduces the effective face velocity (and hence pressure differential), both effects giving a longer on-stream life. It will be seen later that the production methods for metal filters are often determined by the need to attain a large surface area of filter medium within a small working volume.

Equation (3) also indicates how, after a period of uniform operation at constant face velocity, the pressure drop across a depth filter increases rapidly as the filter blocks (i.e. as dr and e both become smaller due to the presence of the particulate).

3. Porous filter media

The very extensive range of practical filtration applications means that a wide variety of different materials and processing methods have evolved to provide a suitable product at minimum cost. The most obvious way of making a porous material is by forming an agglomerate from small particulate, i.e. powders or fibres of a specified size. Paper-making processes, using fibrous starting materials, offer the cheapest method of producing large quantities of sheet material. The fibres may be naturally occurring, such as cellulose, or they

Filtration mode	Flow pattern through medium	Examples
Depth filtration	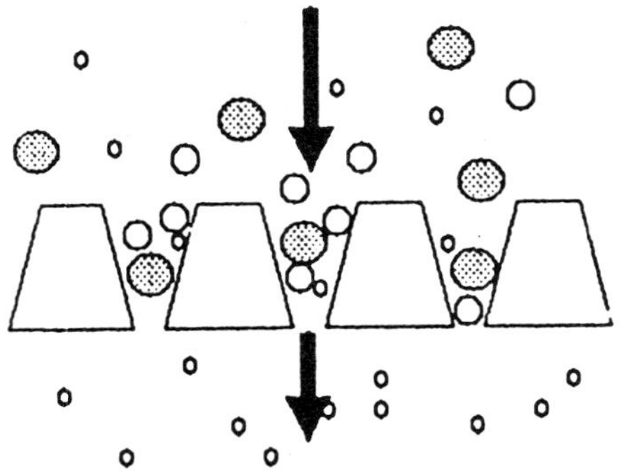	Hydraulic fluids Fuels, lubricating oils Process industry separations Water clarification
Surface filtration	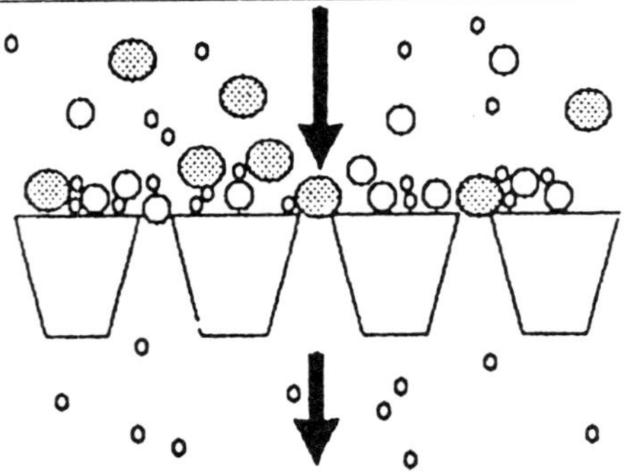	Gas cleaning Product recovery
Crossflow filtration	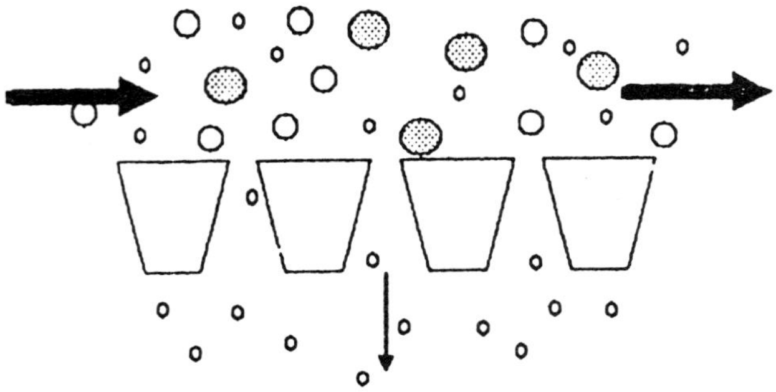	Dairy processing Fruit juice concentration Waste treatment

Figure 1. Different modes of filtration, with examples from commercial practice.

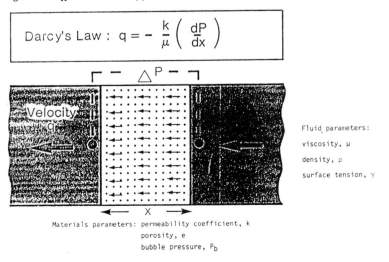

Darcy's Law : $q = - \dfrac{k}{\mu} \left(\dfrac{dP}{dx} \right)$

Velocity, q

Fluid parameters:
viscosity, μ
density, ρ
surface tension, γ

Materials parameters: permeability coefficient, k
porosity, e
bubble pressure, P_b

Figure 2. Parameters affecting viscous flow through a porous medium.

may be manufactured from synthetic polymers or glass. Ceramics and metals are also available as fibres, but these are quite expensive to produce; such materials can be produced relatively more cheaply as powders, which are then converted into porous products by standard powder metallurgical techniques.

The particular filtration application determines what type of material can be used as the porous medium. Thus, natural and thermoplastic polymer fibres will be unable to withstand high temperatures or high stresses; glass fibres and sintered ceramics will be susceptible to brittle fracture. Metals, on the other hand, possess a unique combination of properties, which means that their very high cost (up to several hundred times more, per unit area, than the cheapest paper products) can be justified for critical applications.

Metal filters can withstand high temperatures, high pressures, corrosive environments and high levels of radioactivity. Because porous metals are mechanically tough, they can be fabricated into a wide variety of shapes, and may be joined by brazing or welding. A selection of porous metal filter products is shown in Fig. 3, and a list of some of the standard applications of porous metals is given in Fig 4. Again, in practice, the the most cheaply produced metal is used in the form of a filter product which will perform effectively for an acceptable length of time. Typical materials are tin-bronze, stainless steel, nickel-base alloys, titanium and precious metals, in increasing order of cost. It may be noted that in some cases, metal filters can be chemically or thermally cleaned for re-use, so that the high initial filter cost can be amortised over an extended period of time.

The production of porous metal filter media is aided by the ability to self-bond the materials by sintering at high temperature, without any requirement for additional bonding agents. However, in contrast to conventional powder metallurgical processing, subsequent removal of porosity must be avoided. With powder starting materials, the porosity is maximized by using powders with a narrow particle size distribution. The powders are invariably produced by atomisation from the melt, and a range of filter grades is produced from powder which has been classified into narrow sieve fractions. Powder diameters could extend from as coarse as 1 mm down to as fine as 20-40nm. Some of the relevant properties of sintered bronze and stainless steel powders are included in Fig. 5. Stainless steel is the metal most commonly available in the form of wire or as fibre. Wire of diameter down to about 50μm can be processed into filter mesh in a variety of different weaves; fibre suitable for filter manufacture is available from about 25μm down to as low as 2μm. Since the fibres are produced by a repetitive drawing, rebundling and drawing technique, the diameters of any particular fibre grade are extremely uniform, which is beneficial for use in filters.

As may be seen from the data listed in Fig. 5, the porosities of fibrous media are significantly higher than those achievable with powder materials. The marked contrast between the internal pore structures of powdered and fibrous media is shown by the cross-sections in Figs. 6 and 7 respectively. Furthermore, the powder diameter required to give a particular pore size (in low porosity product) is much greater than the fibre diameter required to give similar pore size in a high porosity product. This relationship may be expressed quantitatively using the Kozeny Carman analysis, and is summarized by the curves in Fig. 8 which, to a first approximation, are applicable to both powders and fibres.

4. Production of Porous metal filters

Although there are two aspects to the production of metal filters, namely the preparation of the porous medium and its conversion to a practical filter product, wherever possible these two aspects are combined to produce a finished component which can be directly inserted into a process vessel, or filter housing, which is itself incorporated in a fluid processing line. Outlines are given below for the three most common types of metal filters.

4. 1 Bronze powder products

The alloys are single-phase solid solutions of between 8 and 12wt%. tin in copper, with controlled additions (0.1 - 0.4wt%) of phosphorus. Air atomisation of the molten alloy results in a spherical powders which are classified into narrow size fractions by sieving. The bronze powder is loose packed often vibrated into graphite or stainless steel moulds and sintered under a reducing gas atmosphere at a temperature (below the solidus

Figure 3. A selection of porous metal filter products.

General applications	Filtration applications
Sparging, fluidising media	Industrial and aerospace hydraulics
Flow controlling (eg. de-icing fluids)	Molten polymer processing (film and fibre production)
Porous electrodes	Process industry (eg. ammonia synthesis, catalyst recovery)
Self-lubricating bearings	Nuclear power plant operation and waste treatment
Surgical implants	Food and drink manufacturing
Sound absorbers	Hot gas cleaning
Heat pipes	

Figure 4. Some applications of porous metal products.

Material	Particulate diameter µm	Porosity	Viscous permeability coefficient, k $10^{-12}m^2$	Bubble pressure pore diameter µm
Sintered bronze powder	24*	0.38	0.53	11.0
	55*	0.36	1.96	22.5
	76*	0.35	4.35	32.1
	127*	0.37	12.7	56.2
	212*	0.37	22.2	71.1
Sintered stainless steel powder	50	0.32	1.0	19.0
	10	0.32	2.0	34.0
	20	0.42	6.0	51.0
	30	0.44	13.0	83.0
	80	0.50	45.0	143.0
Sintered stainless steel fibre	4	0.67	0.74	10.1
	4	0.80	3.20	18.1
	8	0.76	4.37	24.2
	8	0.83	9.39	35.4
	12	0.56	1.00	12.8
	12	0.84	35.50	60.1

* Mean diameter within sieve range

Figure 5. Properties of a range of powdered and fibrous microporous metals.

50 µm

Figure 6. Transverse section through a bronze powder filter medium.

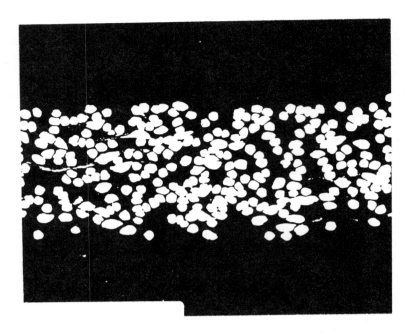

Figure 7. Transverse section through a stainless steel fibre medium.

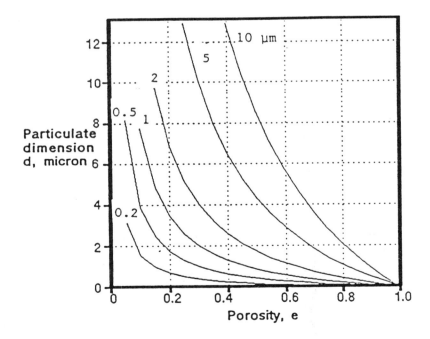

Figure 8. Dependence of mean pore diameter,d_r upon porosity and dimensions of particulate (powder or fibre).

at around 800°C) which is critically dependent upon the alloy composition the powder particle size and the component geometry. The aim of the process is to minimize the overall volume shrinkage while ensuring that the size of the sintered necks between adjacent particles (Fig. 9) results in adequate strength of the sintered component. A lower sintering temperature is required to produce the optimum structure in finer powders because of the greater activity of surface, relative to volume, diffusion.

There is always shrinkage upon sintering, and the magnitude of this effect determines both the size of the moulds and their shape because the product must be readily removed after sintering. The precise external dimensions may be established through a final cold-coining opeation. This action may also be applied, not for dimension control, but for precise control of air permeability which is an important quality control parameter in production.

4.2 Stainless steel powder products

The most common alloy is type 316L stainless steel, Fe-17Cr-l2Ni-2.5Mo (0.03C max), although other stainless steel alloys are processed. Powders are produce by gas or water atomisation and particle shape is generally described as being "irregular". Since the powder is covered by a stable oxide film, sintering between loose powder particles is more difficult to control than is the case with bronze powders. Nevertheless, some manufacturers use loose sintering of powder, for example, spread out on large sheets with a doctor blade, in order to ensure that the final porosity value is a maximum. Other manufacturers prefer to give their powders a certain amount of initial cold compaction, in order to rupture the oxide films and allow sintering to proceed more controllably; the uniformity of such a product is likely to be higher than in a loose-sintered material, but the porosity is likely to be lower. Cold compaction may be achieved in a metallic die, or in an isostatic press, the latter being particularly well suited to the production of seamless tubular products or large pieces in which the achievement of a uniform green density is important.

Powder sintering is performed in a hydrogen atmosphere or vacuum furnace under conditions governed by the same factors discussed above for bronze powders; sintering temperatures are usually in excess of 1200°C. The as-sintered product may again be cold deformed to control the dimensions or the final permeability. Since sintered stainless steel powder sheet is relatlvely plastic it can be readily fabricated into various shapes; for example, tubes in which the seams are subsequently welded.

4.3 Stainless steel fibre products

Stainless steel fibres, originally developed for antistatic textile applications have, in recent years, been finding increasing application in filtration products. The porous fibre media are produced in the form of thin sheets with very high porosity so that, despite the relatively high cost of fibre production compared with powder production, the eventual cost/unit area is very competitive. Furthermore, the fibre media is highly plastic and can, for example, be pleated like paper, to give metallic filters with a very large surface area.

The stainless steel fibres are produced by a lengthy process of repetitive drawing and bundling of copper clad rods, with final chemical dissolution of the copper to release the fibres. Depending upon the extent of processing, fibres are available for use in filtration products having exceedingly uniform diameters at fixed sizes from 25μm down to 2μm. The continuous fibres are chopped to length and deposited upon a porous substrate by air or wet laying in the manner of paper or textile processing. The resulting web is then sintered in the same manner as for stainless steel powder, and subsequently cold calendered between hydraulic rolls to give the desired density or permeability; the surface structure of a fibre medium is shown in Fig. 10. If the fibres are "loose sintered" at a very low initial density, then there will be a low proportion of sintered inter-fibre bonds (Fig. 11) and the final product will be soft and floppy. If the web is compressed and sintered under a dead load, the higher density of inter-fibre bonds means that the resulting product is much more rigid, having the feel of cardboard. Stainless steel fibre media can be readily fabricated into a variety of shapes which can be joined or sealed by welding.

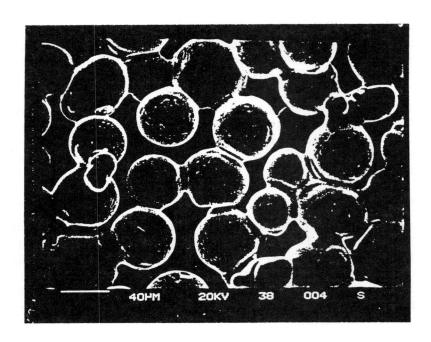

Figure 9. Surface of bronze powder filter medium.

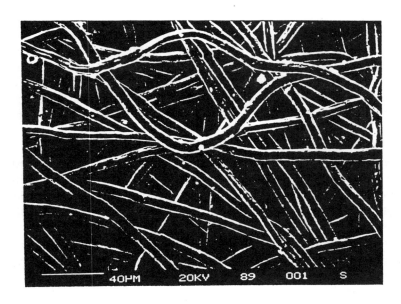

Figure 10. Surface of stainless steel fibre filter medium.

Figure 11. Sintered bonds in stainless steel fibre medium.

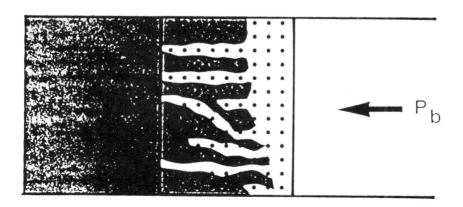

Figure 12. Diagram showing displacement of fluid in bubble pressure test.

5. Performance of metallic filters

There are a number of tests which can be performed to characterise metallic filter media (or fabricated filters).

5.1 Permeability

A permeability test involves measuring the pressure drop across the filter for a given gas flow rate; the procedure is described in a standard ISO test. If proper precautions are taken to eliminate edge effects, to correct for gas pressure and temperature, and to eliminate non-viscous inertial losses, then the results can be described quantitatively by equation (1), leading to the calculation of the material parameter, k, the viscous per-meability coefficient. Often, however, the test results are described simply by curves of pressure drop versus gas or liquid flow rate, from which a measure of "permeability" for that particular component can be read off.

5.2 Bubble pressure

A bubble pressure determination is a simple yet powerful means of measuring a pore size, and the procedure is again the subject of a standard ISO test . The test involves impregnating the porous medium with a fully wetting liquid such as isopropanol, and measuring the gas pressure required to displace the liquid and produce a stream of gas bubbles from the surface (Fig. 12). The first appearance of bubbling can indicate a large defect in a fabricated filter, or may simply reveal the location of the largest "through-pore" in the medium (having originated at the point of minimum cross-section along this pore). The pressure at which generalised bubbling occurs (so-called "mass bubble pressure" P_b) gives a good measure for an average pore-size in the medium (d_r), through the relation:

$$d_r = \frac{4\gamma}{P_b} \qquad\qquad (4)$$

where γ is the surface tension of the wetting liquid. Equation (4) applies strictly to circular pores having no inter-connectivity, for example as in a thin membrane having cylindrical through-pores. However, it is becoming increasingly popular to determine a "bubble pressure pore-size distribution" in automated equipment which measures pressure differentials at increasing gas flow rates after initial bubbling. The interpretation of such data, through the use of equation (4), particularly at high gas flow rates in thick media with inter-connected pores, is considered highly problematical. The resulting "average bubble pressure pore-size" will always be much less than a "volume average pore-size" corresponding to the pressure required to displace half the volume of wetting fluid from the pores. In metal filters, this latter pressure is very close to the "mass bubble pressure", which means that equation (4) itself actually gives a good measure of average pore size.

5.3 Separation efficiency

The above tests are used to characterize the porous medium, but they give no indication in themselves of the ability of the filter to remove particles of a particular size. In a separation efficiency test, a particular test dust (suspended either in a gas or liquid) is passed through the filter or porous medium, and the particle size distribution upstream is compared with the distribution downstream, as indicated schematically in Fig. 13. Since the selection of test dust and fluid must relate to the intended filter application there is clearly no universal test for separation efficiency. In its simplest form, a suspension of fine glass beads is passed through the filter, and the largest size to have passed through is observed by examination of the filtrate in a microscope. The hydraulics industry has established a more sophisticated test employing optical particle counters and a suspension of "AC fine test dust" in continuously recirculating hydraulic oil. Modification of this test, involving a single pass of test dust suspended in liquid or gas, gives a separation efficiency curve of the type shown in Fig. 14, which can be related to many of the applications of metallic filters. In such a test, it is also possible to determine the actual amount of test dust entrained upon or within the filter (the so-called "dust holding capacity"), which is a measures on-stream life.

Figure 15 includes filtration test results for a selection of different metallic filter media of different pore sizes. Separation efficiency test results always show that the medium is capable of removing appreciable

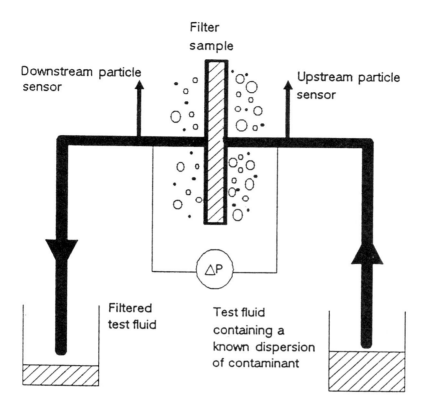

Figure 13. Principle of filtration efficiency test.

Material	Sample thickness (mm)	Bubble pressure pore size (μm)	Particle size (μm) for given cumulative retention by number			Dust holding capacity (mg/cm²)
			50%	90%	99%	
Sintered bronze powder	1.49	11.0	2.0	4.3	5.6	2.19
	1.42	22.5	4.0	9.5	10.7	3.54
Sintered stainless steel fibre	0.45	18.1	2.0	5.3	8.0	4.25
	0.16	24.2	2.8	8.2	11.1	4.54

Figure 15. Filtration properties of selected powder and fibre media.

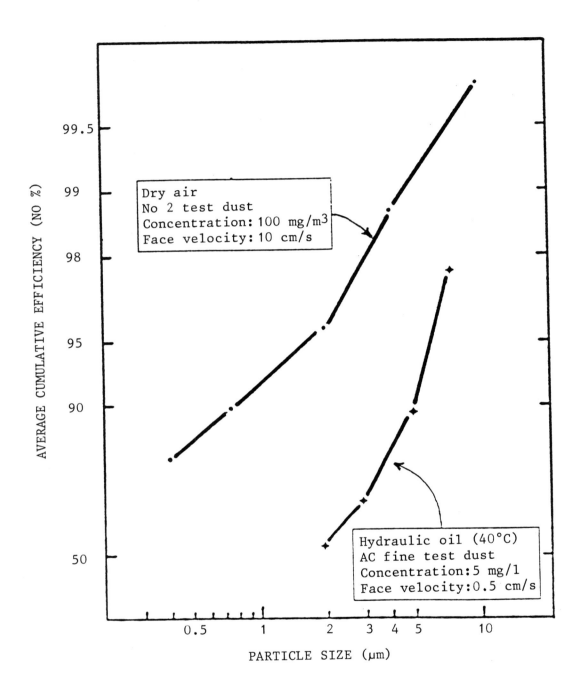

Figure 14. Filtration efficiency of fibre medium for separation from liquid and gas.

amounts (whether on the basis of particle weights or numbers, or on a differential or cumulative size basis) of particles which are substantially smaller than the dimension for, say, the bubble pressure pore size.

However, in solid-liquid separations using similar types of porous media, it is often possible to correlate the results of these two tests over a large range of pore sizes. For this reason, filter suppliers will often simply quote a "filter micron rating" which is a particular fraction (typically 0.2-0.5) of the bubble pressure pore size. Users of filters should be cautious of filter ratings when the value of this fraction, or the details of the test method, have not been specified. In particular, it should be noted that the separation efficiency of particular sized particles from a gas stream is invariably much higher than that of a liquid (Fig. 14).

Another consequence of the above observations is that a micron size which is given as a measure of the efficiency of depth filtration, will be much smaller than the actual surface pore size, which may control the efficiency of separations in the cross-flow mode.

5.4 Other tests

Other tests on metallic filter media may be specified for particular applications. These include mechanical strength, which may affect whether particles of metal could break away from the medium in service and contaminate the filtrates or chemical analysis of the metal or alloy, which may affect the corrosion resistance of the filter.

Manufacturers are usually reluctant to reveal the structural parameters of the products, e.g. particulate sizes employed and effective porosity values. It is worth noting, however, that if these parameters are known, or can be assumed, it is possible to calculate the permeability and bubble pressure of the materials, using a Kozeny Carman analysis, to a good level of accuracy.

6. New developments

The market for porous metal filters is small relative to the total market for filtration products, but it is growing steadily as the need to achieve more critical and specialized separations becomes apparent.

Thus there are opportunities to operate in more critical and aggressive environments, where novel alloys can be applied on the basis of their resistance to chemical attack to high temperature oxidation or to hot corrosion. Improved methods of producing both metal powders and metal fibres will also extend the range of porous metal filters which are available.

There are always opportunities for increasing performance (on-stream life and separation capability) by better design of the microporous structures. The solution here is to produce composite structures in which the pore size changes throughout the thickness of the medium. Thus it is possible to emulate in practice the schematic pore structures shown in Fig. 1, in which the surface pores are shown to be coarse for a depth medium, and fine for a surface medium. Fibre processing, in which a series of different layers are combined (Fig. 16), often with woven meshes, is a very powerful approach to the preparation of composite structures with significant levels of complexity.

A final area of new development is to extend the range of pore sizes in metals down to finer levels, which are normally typical of organic polymers (and some specialised ceramics). Figure 17 shows membrane tubes made entirely from stainless steel, with a fine sub-micron pore size on the inner surface. These tubes, which are being employed in radioactive and toxic waste treatment, are used in the crossflow mode and are capable of being welded in parallel arrays between tube plates, rather like the configuration of a heat exchanger. In such applications, it is possible that another unique characteristic of metals their electrical conductivity, could also be exploited. If the metallic membrane is made the cathode of an electrolytic cell, the membrane surface can be cleaned periodically by the *in situ* generation of gas bubbles at the metal surface.

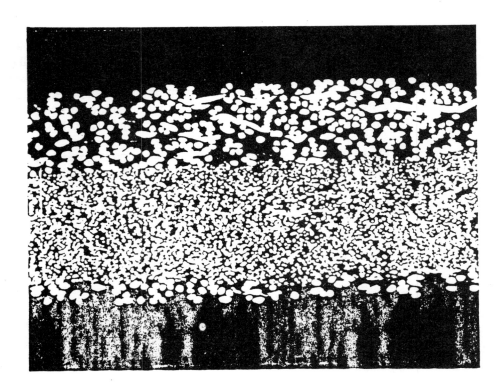

Figure 16. Transverse section through composite fibre medium.

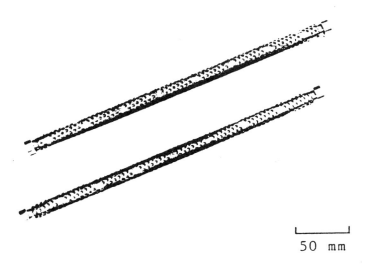

50 mm

Figure 17. Microporous stainless steel membrane tubes for crossflow separations.

7. Conclusion

Porous metals, produced by a variety of powder metallurgical processing techniques, have a number of unique properties which ensures their continuing (and expanding) application in difficult or critical industrial separations. The description of filtration mechanisms and of porous metal products which have been given in this Chapter, should provide practising engineers with sufficient understanding and confidence to discuss potential applications with filter manufacturers in a more objective manner than has, perhaps, been the case in the past.

Case Study 8
Rare Earth Permanent Magnet Components

J. ORMEROD
Previously at Philips Components Ltd, Southport

Abstract

Rare earth permanent magnets today account for more than 10% of the total world permanent magnet market, valued at £950 millions in 1987, and projected to increase at 10% per annum over the coming years.

The important permanent magnet properties of coercivity, remanence and temperature stability are all influenced by microstructure and phase chemistry. Hence the processing route used to fabricate the permanent magnet is critical in determining the final magnetic performance. To date powder metallurgical processing has yielded the optimum microstructure resulting in the best translation from the intrinsic properties of a rare earth - transition metal compound to the characteristic parameters of a permanent magnet.

Rare earth permanent magnets are used in a wide range of industrial, domestic, automotive and aerospace application areas. The specific applications make use of the weight and volume reduction of the magnetic circuit and associated components made possible by the high magnetic energy available.

1. Introduction

Permanent magnets today are used in a wide range of industrial, domestic, automotive and aerospace applications. Their special technological importance derives from the ability to act contactlessly on ferromagnetic material, either by attraction or repulsion, and to provide a permanent magnetic flux with no energy input and hence at no operating cost. The current usage of permanent magnets in domestic applications averages 50 per household in Western Europe.

Perhaps the most surprising range of permanent magnet uses are the numerous applications in a modern passenger vehicle. These applications include an array of D.C. electric motors such as the starter, heater and air conditioner blower, windscreen wiper, window lift, door lock and fuel pump motors.

A fully equipped car can have more than 30 D.C. electric motors. Other uses include actuators, gauges and sensors. In all these examples higher performance magnetic materials may afford the advantages of increased operating efficiency and reduction in size and weight.

Figure 1 shows the total permanent magnet market split by material type. This total market is valued at £950 millions in 1987. The market, in terms of volume, is totally dominated by the ferrite class of material (>97%). However, in terms of value the rare earth permanent magnet share is significant (>10%).

Two significant areas of market growth have occured. Firstly, the introduction of ferrites in the early 1950s has led to market domination today. Secondly, market penetration by rare earth permanent magnets has been dramatic since their introduction in the early 1970s. The growth rate of the total market is around 7% per annum with the rare earth magnet sector growing in excess of 10% per annum. It is predicted that future usage of permanent magnets will expand faster than the historical rate, with ferrite and rare earth permanent magnets being the dominant materials.

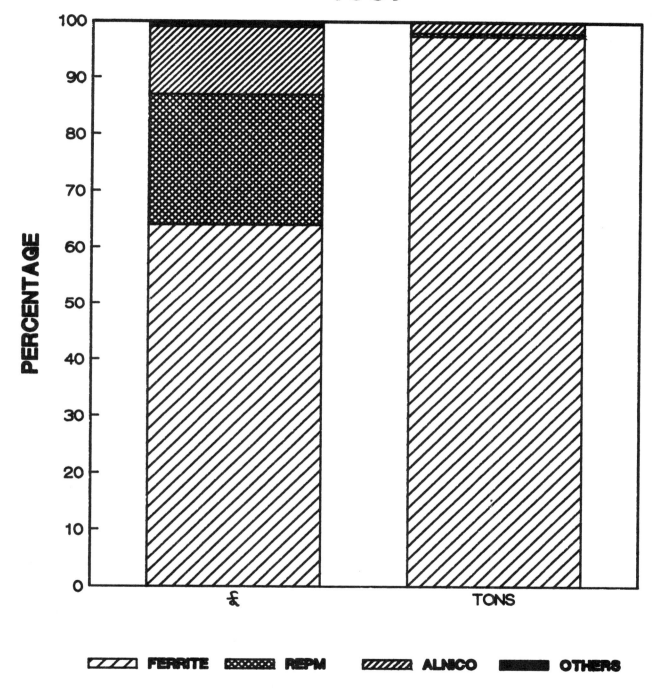

Figure 1. Total permanent magnet market on the basis of value and tonnage.

The vast majority of rare earth permanent magnets are produced by powder metallurgical processing routes.

Commercial rare earth permanent magnets, based on the $SmCo_5$ intermetallic compound, have been produced since the early 1970s. Shortly after the development of $SmCo_5$ permanent magnets, alloys containing copper as well as the rare earths and cobalt emerged. These become known as the precipitation - hardened family of R(CuCo) alloys and eventually led to the development of high energy Sm(Co,Cu,Fe,TM)7-8 magnets (where TM = Zr, Ti or Hf).

Since the middle of 1983, several permanent magnet manufacturers, in Europe, the U.S., and Japan, have announced their intention to begin commercial production of permanent magnets based on the $Nd_2Fe_{14}B$ intermetallic compounds. These new materials combine high polarization coercivity, HcJ, with the highest known maximum energy product, (BH) max. These parameters are considered to be the two most important indicators of permanent magnet performance.

The improvement in primary magnetic properties of the NdFe - based magnets over the existing high energy SmCo - based magnets is illustrated in Table 1.

As a comparison, the properties of a typical ferrite permanent magnet, the type of permanent magnet material produced in the largest tonnage, are included in the table. Of course, not only performance of the permanent magnet material but also the costs of production determine their relative market shares. Figure 2 shows the relative production costs of typical magnet geometries for three rare earth materials and a ferrite magnet. The comparison is made on the basis of unit mass. As can be seen the ferrite material is an order of magnitude cheaper than the rare earth materials.

The much enhanced magnetic properties of the NdFe based materials will allow the further miniaturization of permanent magnet circuit designs and broaden the range of permanent magnet applications. In addition, the basic raw materials required for NdFe - based magnets have considerable price advantages and fewer supply restrictions than either Sm, or Co, which together, form the main components of the established rare earth permanent magnets. This could allow NdFe - based magnets to be produced for, and used in, large volume applications.

Philips Components Limited manufacture a wide range of REPM grades based on either the Nd2Fe14B system or $(NdDy)_2Fe_{14}BNb$ system and marketed under the trade name Neodure. Table 2 illustrates the typical magnetic characteristics of the Neodure grades currently available. Figure 3 indicates the range of REPM products manufactured by Philips Components Limited.

2. Historical development of rare earth permanent magnets

Several comprehensive reviews [1-6] exist which extensively cover the development of rare earth magnets and the factors determining their magnetic properties.

Rare earth permanent magnets can be defined as a group of permanent magnet materials containing the magnetically active components rare earth transition metal (R - T) where R is one or more of the elements having atomic numbers 57 (La) to 71 (Lu) and the group 3B element of atomic number 39 (Y). Up to the advent of NdFe - based materials, the commercially most important rare earth permanent magnets were based on Sm and Co.

Rare earth - Co magnets can be divided into four types depending on whether the primary phase is of the RCo_5 or R_2Co_{17} type and whether a precipitate phase (for domain wall pinning) within the grains is present or absent. The latter types are referred to as multi-phase and single-phase magnets respectively, although in practice all commercial sintered permanent magnets have complex multi-phase microstructures. All four types are generally prepared by powder metallurgical processing.

Table 1. A comparison of the composition and properties of some permanent magnets manufactured by powder metallurgy

COMPOSITION	Nd2Fe14B	SmCo5	SrFe12O19	
MATERIAL GRADE	RES270	RES190	FXD380	
Br typical	1.1	0.89	0.39	T
BH max typical	215	154	28.2	kJ/m3
HcJ typical	1000	1100	275	kA/m
Temperature coefficient of Br (20 to + 150°C)	-0.13	-0.04	-0.2	%/K
Temperature coefficient of HcJ (20 to 150°C)	-0.6	-0.05	0.34	%/K
Recoil permeability	1.05	1.05	1.1	
Curie point	310	720	450	°C
Max continuous operating temperature.	120	250	350	°C
Density	7.4	8.3	4.75	x10 3 kg/m3

COST COMPARISON

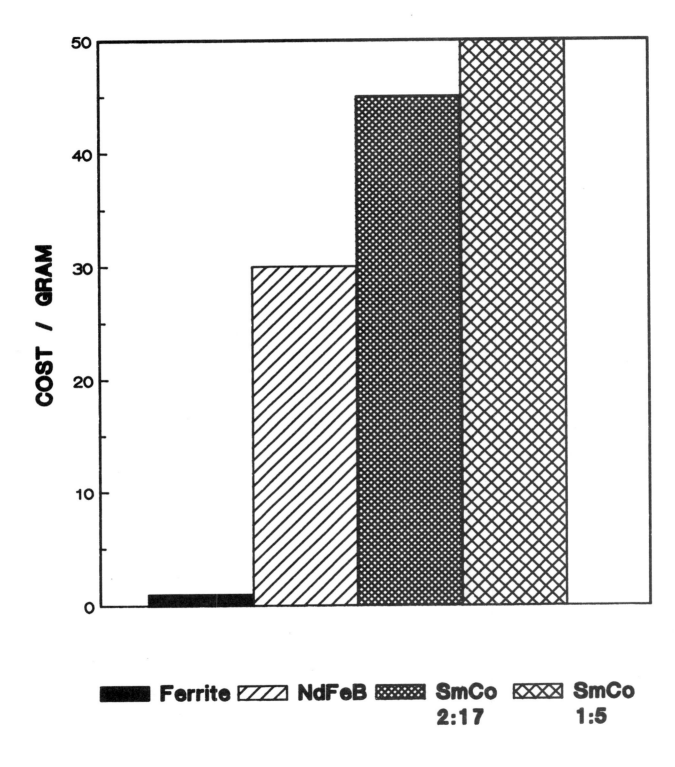

Figure 2. Relative production costs of various permanent magnet materials.

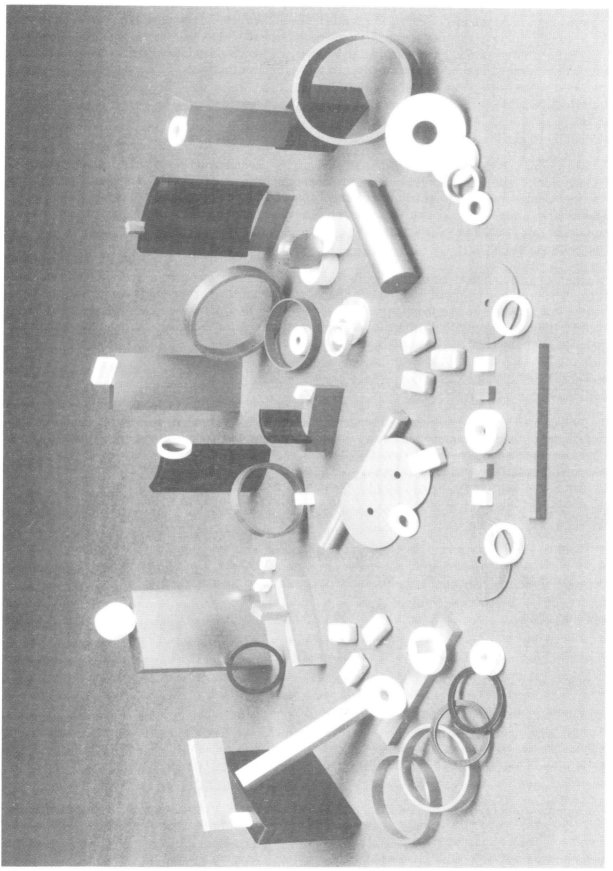

Figure 3. Example of the REPM product range manufactured by Philips Components Limited.

Historically, the development of RFe - based permanent magnets, by powder metallurgical processing, has been hindered for several reasons. First, Fe forms much fewer intermetallic compounds with the rare earths than Co. Secondly, stable compounds of the RFe_5 composition are absent. Thirdly, compounds which are stable, e.g. R_2Fe_{17}, have low Curie temperatures and planar preference anisotropy. However two alternative approaches have been used in the search for RFe permanent magnet materials, These are by:

1. Extending the study to metastable non-equilibrium phases instead of being limited to the equilibrium phases.
2. Extending the study to ternary / quaternary systems for stable phases.

These two approaches have been followed, independently, by several workers [7 - 10]. The former method takes its lead from Clark [11], who demonstrated that amorphous materials provided a starting point from which a fine grained metastable structure could be obtained by an annealing treatment. Most of the investigators who followed this approach, used a technique called melt-spinning, to produce the amorphous precursor or the fine grained metastable structure directly. A schematic diagram of a typical melt-spinning apparatus is shown in Fig. 4.

This method of melt-spinning consists of melting the alloy or elements in a quartz tube either under vacuum or inert gas. The melt, under argon pressure, is ejected through an orifice in the quartz tube onto a rotating, water cooled, copper wheel or disc. Cooling rates in excess of 10^6 K/s are produced. This technology has been developed by Delco Remy (GM Corporation) to produce a range of NdFeB-based magnets known as Magnequench. The Magnequench process is shown schematically in Fig. 5.

More recently the search for new RFe compounds has shifted to a study of stable phases formed in the ternary / quaternary system based on NdFeB.

At the 29th Conference on Magnetism and Magnetic Materials, Sagawa and co-workers [12] reported their results of studies of the light rare earths, Fe and B ternary systems. In particular a ternary compound in the NdFeB system, with a composition in the range 12 at.% Nd, 6 at.% B and 82 at.% Fe, was found to have excellent potential as a permanent magnet material. The compound was found to have a tetragonal structure, with a high uniaxial anisotropy and a Curie temperature of 585K. Permanent magnets were produced by standard powder metallurgical processing, from an alloy composition of 15 at.% Nd, 8 at.% B and 77 at.% Fe, with (BH) max value in excess of 279 kJ/m³.

3. Microstructure

The important properties characterising a permanent magnet component are:

Remanence, Br;

Polarization coercivity, HcJ;

Maximum energy product, (BH) max, and,

Temperature dependence of Br and HcJ, Tk.

All these parameters are largely influenced by the microstructure and phase chemistry. Hence the processing route used to fabricate the permanent magnet is critical in determining the final magnetic performance.

The requirements of a rare earth transition metal compound to be a potential permanent magnet material are:

The compound must be ferro-or ferri-magnetic with a high Curie temperature, Tc;

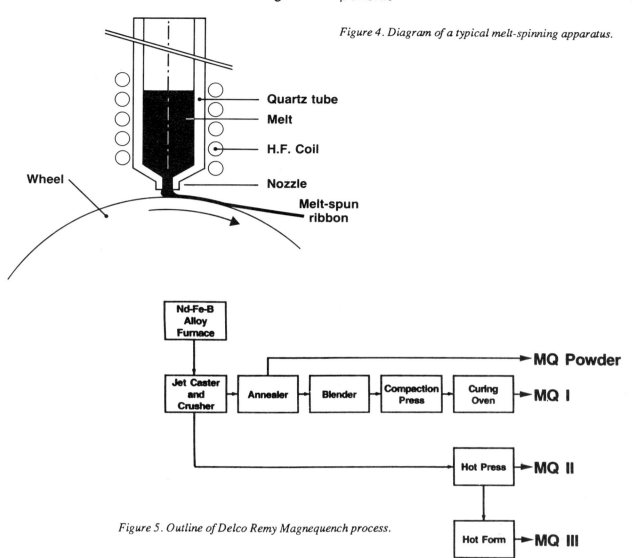

Figure 4. Diagram of a typical melt-spinning apparatus.

Figure 5. Outline of Delco Remy Magnequench process.

Table 2. Typical magnetic characteristics of Neodure magnets measured at 25°C

NEODURE GRADE	REMANENCE Br(T)	COERCIVITY HcB(kA/m)	INTRINSIC COERCIVITY HcJ(kA/m)	MAXIMUM ENERGY PRODUCT (BH) MAX (kJ/m3)
RES 270	1.10	700	1000	215
RES 300	1.15	750	1000	240
RES 350	1.20	800	1000	280
RES 255	1.05	750	1500	200
RES 275	1.10	800	1500	215
RES 305	1.15	850	1500	240

The compound must be ferro-or ferri-magnetic with a high Curie temperature, Tc;

Room temperature magnetisation (Ms) must be high;

The compound must have a large magnetocrystalline anisotropy, H_A and a magnetically unique crystal lographic axis.

The relationship between these so called primary magnetic properties and the characteristic parameters of a permanent magnet, the secondary properties, is shown diagramatically in Fig. 6. To date powder metallurgical processing has yielded the optimum microstructure resulting in the best translation from primary to secondary magnetic properties.

Magnetisation reversal in rare earth permanent magnets occurs by the nucleation and growth of reversed magnetic domains at fields well below the anisotropy field, H_A. Both reverse-domain nucleation and domain - wall motion are influenced by microstructure making HcJ, Br and (BH) max sensitive to grain size, texture, second-phase particles and grain boundary characteristics.

In considering grain size, an important parameter is the so-called single domain particle diameter, Dc, typically 0.2 - 2 μm in rare earth compounds. The microstructure of most current sintered rare earth magnets approximates one of two idealised types:

(A) - Single phase, aligned grains with D>>Dc or
(B) - Aligned grains with D>>Dc containing a finely dispersed precipitate.

In type (A) domain wall motion is easy within the grains once a reverse domain is nucleated. To achieve high coercivity it is necessary that grain boundaries block domain wall motion from grain to grain. Otherwise, one nucleating defect could lead to reversal of an entire magnet. In type (B) each grain contains a finely dispersed precipitate of a second phase, with properties different from the matrix, resulting in the pinning of domains. Texture, specifically the degree of alignment of magnetic easy axes, determines the maximum Br, which in turn limits (BH) max.

Rare earth magnets generally contain a few per cent of voids and rare earth oxide particles. These and other second-phase particles lower the packing fraction of the majority phase, thereby lowering Br and (BH) max. They may also serve as sites of easy nucleation of reverse domains thereby lowering HcJ in magnets of type (A).

Since grain boundaries are generally sites of composition deviations, preferential precipitation, voids and enhanced demagnetising fields, they are often the site of reverse domain nucleation. The weakened exchange forces at grain boundaries, produced by disorder and segregation, also provide domain wall pinning important to high HcJ in magnets of the type (A).

4. The powder metallurgical processing of rare earth permanent magnets

The processing of the various types of rare earth permanent magnet materials can be carried out by a broadly similar powder metallurgical process. In this section the process steps are outlined.

The high reactivity of the rare earths and their alloys and the critical dependence of the magnetic properties on the chemical composition requires the effective suppression of contamination during the alloy preparation and subsequent powder metallurgical processing. In particular oxidation of the rare earth components by O_2 / H_2O must be kept to a minimum through all fine powder handling and heat treatment stages.

The main process steps taken during the production of REPM's are shown in Fig. 7. The general process consists of alloy preparation, pre-milling, milling, composition control and adjustment, particle alignment and pressing, sintering and heat treatment, machining, coating and finally magnetising.

4.1 Alloy preparation

Rare earth - 3d transition metal alloys can be produced by two methods on an industrial scale. These are vacuum induction melting and calciothermic reduction.

The vacuum induction method has the advantage that it can produce a wide range of rare earth alloy compositions with very low oxygen contents (<200 ppm). The typical microstructure of an as-cast ingot of the alloy $Nd_{16}Fe_{76}B_5$ is shown in Fig. 8. The structure consists of three main phases; primary columnar grains of the hard magnetic phase $Nd_2Fe_{14}B$, a boron rich phase $NdFe_4B_4$ and a Nd rich grain boundary phase.

The calciothermic production of rare earth alloys was developed independently by two groups working at General Electric, U.S. [13] and Th. Goldschmidt, W. Germany [14]. In the General Electric process cobalt powder, calcium granules and rare earth oxide powder are blended together and then reacted under hydrogen at 1423K. The reaction can be represented by the equation:

$$R_2O_3 + 10Co + 3Ca \xrightarrow[\text{3 hours}]{1423K, H_2} 2RCo_5 + 3CaO$$

After cooling, the excess calcium and calcium oxide are removed from the reacted product by reacting with moist nitrogen, then washing with water and dilute acid. This process is known as the reduction - diffusion (R - D) process.

The Goldschmidt process, known as co-reduction, is a variation of the R - D process in that the reaction is carried out under vacuum at 1273K and both cobalt powder and cobalt oxide powder are used as raw materials.

The main advantages of the calciothermic reduction process are the use of rare earth oxide as raw material and the direct production of alloy powder suitable for milling. However, both the oxygen content and calcium content are higher than alloys prepared by melting.

4.2 Pre-milling

Depending on the method used to prepare the alloy, the material may require a size reduction stage prior to final milling. For example, after vacuum melting and casting, the NdFeB alloy is in the form of chill cast lumps. These are crushed, under a nitrogen atmosphere in a high energy hammer mill, to a particle size range <500 micron.

An alternative chemical method of pre-milling the alloy has been developed in co-operation with the group of Prof. Rex Harris at the University of Birmingham. This process is known as hydrogen decrepitation. It has been shown that NdFeB alloys react readily with hydrogen at moderate pressures exhibiting a strongly exothermic reaction [15]. Measurements on the desorption behaviour of hydrogen from a $Nd_{16}Fe_{76}B_5$ alloy indicated the vacuum degassing consisted of two stages whereby hydrogen was first desorbed from the $Nd_2Fe_{14}B$ matrix phase below 300°C with the remainder being evolved from the Nd rich phase at higher temperatures [16]. The formation of two hydrides is consistent with the observed decrepitation behaviour where the initial activation process corresponds with the hydriding of the intergranular neodymium rich material resulting in transgranular fracture. This is followed by the hydriding of the matrix phase with the attendant transcrystalline cracking of the individual crystallites. Figure 9 shows a micrograph of a hydrided NdFeB particle exhibiting intergranular fracture. This technique of hydrogen decrepitation is exploited to produce a friable pre-milled material with a particle size less than 500 microns directly suitable as input material for the fine milling stage.

4.3 Milling

The object of milling the rare earth permanent magnet alloys is to produce a narrow size distribution of single crystal particles, i.e. individual particles containing no grain boundaries and therefore only one preferred axis

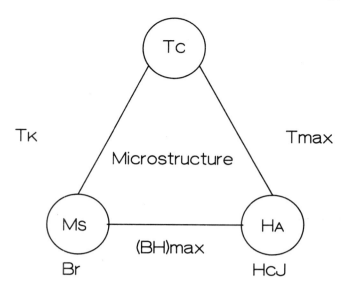

Figure 6. Relationship between the primary and secondary magnetic properties and microstructure.

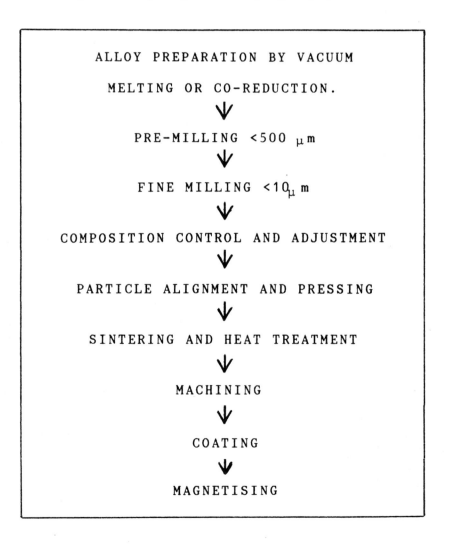

Figure 7. General process steps for the powder metallurgical production of REPM's.

Table 3. Major application areas of REPM's

APPLICATION GROUP	EXAMPLES	SYSTEM FUNCTION PROPORTIONAL TO
ACOUSTIC TRANSDUCERS	LOUDSPEAKERS HEADPHONES TELEPHONE RECEIVERS MICROPHONES PICKUPS	B
PERMANENT MAGNET MOTORS & GENERATORS, ELECTRO-MECHANICAL TRANSDUCERS	D.C. MOTORS E.C. MOTORS SYNCHRONOUS MOTORS STEPPING MOTORS GENERATORS LINEAR MOTORS MOVING-COIL MOTORS TORQUE TRANSMITTERS	B
MAGNETO-MECHANICS	COUPLINGS SEPARATORS ATTACHMENT SYSTEMS MAGNETIC CONVEYORS BEARINGS TRANSPORT SYSTEMS	B^2
MAGNETIC FIELD AND FOCUSSING SYSTEMS	DIPOLES QUADRUPOLES HEXAPOLES UNDULATORS WIGGLERS CIRCULATORS MASS SPECTROMETERS NMR SYSTEM	B

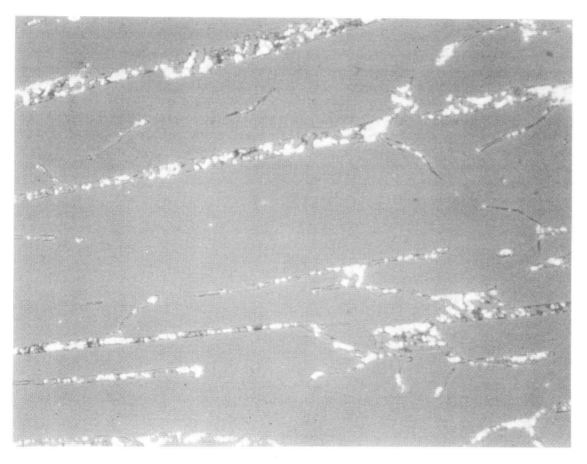

Figure 8. Typical microstructure of an as-cast ingot of the alloy $Nd_6Fe_{76}B_5$. (Magnification x 200)

of magnetisation. In addition, sufficient particle surface area must be present for high sinter reactivity. For single phase magnets, where the coercivity is controlled by domain nucleation and wall pinning at grain boundaries, the particle size and particle surface condition play a critical role in determining the coercivity of the sintered magnet. The critical parameters to be controlled during milling are particle size, particle size distribution, damage to crystal structure and oxidation.

The milling process can be carried out by either ball milling in an organic liquid under an inert gas e.g. attritor milling in cyclohexane, or by jet milling. The jet mill is a dry milling process in which the attrition action is mainly due to high velocity particle - particle collision. A typical manufacturing jet milling facility is shown in Fig. 10.

Figures 11 and 12 shows micrographs of typical NdFeB powders produced by attritor milling and jet milling respectively. The classifying action of the jet mill system is evident from the narrower particle size distribution shown by Fig. 12.

4.4 Compositional control and adjustment

As previously mentioned the magnetic properties of rare earth permanent magnets are critically dependent on the chemical composition. Any contamination, particularly oxidation, of the alloy occurring during processing depletes the alloy of the rare earth components. This results in a shift in composition to the T-rich side of the phase diagram, which may cause a magnetically unfavourable phase distribution.

In the case of $SmCo_5$ magnet production the optimum properties are found to occur over a composition range of 0.5wt % Sm; this corresponds to a mere 0.08 wt % oxygen pick up. To prevent excessive dilution of the magnetic material by Sm_2O_3 a maximum oxygen content of 0.6 wt% should not be exceeded in the finished magnet. The Sm_2O_3 formation is compensated for by introducing a corresponding excess of Sm over the stoichiometry of $SmCo_5$.

This can be done during the alloy preparation stage or by blending a Sm - rich milled alloy with the $SmCo_5$ milled alloy. The latter method is used during the manufacture of RES 190 magnets since it allows easier correction for slight variations in oxygen pick-up from batch to batch of milled powder.

For NdFeB the composition range for optimum magnetic properties is less critical than that for $SmCo_5$. The critical R content for NdFeB magnets is about a factor of 10 greater than the critical range for $SmCo_5$ magnets. This enables NdFeB magnets, with careful processing control, to be prepared by the single powder method.

4.5 Particle alignment and pressing

To obtain a powder compact with maximum magnetisation the powder particles are magnetically aligned and pressed such that the easy axes of magnetisation of the particles are parallel.

The powder compaction is performed by die pressing or by isostatic pressing. In the first method, the aligning magnetic field is set up in the cavity of a non magnetic die with its axis lying either in the direction of pressing or at right angles.

In large scale production multi-impression tooling is generally used. High homogeneous field levels are required to produce a high level of uniformly aligned particles. A typical uniaxial pressing system is shown in Fig. 13.

The applied field can be D.C. or some combination of D.C. and pulse. The degree of alignment is influenced by particle shape and the particle size distribution, magnitude of aligning field and pressing pressure. The pressing pressure should be sufficient to give the powder compact enough mechanical strength to withstand handling but not high enough to cause particle misorientation.

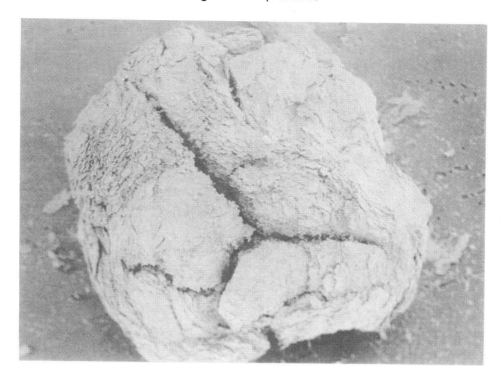

Figure 9. Micrograph of hydrided NdFeB particle. (Magnification x 1500)

Figure 10. Jet milling facility.

Figure 11. Scanning electron micrograph of attritor milled NdFeB powder. (Magnification x 1000)

Figure 12. Scanning electron micrograph of jet milled NdFeB powder. (Magnification x 1000)

Isostatic pressing is normally carried out on powders pre aligned in a pulsed magnetic field of a level 3 or 4 times that used in uniaxial die pressing. This improves the degree of particle alignment, which is then maintained during isostatic pressing and results in higher Br and (BH) max values than for die pressed pieces.

Figure 14 shows the effect of varying the aligning field and pressing method on the remanence of a rare earth permanent magnet material (RES 190).

4.6 Sintering and heat treatment

The sintering of rare earth permanent magnets is undertaken in inert gas atmospheres, reducing atmospheres or under vacuum. The sintering treatment should result in a magnet with a high density, and for magnets with a nucleation and grain boundary pinning coercivity mechanism, no appreciable grain growth. A constant and well defined sintering temperature is necessary in order to ensure the magnet has no open porosity which could lead to oxidation and ageing during use. This requires the density to be greater than 95% of theoretical density. The optimum temperature range for sintering RES 190 magnets has been found to be centered on 1428K with a range of 15K. The as-sintered coercivity of $SmCo_5$ is very low and a post sintering heat treatment is necessary.

However, the optimum sintering temperature range of NdFeB magnet is much wider and a constant properties can be achieved over a range of 80K. The coercivity can again be increased by means of a post sinter heat treatment in the region of 903K for 1 hour. It was suggested by Sagawa et al.[12] that the enhancement of coercivity is due to the removal of damaged particle surfaces by the action of a grain boundary liquid phase.

4.7 Machining

During the sintering operation the pressed product volume reduces to the final magnet body. This shrinkage depends upon production factors and the product final magnet shape and size. This results in some variation in magnet size and therefore a machining operation is necessary.

Rare earth permanent magnets are in general hard and brittle, although NdFeB magnets are rather tougher and less susceptible to breakage and chipping. Magnetic chucks are not used to hold pieces down directly. Small series items are fastened by special adhesives to steel backing plates, then ground on conventional grinding machines fitted with either silicon carbide or diamond grinding wheels. Large series production is ground on double disc machines where the pieces are moved between two grinding wheels set the required distance apart. A typical system is shown in Fig. 15. Small blocks tend to be slit using diamond impregnated wheels. Machined surfaces are required either to give the required magnetic contact with the associated components in the final assembly or for dimensional reasons.

4.8 Coating

Magnets based on the $Nd_2Fe_{14}B$ intermetallic are susceptible to corrosion and require a corrosion resistant coating for normal applications. The optimum coating and coating technology has to fulfil several criteria:

1. The coating must be thin to minimise air gaps in the magnetic circuit.

2. The coating must be uniform and provide complete coverage of all magnet surfaces.

3. The coating must be glueable to other parts of the magnetic circuit.

4. The coating technology must evolve little or no hydrogen.

5. The coating technology has to be applicable to a wide range of magnet shapes and sizes.

These criteria have been met by two coating techniques which are applied to the Neodure range of magnets. These are:

Figure 13. Uniaxial pressing system.

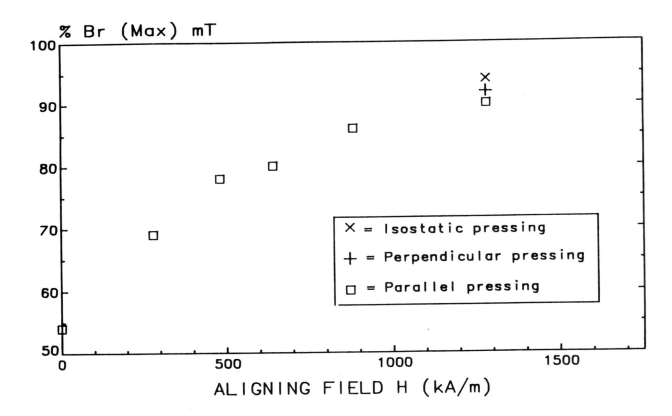

Figure 14. The effect of aligning field and pressing method on remanence of RES190.

- Ion vapour deposition of aluminium which produces a coating thickness of 10 ± 3 μm. The products can either be barrel or jig coated during this process.

- Cathodic electropaint (epoxy) with produces a thicker coating of 23 ± 5 μm and can only be applied to jigged products.

Both these coatings have guaranteed performance of 7 days resistance to accelerated humidity testing.

4.9 Magnetisation

Since most rare earth permanent magnets combine relative recoil permeabilities close to unity and high coercivity, then, they may be magnetised prior to assembly without flux loss. However, because of the difficulty of handling magnetised and brittle material it is usual for the user to carry our magnetisation during the system assembly.

5. Quality assurance

Conformance with specification must be assured for all products by an effective Quality Assurance System. At Philips Components Southport this is based on ISO9000 which integrates the different quality management activities. Such activities are not just product related but also embrace support functions including calibration, design and development, engineering, training, logistics and systems reviews. Quality plans are normally prepared for individual customers. These define specifications, manufacturing methods, inspection procedures and agreements made relevant to a particular product.

Product quality is achieved by close monitoring of all manufacturing operations utilising SPC techniques where appropriate.

6. Effect of temperature on magnetic properties

The working induction of a magnet falls with increasing temperature. This reduction can be caused by three effects; reversible, irreversible and irrecoverable changes.

Reversible changes occur because the relevant structure - insensitive properties of saturation magnetisation and anisotropy constant are both temperature dependent. In the case of NdFeB magnets the temperature coefficient of remanence is $-0.13\%/$ K^{-1} and the average temperature coefficient of coercivity is $-0.6\%/$K^{-1}.

The effect of temperature on the demagnetisation characteristics of a RES 255 magnet can be seen in Fig. 16.

Irreversible changes are due to thermal fluctuations causing domain reversal by irreversible rotations or wall movements. Remagnetisation is required to restore the original value. Irrecoverable changes cannot be recovered by remagnetisation and are caused by structural changes such as oxidation, phase changes or grain growth. As remagnetisation is rarely practical the maximum recommended temperatures of operation for the various magnet grades should never be exceeded.

7. Applications

The earliest commercial applications of rare earth magnets were in stepper motors for electronic watches, in the replacement of AlNiCo magnets in electron beam focussing systems such as travelling wave tubes and in some medical applications. Subsequent applications made greater use of the potential weight and volume reduction made possible by the higher magnetic energy.

Typical new applications were in magnetic bearings, servomotors, switches and actuators. The real breakthrough happened after 1975 when many new types of motor, generator, couplings, etc, were designed to use rare earth permanent magnets. Over the past few years, the application of rare earth permanent magnets, particularly in the Far East, in audio-visual and other consumer products has started to open new market opportunities.

Figure 15. Double disc grinding system.

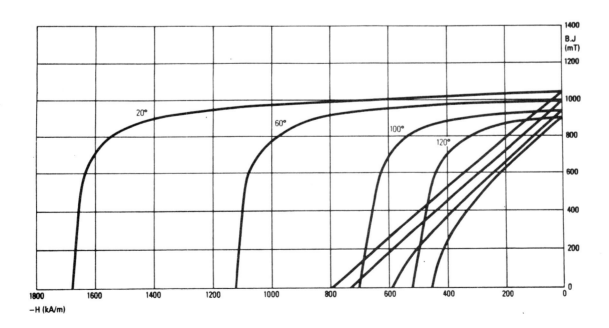

Figure 16. Effect of temperature on demagnetisation characteristics of RES 255.

Recently, a new market opportunity has developed due to the growth in Information Technology. Disk file systems have been developed which utilise a voice coil motor actuator to position the read /write head over the hard disk. The use of rare earth permanent magnets in these devices has enabled access times to be dramatically reduced.

It is impossible here to describe in detail all the many applications in which rare earth permanent magnets are expected to provide an innovative edge. The major applications are listed in Table 3 and characterized by their dependence on flux density B.

8. Conclusion

The powder metallurgical processing of REPM's produces materials with the highest known magnetic properties. At their present stage of development NdFeB magnets are distinctly superior to SmCo materials in terms of their performance at room temperature. However, at temperatures in excess of 140°C they are inferior. In order to ensure NdFeB magnets find applications in as many fields of modern technology as possible their operating temperature must be extended to 200°C without risk of demagnetisation. Improvements in the temperature dependence of magnetic properties requires both an increase in the Curie temperature and improved thermal stability of the coercivity.

Increases in Curie temperature can be achieved by substituting some Fe by Co, e.g. a substitution of 10% of the Fe by Co produces an increase in Curie temperature from 585K to 671K with a reduction in TK Br to 0.08% /K.

Increases in HcJ can be obtained by the addition of certain heavy rare earths, e.g. Tb, Dy or Ho. The addition of other elements, such as Ti, Mo, Zr, Nb and Hf, all produce increases in HcJ.

Corrosion and oxidation problems are mainly associated with the free Nd present in the grain boundary eutectic phase. It may be possible to reduce the amount of free Nd by the addition of Co or a heavy rare earth which forms a rare earth compound in favour of free Nd in the eutectic phase. However, currently available coatings e.g. Ion vapour deposited aluminium, have guaranteed performance in excess of 200°C.

Finally, increase usage of all REPM's will be achieved by the economics of reducing manufacturing costs during powder metallurgical processing. Since all rare earth permanent magnets exhibit high values of HcJ this results in magnetic circuit design requiring components with short magnetic axes.

Such components present particular problems in minimising grinding allowances. This requires the careful control of pressing conditions and powder dosing in the die cavities, the minimisation of distortion during sintering and heat treatment and the choice of suitable finishing methods. Similarly, because of the high raw material costs, the process control at all process steps must be such that a zero defect failure rate is guaranteed.

9. References

1. E.A. Nesbitt and J.H. Wernicke, Rare Earth Permanent Magnets, Academic Press, New York, 1973.

2. K.J. Strnat , J. Magn. Magn. Mater. 7, 1978, 351.

3. A.Menth, H. Nagel and R.W. Perkins, Ann. Rev. Mat. Sci. 8, 1978, 21.

4. J.D. Livingston, Gen. Electric Company, Report No. 80 CRD 139, 1980.

5. J. Ormerod , J. Less Common Metals 111, 1985, 49.

6. J. Ormerod, Metals and Materials, August 1988, 478.

7. N.C. Koon and B.N. Das, J. Appl. Phys. 55, 1984, 2063.

8. J.J. Becker, J. Appl. Phys. 55, 1984, 2067.

9. G.C. Hadjipayonis, R.C. Hazelton and K.R. Lawless, J. Appl. Phys. 55, 1984, 2073.

10. J.J. Croat, J.F. Herbst, R.W. Lee and F.E. Pinkerton, J. Appl. Phys. 55, 1984, 2078.

11. A.E. Clark, Appl. Phys. Lett. 23, 1973, 642.

12. M. Sagawa, S. Fujimura, N. Togawa, H.Yamamoto and J. Matsuura, J. Appl. Phys. 55, 1984, 2083.

13. R.E. Cech , J. Met. 26, 1974, 32.

14. C. Herget and H.G. Domazer, Goldschmidt Informiert 35,1975, 3.

15. I.R. Harris, C. Noble and T. Bailey, J. Less Common Metals, 51, 1985, 106.

16. E. Rozendaal, J. Ormerod, P.J. McGuiness and I.R. Harris, Proc. 9th Int. Workshop RE Magnets, Bad Soden, W. Germany 275, 1987.

Case Study 9
Soft Magnetic PM Materials

B. WEGLINSKI

Institute of Electric Machine Systems, Technical University of Wroclaw, W. Wyspianskiego 27, 50-370 Wroclaw, Poland

1. Introduction

The history of PM materials applications for manufacturing of magnetic cores is as old as the use of iron sheets for magnetic cores. Both ideas appeared almost simultaneously in the early 1880s. Edison's proposal was to apply sheets of thickness 0.4 to 0.8mm for magnetic cores working in alternating magnetic fields, while Fritts's idea was to build magnetic cores of iron particles bound with wax. The sheet structure of magnetic cores was used in electrical machines whilst the powder structure of cores was used in radio engineering and telecommunications until soft magnetic ferrites replaced it. Present dynamic development of automation and robotics, as well as promoting miniaturization of all kinds of technical devices, generate growing requirements for micro-motors of different types. This is the main reason why PM materials have come back as soft magnetic materials for magnetic cores for electrical devices (electric motors, relays, chokes, transformers etc.) [1, 2].

The reasons for the application of PM cores are:

- economic, because they offer attractive technology for long series and mass production of cores, which are produced without waste of raw material, and are to shape with quite acceptable dimensional tolerances, which avoids finishing operations,

- technical, attributed to the functioning of devices and required material properties.

Generally, magnetic properties of PM materials are comparatively lower than commonly used electrical steel sheets, although the sheet confines the distribution of magnetic flux in planes parallel to the sheet surfaces. In many electrical machines, such as for instance: stepper or disc motors, rotating-linear or linear-tube motors, a spatial distribution of magnetic flux is a favourable one. PM materials enable such distribution and secure satisfactory magnetic conditions for magnetic flux. Additionally, using sheet, there are difficulties with miniaturization of magnetic cores and the magnetic properties of cores are diminished due to effects of stresses which are introduced into parts during their punching. Waste of material by punching, for some types of electric motors, can reach 60% and even 80%.

On the other hand, the recent development of new types of iron powder with high chemical purity and high compressibility, as well as research on soft magnetic PM materials, has enabled improvement of their magnetic performance. These ensure that PM materials are competitive with electrical sheet in many applications.

Additionally, PM materials enable creation of integrated magnetic elements. The integrated element can serve different functions in electric converters and is an assemblage of parts made of different materials such as: soft magnetic, hard magnetic, electrically conducting, mechanically strengthening and so on.

Soft magnetic PM materials can be divided into the following:

1. Soft magnetic sinters [3].

2. Dielectromagnetics [4].

3. Magnetodielectrics [4].

Dielectromagnetics and magnetodielectrics are names referring to PM materials consisting of the same basic components: ferromagnetic material (predominantly iron powder) and dielectric (predominantly plastics like epoxy resin) [4]. The main functions of dielectric are insulation and binding of ferromagnetic particles. In dielectromagnetic, magnetic features prevail over dielectric ones, whereas it is quite opposite in magnetodielectrics. According to the dielectric content a material can belong to one of these groups [5]. Practically, materials with up to 2 wt% of dielectric content can be considered as dielectromagnetics, and those of higher dielectric content as magnetodielectrics.

Soft magnetic sintering technology is the same as common sintering, but for changing their properties such alloying elements as silicon, phosphorus and nickel are usually added.

2. Magnetic properties

Magnetic materials are conventionally divided into two primary groups:

- soft magnetic,

- hard magnetic.

Soft magnetic, or low coercivity materials are capable of reaching saturation even in weak magnetic fields, due to comparatively high magnetic permeability, and exhibit low hysteresis loss. Magnetization of these materials occurs mainly due to the displacement of domain walls.

Hard magnetic, or high coercivity materials are used for permanent magnets. They possess high specific energy, which varies in proportion to the remanence (Br) and coercivity (Hc). Magnetization of these materials occurs by the dominant role of magnetization vector rotation, which requires more energy than displacement of domain walls and thus their hysteresis loss is large. In other words, soft magnetic materials have a narrow hysteresis loop with low coercivity and hard magnetic materials have a wide loop with high coercivity.

Magnetic properties which determine magnetic material from the point of view of its application for magnetic cores are usually described in terms of magnetic induction (or magnetic flux density) B, magnetic intensity (or magnetic field strength, or magnetising force) H, and total energy loss ΔP which depends on induction and frequency. The plot of B versus H is called the magnetization curve (B = f(H)). The initial or normal magnetization curve is used as the basic characteristic of magnetic material.

The initial magnetization curve (Fig. 1) relates magnetic induction to monotonically increasing magnetic intensity, starting from the demagnetized state of a specimen.

The normal magnetization curve represents geometrical location of the peaks of hysteresis loops for different magnetic intensities. Cyclical magnetization of a test specimen results in a closed magnetization curve, named a hysteresis loop (Fig. 1). The basic parameters of a hysteresis loop are:

- remanence (Br) being the magnetic induction remaining in the specimen after the magnetic field is removed,

- coercivity (Hc) being the magnetic intensity required to reduce the remanence to 0.

- hysteresis loss (ΔP_h) whose value is proportional to the loop area.

The relationship between magnetic induction and magnetic intensity can be described, apart from B = f(H) curve, by means of absolute permeability - μ_a = B/H by the relative permeability - μ = B/μ_oH, where μ_o is the permeability of a vacuum. Of many different kinds of permeability, maximum permeability μ_{max} is in most frequent use.

Magnetization of material in alternating fields causes energy losses named total loss Δp, whose value depends on magnetic induction and frequency for a finite sample. Measurement of energy loss as function of frequency (Δp = f(f)) enables division of total loss into Eddy current loss (ΔP_e) and hysteresis loss (ΔP_h). Eddy current loss depends on magnetic and electrical properties (e.g. High Resistivity = low ΔP_e), and dimensions of the core.

The resistivity of material strongly determines the operating frequency range. The greater the resistivity of the material, the higher the frequencies at which it can operate. Good soft magnetic material should exhibit high values of Bs, B for definite values of H and μ_{max}; low values of Hc, Δp, ΔP_h and ΔP_e.

3. Processing of soft magnetic materials by powder metallurgy

Some of the basic technological processes for making soft magnetic PM materials are shown in Fig. 2. They are based on typical operations used in powder metallurgy. Processes leading to an increase of density of PM materials may be used for manufacturing of soft magnetic PM materials. Since density is the main factor influencing magnetic properties.

Powders used for soft magnetic materials are atomized iron powders of extreme chemical purity and very good compressibility, which ensures good compact density. The presence of carbon, sulphur and nitrogen is particularly unfavourable due to the increase in coercivity.

3.1 Soft magnetic sintered components

Soft magnetic iron matrix sinters of importance for magnetic applications can be divided into the following groups [6]:

- sintered iron,

- iron - silicon sinters,

- iron - phosphorus sinters,

- iron - nickel sinters.

Sintered iron exhibits average magnetic properties and high energy losses. This material is extensively described in the scientific literature due to its applications for structural components. The basic difference magnetic sintered iron is in the chemical purity and large grain structure required. It is expected that its importance as magnetic material will decrease.

Iron-silicon sinters exhibit comparatively high resistivity that decreases the energy loss considerably. It ensures that these sinters may be considered for magnetic cores working in alternating magnetic fields. Admixture of silicon to iron should be in the range 3 to 5 wt%. Their processing is very sensitive to sintering parameters and non-metallic inclusions which makes repeatability difficult to obtain. The most favourable silicon admixture is in elemental form and particle size below 0.06mm [2], though its introduction in the form of ferro silicon or master alloy is also used [6].

Iron - phosphorus sinters are very attractive materials for A.C. applications, due to their good magnetic properties. Optimum admixture of phosphorus lies in the range 0.8 to 1.2 wt%. The best results are obtained when phosphorus is introduced into iron in the form of iron phosphide (Fe_3P). Good magnetic properties are attributed to high density, resulting from liquid phase sintering and a structure characterized by large grains and coagulated spherical pores (7).

Iron - nickel sinters are usually used as alloys of 50% Fe and 50% Ni [8]. For their manufacture alloyed powder 50% Fe - 50% Ni is employed. These sinters are used for special applications. For general applications they are too expensive due to the high price of nickel.

Powder particle size distribution does not play an essential role in the case of sinters. Their magnetic properties depend on grain size which are present in material after recrystallization during sintering. Methods of admixtures and lubricant addition to mixtures, mixing and compacting do not differ from typical processes used in powder metallurgy [9, 10]. Double pressing is very effective for improvement of magnetic properties, particularly if powder of poor compressibility is used. In the case of integrated magnetic elements, consolidation of powder into a porous skeleton, which is afterwards infiltrated with copper, may be conducted during sintering, without previous compacting. By production of integrated elements, additions of different properties (fillers) may be inserted into the powder mixture before compacting [11].

Sintering in hydrogen is a basic operation for consolidation of a compact. The sintering temperatures are determined more by the technical possibilities of furnaces. The rate of cooling after sintering should be slow to ensure creation of a structure with coarse grains. Any additional treatment, which leads to improvement or change of sinter properties or dimension tolerance, like redensification, sizing, annealing, etc., is advantageous for soft magnetic sinters.

3.2 Dielectromagnetics

The application of a dielectromagnetic determines the particle size of iron powder used. To reach high magnetic properties, coarse powder particles within the range 0.15 to 0.6mm should be used. For high frequency applications, fine powder such as the carbonyl iron powder with spherical shaped grains and a size below 0.06mm should be used. This ensures complete insulation of grains and leads to decrease of Eddy current loss.

Powder particles should be spheroidal or granular with possibly low open porosity. This ensures good insulation of particles with a small amount of dielectric. Powders of nickel, cobalt and ferromagnetic alloys like alsifer (6 to 8% Al, 9 to 11% Si, rest Fe), molybdenum permalloy (80% Ni, 2% Mo, 18% Fe) and the like, may also be employed in dielectromagnetics.

The dielectrics role is to ensure good electrical insulation and mechanical binding of ferromagnetic powder particles. The amount in dielectromagnetics is within the range 0.1 to 2wt%. Epoxy resin which exhibits supreme adhesion to many materials is used predominantly. However epoxy resin and other organic dielectrics have a low temperature of disintegration (below 500K). Sometimes dielectromagnetics should be thermally recrystallized, within the range of 850 to 1060K, to relieve stresses generated during compacting with iron particles. In such case inorganic dielectrics like: phosphates, oxides, silicon dioxides, glass etc. can be used. Fillers can also be employed for mechanical strengthening of material. For strengthening purpose various kinds of fibres, like glass or carbon can be used. Electrically conducting or magnetic fillers may be in the form of rods, wires, fibres, foils, sheets and the like [4].

The aim of mixing is to ensure uniform deposition of the dielectric on the surface of ferromagnetic particles. Selection of mixing equipment and procedure depends on the form of the dielectric. If the dielectric is a liquid phase, as solution in a solvent, (e.g. epoxy resin,) a blade mixer can be used. In such a case mixing is carried out to complete evaporation of the solvent, mostly at an elevated temperature, to coat loose powder ready for compacting. In this way, more than one layer of dielectric may be deposited on ferromagnetic particles [12].

Uniaxial die compacting is the basic procedure used in forming. High compacting pressures - over 600 MPa (mostly 800 MPa) should be employed to reach a high density compact. Lubrication is an essential problem of dielectromagnetic compacting, and the only acceptable solution seems to be the lubrication of the die wall, mandrels and punches using oil in liquid or spray form.

Curing is the basic thermal treatment used for final consolidation of the compact. The temperature of this treatment depends on the dielectric used. In the case of organic dielectric, this is between 370 and 470K, and for inorganic dielectric between 1000 and 1300K. Sintering time depends on temperature and type of dielectric; usuallym it is in the range 0.5-2 hours. If necessary, to secure dimensional stability or full cross-linking in the polymer used as dielectric, thermal stabilizing may be used.

An important advantage of dielectromagnetics is the close tolerances of dimensions which may achieved.

3.3 Magnetodielectrics

Raw materials and processing of magnetodielectrics are similar to processing of dielectromagnetics but other methods of forming like casting, centrifuging and luteing can also be employed. Forming by centrifuging may be used for pipe fitting production, e.g. semimagnetic partitions for electric motors [13]. Forming of magnetodielectric by luteing is used for groove closures. These were formed from magnetodielectric putty directly in open grooves by luteing and injecting the putty under pressure [14]. These methods may be employed in the forming of magnetodielectrics due to a high dielectric content - usually over 10wt%.

4. Properties of soft magnetic PM materials

Properties of the materials discussed depend on:

- the powders used, including their compressibility and chemical purity,

- admixtures,

- impurities introduced during processing,

- the processing parameters the material.

The above will determine the density, structure and the magnetic properties of material. Density is a fundamental parameter which determines the magnetic properties of the material. Dependence of magnetic induction on density, for definite values of magnetic intensity can be approximated by straight lines, called "lines of standard induction" (Fig. 3), both for sinters (Fig. 3) and dielectromagnetics (Fig. 4) [15]. These lines (Fig. 4) are independent of powder type, dielectric content and the method of a predetermined density level. They can be employed for the monitoring of soft magnetic PM materials processing. This can be carried out by measurement of magnetic induction and density. Measured values are compared with values of induction for specific density taken from lines of standard induction. Other magnetic properties do not display linear correlations with density, and their behaviour is sometimes very different - due to the type of material, the powder or dielectric used (Fig. 4).

4.1 Sintered iron

According to Moyer et al. [16] the porosity of sinters made of high purity atomized iron powder essentially influences their magnetic properties. When samples were hot repressed so that no porosity was present, the magnetic properties were as good or even better than conventional high purity solid iron. A linear decrease of induction and remanence and increase of resistivity with decrease of sintered density were also observed. Porosity restricts grain growth, and small, closely spaced pores cause the greatest degradation of properties [16]. This is in agreement with research results carried out by the author [1, 2]. Dependence of some magnetic properties on density of sinters made of ASC 100. 29 and NC 100. 24 iron powders are shown in Fig. 5. Thermal treatment essentially influences coercivity and permeability which are the most sensitive magnetic

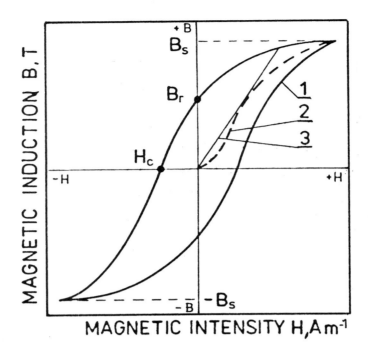

Figure 1. Hysteresis loop (1), initial magnetization curve (2) and maximum magnetic permeability u_{max} (3); Bs - magnetic induction of saturation, Br - remanence, Hc - coercivity.

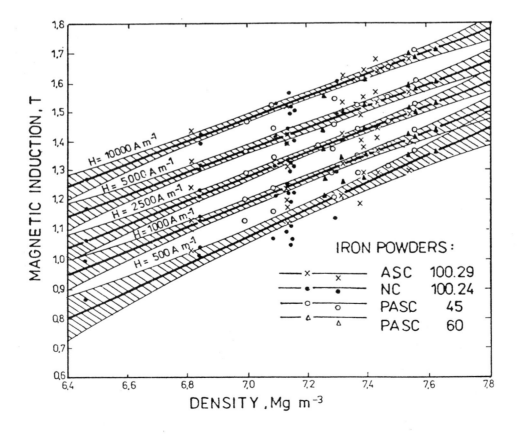

Figure 3. Lines of standard induction for soft magnetic sinters (hatched areas indicate 99% confidence limits) [1].

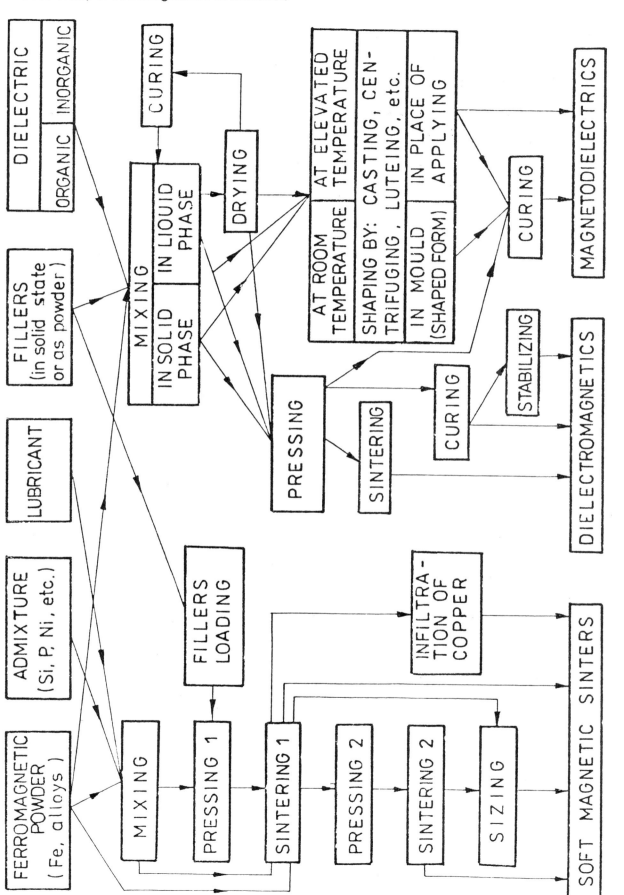

Figure 2. Basic processing routes of soft magnetic PM materials.

parameters of the material. For instance, anealing for 24 h at 1473 K in dry hydrogen caused over 50% increase in permeability and about 25% decrease in coercivity for sinters made of ASC 100. 29 iron powder.

Considering the influence of processing parameters on magnetic properties of sintered iron, the following points can be made[18, 19]:

1. Compacting pressure has a major influence on magnetic properties.

2. To reach maximum magnetic properties double pressing should be employed.

3. Sintering temperatures in the range 1323 to 1623 K for 3h and sintering time in the range 1 to 24 h at a temperature of 1473 K have no significant influence on most of the magnetic properties with the exception of permeability and coercivity.

4. Particle size distribution of powder has minor influences on magnetic properties.

4. 2 Iron - silicon sinters

Addition of silicon is unfavourable for magnetic induction whose values for finite sintered density are smaller than values found from lines of standard induction (Fig. 3). This is compensated by improvement of other magnetic properties. Admixture of 4wt% Si results in a 400% increase of resistivity, a 60% decrease of losses, and a 50% decrease of coercivity [20].

Processing parameters have an major influence on properties of Fe - 4% Si sinters. An example of changes of density are shown in Fig. 6. Changes of permeability and coercivity for processing parameters of up to 100% are indicated in Fig. 6. The influence of sintering temperature and time is more significant than compacting pressure. From studies [21], it was found that Fe - 4% Si sinters of good and comparable magnetic properties can be obtained by application of:

- low compacting pressures (600 MPa) and longer sintering times (24 h),

- low compacting pressures (600 MPa), high sintering temperatures (1550K) and medium sintering times (8 h),

- medium compacting pressures (800 MPa), high sintering temperatures (1550K) and short sintering times (2 h).

4.3 Iron - phosphorus sinters

Addition of phosphorus has a favourable influence on density and magnetic properties of sinters. Phosphorus introduced in amounts of 0.8 wt%, in the form of Fe_3P, result in the increase of density (4.7%); resistivity (90%); permeability (136%), and decreases of coercivity (52%); total loss (51%), and hysteresis loss (61%) [22]. Magnetic inductions for finite densities are greater than those found from lines of standard induction (Fig. 3). Good magnetic properties of Fe - 0.896P sinters are attributed to high density, resulting from liquid-phase sintering and a structure characterized by large grains and small amounts of coagulated and round pores [23]. The affect of the processing parameters on the magnetic properties of Fe - 0.8%P sinters is great, particularly in changes of permeability (Fig. 7) and coercivity.

It is possible to obtain comparable magnetic properties of Fe - 0.8%P sinters using the appropriate combination of processing parameters [24]. The following values can be considered as optimized properties of Fe - 0.8%P sinters:

- minimum density - 7. 7 Mg m^{-3},

- minimum permeability - 14000,

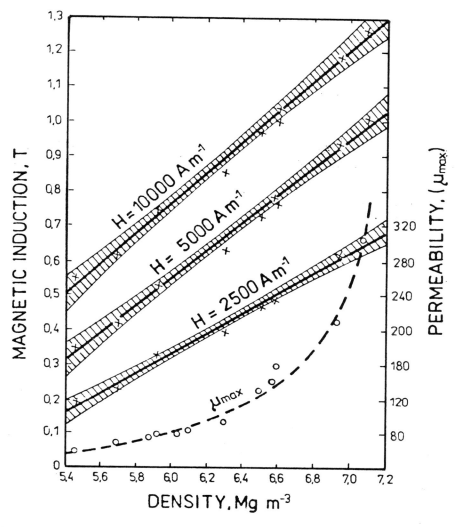

Figure 4. Lines of standard induction and permeability versus density for dielectromagnetics made of ASC 100.29 iron powder and epoxy resin in amount 1 wt% and 3 wt% (hatched areas indicate 99% confidence limits) (2).

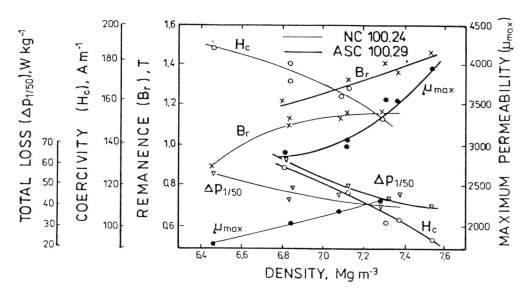

Figure 5. Relationship between magnetic properties and densities of sinters made of ASC 100.29 and NC 100.24 iron powders (17).

- minimum magnetic induction of saturation - 1. 83 T,

- maximum coercivity - 32 A m^{-1},

- maximum total energy loss (at 1 T and 50 Hz) - 21 W. kg^{-1}.

4.4 Iron - nickel sinters

Fe - 50% Ni sinters are characterized by high permeability and low coercivity which make them useful in special applications. The permeability and coercivity are very sensitive on sintering parameters. By compacting at 800 MPa and sintering at 1450 K over 8 h the following properties should be reached [25]:

- minimum density - 7 . 75 Mg m^{-3},

- maximum resistivity - 0.43 μVm,

- minimum magnetic induction of saturation - 1.4 T,

- minimum permeability - 15000,

- maximum coercivity - 16 A m^{-1},

- maximum total energy loss (at 1 T, and 50 Hz) - 15.2 W kg^{-1}.

4.5 Dielectromagnetics

Properties of dielectromagnetics depend, on processing parameters and particularly on dielectric content, compacting pressure, and properties and the structure of ferromagnetic powder used. The influence of dielectric content on some properties of dielectromagnetics made of ASC 100.29 iron powder and epoxy resin, compacted with pressure 600 MPa, are presented in Table 1. The values of magnetic induction for finite densities can be found from lines of standard induction (Fig. 4). Dielectromagnetics are characterized by high values of resistivity and low energy loss. That is why they are suitable material for magnetic cores for alternating magnetic flux (27).

Different behaviour of magnetic materials in static and dynamic (alternating) magnetic fields are caused mostly by Eddy currents. In the case of dielectromagnetics and magnetodielectrics, Eddy currents are seriously limited by insulating barriers of dielectric. In effect there are practically no differences between dynamic and static magnetic parameters which are independent of the dimensions of samples used for measurements. There are no differences between energy loss of a real magnetic element and conventional loss of material (measured on samples of specified dimensions) [28]. In the case of sinters magnetic parameters are markedly affected by the frequency of the imposed magnetic flux and the dimensions of magnetic element used for measurements.

Magnetic properties of dielectromagnetics can be changed by use of powder particles with different shape. The particles can be grains, flakes [29] needles, fibres etc., and these can be exploited for relative ease of producing magnetic anisotropy.

4.6 Magnetodielectrics

The level of magnetic properties of magnetodielectrics, due to their supplementary function in a magnetic circuit, is low. Sometimes their magnetic properties may be limited because too high a value of permeability may worsen the performance of the magnetic circuit, if part of it is made of magnetodielectric. Such a situation is found in the case of magnetic wedges. An example of magnetodielectric properties that can be found in cast magnetodielectrics is as follows [30]:

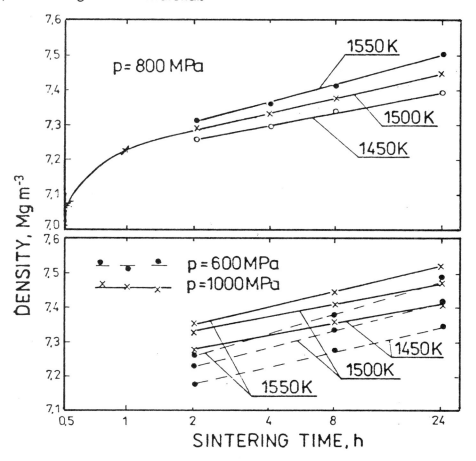

Figure 6. Effect of sintering temperature and time on density of Fe - 4% Si sinters compacted at: 800 MPa, 600 MPa, and 1000 MPa [3].

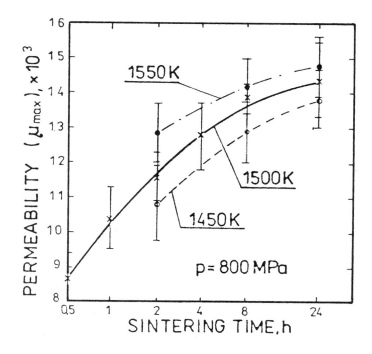

Figure 7. Effect of sintering parameters on permeability of Fe - 0.8%P sinters pressed at 800 MPa (99% confidence limits of mean values are indicated) [24].

- permeability 4 to 20,

- resistivity - over 0.1Vm,

- bending strength over 100 MPa.

5. Magnetic core design criteria by application of PM materials

Two basic criteria influence the application of soft magnetic PM materials for magnetic cores with alternating magnetic flux [7]. They are:

- electrodynamic,

- technological.

According to electrodynamic criterion, the width of the transverse section of solid rectangular core (b) penetrated by alternating magnetic flux cannot exceed twice the value of the electromagnetic wave penetration depth [7]. The values, in the case of dielectromagnetics and magnetodielectrics employed in alternating fields of frequency 10 to 1000 Hz, range from centimetres to metres. It means that any magnetic core designed in a dielectromagnetic is not limited by electrodynamic criterion. In the case of sinters, their wave penetration depth is in the lower range from 0.001mm to several millimetres, which certainly imposes constraints on the transverse - section dimensions (b) of designed cores. If the electrodynamic criterion is disregarded then eddy current loss increases excessively [7].

Technological criteria come from compacting options and particularly from the possibility of compacting slender elements with a maximum height to minimum thickness ratio. The upper limit is the value of slender for which it is possible to make a compact with a proper density distribution and which, after sintering, properly fulfills its function as a magnetic core. Its precise value depends on several factors, such as the powder used, the lubricant and the processing parameters, and is determined experimentally [7].

Fulfilment of both criteria, and particularly the electrodynamic one is difficult, especially for the design of magnetic cores made of sinters. The most effective solution which enables fulfilment of both criteria is the partition of a core into layers, segments or other elements.

The elements can be shaped into (Fig. 8):

- rings,

- sectors with trapezoidal transverse section,

- discs,

  or other shapes.

The soft magnetic PM materials are quite different from commonly used electrical sheet. They create new possibilities for magnetic core construction, but they need further development and new design rules [3,31].

6. Magnetic applications of PM materials

Regarding magnetic applications of PM materials, it is useful to consider the function carried out by magnetic elements in an electrical converter. The magnetic core functions are diverse, but they can be divided into three essential groups [27]:

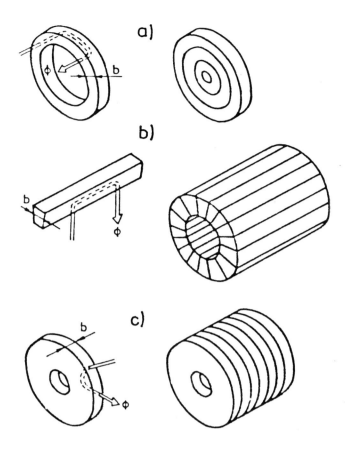

Figure 8. Partition of magnetic cores into elements according to electrodynamic and partially technological criterion:

(a) ring shaped, (b) sector shaped with trapezoidal transverse section, (c) disc-shaped [7].

Table 1. Changes of density (d), resistivity (r), total loss (for 1 T and 50 Hz) (Δp), and bending strength (Rg) for different dielectric content in dielectromagnetics made of ASC 100.29 iron powder [26]

Dielectric content wt%	δ Mg m^{-3}	ρ $\mu\Omega$m	Δp W . kg^{-1}	Rg MPa
0.2	7.13	500	8.9	105 ± 16
0.6	7.07	1000	9.0	121 ± 29
1.0	6.99	1200	9.4	122 ± 10
1.4	6.93	1600	9.2	168 ± 20
2.0	6.80	4300	9.3	206 ± 10

- basic,

- complementary,

- supplementary.

The basic function is carried out by magnetic cores penetrated by the main magnetic flux. Materials for such cores should essentially have high permeability and saturation induction and low Eddy current loss. These conditions are fulfilled by dielectromagnetics. Sinters can also be applied if the measures described in section 5 are undertaken. The basic function is carried out by such typical magnetic elements as armatures, yokes, field magnet cores, poles, cores of chokes and relays.

The complementary function is carried out by magnetic cores in which a total or partial main magnetic flux and sometimes leakage flux flows. For this purpose, applied material should have various values of permeability, saturation induction and energy loss, dependent on the type of specific application. Examples of cores performing a complementary function are concentrators and deconcentrators of magnetic induction and different kinds of magnetic shunts. They can be made of dielectromagnetics and sometimes of sinters.

The supplementary function is carried out by magnetic cores through which, as a rule, magnetic leakage fluxes and in some cases main flux flows. Their main function is not a magnetic one, but very often can be mechanical. The required properties of material for supplementary elements are moderate, as even low values of magnetic parameters with good mechanical strength are acceptable. Magnetodielectrics are mostly used for this purpose. Examples of such applications are closures of open or semi-open slots of electrical motor armatures, in the form of putty or cast magnetodielectrics, ready formed grooved wedges, and hermetizing semi-magnetic partitions for asynchronous motors.

The above-mentioned functions can be joined and electrical and mechanical functions may be added. In such cases one can deal with integrated magnetic elements which should become magnetic elements of the future [11]. To build such elements, all the described PM materials can be employed. The research on the applications of soft magnetic PM materials shows that, based on technological and economic grounds, such applications are possible and advisable [32]. Every year, more and more concrete examples of industrial manufacture of such elements can be found, such as those shown in Figs. 9, 10 and 11.

7. Acknowledgements

I am grateful to Professor Andrzej Kordecki for a very fruitful co-operation during the research; generating ideas and encouraging my efforts in the field of PM magnetic materials.

I would also like to express my sincere thanks to Dr Dennis Hadfield for his extended efforts in editing this publication.

8. References

1. B. Weglinski, Development prospects in powder composites for magnetic cores of electrical converters, Pr. Inst. Elektromasz. PWr. 24 (Monograph No. 4), 1977.

2. B. Weglinski, Magnetically soft iron matrix powder composites, Pr. Inst. Elektromasz. PWr .32 (Monograph No. 5), 1981.

3. B. Weglinski, "Sinters for magnetic applications" (submitted for publication in Reviews on Powder Metallurgy and Physical Ceramics).

4. B. Weglinski, "Soft magnetic powder composites - dielectromagnetics and magnetodielectrics" (submitted for publication in Reviews on Powder Metallurgy and Physical Ceramics).

Figure 9. Magnetic cores made of PM materials by the Tecsinter Company [33].

Figure 10. Magnetic elements of printer and fuel pumps made by Aplicationes de Metales Sinterizados. (Courtesy C. A. de M. S. -
Barcelona, Spain)

Figure 11. Magnetic cores made by Aplicationes de Metales Sinterizados. (Courtesy C. A. de M. S. - Barcelona, Spain)

5. A. Kordecki and B. Weglinski, Powder Metallurgy 31 (2), 1988, 113 .

6. B. A. James and G. Williams, Proc. 5th Powder Metallurgy Conference, Poland, Vol. II, 1979, 345.

7. A. Kordecki, B. Weglinski and J. Kaczmar, Powder Metallurgy 25 (4), 1982, 201 .

8. L. W. Baum, Precision Metal (March), 1974, 47.

9. H. Hausner, "Handbook of powder metallurgy", Chem. Pub. Co. Inc., New York, 1973.

10. W. D. Jones, "Fundamental principles of powder metallurgy", Edward Arnold Pub. Ltd., London, 1960.

11. A. Kordecki and B. Weglinski, Proc. 7th Powder Metallurgy Conf., Poland, T. I, 1988, 261.

12. A. Kordecki and B. Weglinski, Powder Metallurgy 31 (4), (in press).

13. A. Kordecki and B. Weglinski, Proc. 4th Powder Metallurgy Conf., Poland, Book III, 1975, 71 .

14. H. Keuth, Siemens-Zeitschr. 12, 1970, 736.

15. W. Rutkowski and B. Weglinski, Powder Metallurgy 22, 1979, 67.

16. K. H. Moyer, M. J. McDermott, M. J. Topolski and D. F. Kearney, Powder Technology 30 (1), 1981, 51.

17. K. Gardela and B. Weglinski, Pr. Inst. Elektromasz. PWr. 23 (5), 1976, 55.

18. B. Weglinski and K.Gardela, Metalurgia Proszkow 1, 1977, 53.

19. K. Gardela and B. Weglinski, Pr. Inst. Elektromasz. PWr. 18 (3), 1975, 33.

20. W. Rutkowski and B. Weglinski, Planseeberichte fur Pulvermetallurgie 3, 1979, 162.

21. J. Kaczmar and B. Weglinski, Int J. Powder Metallurgy and Powder Technology 18 (1), 1982, 25.

22. W. Rutkowski and B. Weglinski, Planseeberichte fur Pulvermetallurgie 1/2, 1980, 39.

23. B. Weglinski and J. Kaczmar, Powder Metallurgy 4, 1980, 210.

24. J. Kaczmar and B. Weglinski, Powder Metallurgy 27 (1), 1984, 9.

25. J. Kaczmar and B. Weglinski, Int. J. Powder Metallurgy and Powder Technology 17 (2), 1981, 117.

26. B. Weglinski, Proc. 3rd. Powder Metallurgy Conf., Varna, Bulgaria, 1978, 32.

27. A. Kordecki and B. Weglinski, Powder Metallurgy 27 (2), 1984, 85.

28. Z. Berkowska and B. Weglinski, Proc. 5th Symp. on Powder Metallurgy, Rydzyna, Poland, 1980, 9.

29. B. Weglinski, Proc. 5th Symp. on Powder Metallurgy, Rydzyna, Poland 1980, 183.

30. A. Gardela, K. Gardela and B. Weglinski, Wiadomosci Elektrotechniczne 8, 1979, 204.

31. A. Kordecki and B. Weglinski, Metalurgia Proszkow 2, 1980, 63.

32. S. Kubzdela and B. Weglinski, Metal Powder Report 37 (1), 1982, 21.

33. Tec Sinter - Information Materials, A company of the Olivetti Group, Italy, 1987.

CASE STUDY **10**
Injection Moulding of Soluble Precision Preformed Ceramic Cores for Hollow Investment Castings
E. M. BRISCOE

1. Introduction

The impetus for further enhancement of the technique of investment casting,which owes its origin to the distant past of the Pharaohs, can be attributed to the needs of the modern Gas Turbine, the first versions of which appeared in practical form in 1937 as a jet engine pioneered by Sir Frank Whittle.Under his leadership a Company — Power Jets Ltd —was formed and produced the world's first Jet Propulsion Gas Turbine.

Though patents for the Jet Engine concept were registered in 1928, well ahead of the competition for that power source, it is said that the first jet powered flight was by a Heinkel He 178 some 18 months before the first British jet aircraft, the Gloster E 28/39.The slower development of the British jet was not purely attributable to technical difficulty but also due to lack of appreciation of the potential by those responsible for funding - a syndrome recognisable in various other fields today. Manufacture of the turbine blades naturally followed steam turbine practice; the blades were solid, forged to approximate shape and subsequently machined. Combustion products from the combustion chambers entered the turbine section at approximately 800K (that being virtually the maximum temperature for operation of the alloys then available for the purpose).The thrust of the Whittle engine was 3800 N for an installed mass of 283 kg.Today we have aero gas turbines generating thrusts of up to $2.5 \ 10^5$N and with a power to weight ratio many times better than the original Whittle jet. Furthermore, the specific fuel consumption has also improved dramatically, spurred on by the quadrupling of oil prices in the 1970s.The most significant factor of these changes is attributable to an increase in thermal efficiency, as forecast in the well known relationship between heat engine inlet and exhaust temperature. This was formulated by Carnot; efficiency is proportional to

$$1 - \frac{T_1}{T_2}$$

where T_2 = heat input temperature and T_1 = heat rejection temperature. Clearly this requires an increase in T_2 at a greater rate than increase in T_1. In a jet engine T_2 can be raised from gasses emerging from the combustion chanbers to a level at which the gas turbine blades can survive the increased duty.Today such designs result in turbine inlet temperatures of the order of 1600K,compared with 800K in the Whittle engine. Development of superior alloys has made a significant contribution but the above temperature is some 300K above the melting point of the Nimonic Alloy blades and vanes. Whilst coating the blades with ceramic insulating materials protects them by approximately 50K, the remainder of the gain results from making the blades hollow and cooling their interiors with external air from the compressor stage. Simple "hollowing" in the first developments was as a result of a clever forging technique, but sophisticated cooling patterns require quite complex internal configuration which today is achieved by casting the alloy around similarly complex ceramic cores which, when removed from the casting, provide the desired effect. Some 20% of compressor air is utilised for that purpose but the net gain in efficiency is significant: it would clearly be of further advantage if air power cooling could be eliminated but it is considered that metal alloys have reached virtually their temperature limit and so attention is now being turned to the possibility of developing ceramic type materials with superior properties. Figure 1 shows the evolution of operating temperatures with time and includes prospective targets for non metal components i.e. certain engineering ceramics probably reinforced by ceramic fibres.That subject however lies outside the scope of this chapter as the objective is to describe how complex hollow blade development became possible by the development of precision complex shape ceramic cores.

The market for efficient and high output gas turbine engines, for both military and civil use has grown from small beginnings 50 years ago to substantial volumes today. In 1960 when the development of ceramic cores commenced, the market was less evident but at that time it was established that there was only one other source of supply — in the U.S.A. and with the prospects for worldwide sales, a decision was made by a U. K. company to support, in the long term if necessary, the development of the appropriate technology. This decision was reinforced by a forecast that engine thrust could be increased by some 30% by using sophisticated cooling techniques derived from ceramic cores. It followed therefore that a satisfactory product would command a relatively high price compared with more traditional ceramics. There were, therefore, two key commercial factors leading to the decision to innovate. Unorthodox ceramic technology was likely to be required which was then unquantifiable in terms of cost, duration and payback. Different services and personnel were likely to be necessary to enhance prospects for success and in the shortest time. Finally, the urgency of the project was influenced by encouragement from the British gas turbine industry to provide a U.K. source especially in support of the defence sector.

2. Technical Requirements — in service

In order to appreciate the technical specification targets for ceramic cores, the following is a brief description of the investment casting process. The first step is to place a core with its ends (termed "prints"), registering in locations in a split die whose *internal surface* dimensions correspond with the desired *external* size of the cast turbine blade (after allowing for metal shrinkage). Wax is then injected into the resultant cavity and when solidified the assembly is removed from the die. This assembly is then coated (invested) with various layers of ceramic (termed "stucco"): this coat, when cured chemically, is handleable and forms what is termed the "shell mould". The next step is to place the assembly into a dewaxing oven (hence the term "Lost Wax") and one is left with an outer ceramic mould containing a ceramic core . The space between the two ceramic forms is then filled, usually under vacuum, with molten alloy at up to 1800K.

When cold, the ceramic shell is removed, leaving behind the core inside the casting, which has contracted on to the core; the core is then removed mechanically if it is of a simple form or chemically if complex. The core therefore has to be soluble in chemicals which do not attack the alloy. The resulting artefact, after some external machining, becomes the finished turbine blade though other additional processes may be applied. The above description sets the scene for the technical requirements for a ceramic core — its material and processing.

3. Technical Requirements — ceramic core material and manufacture

The method of use and broad requirements of a ceramic core for lost wax castings has been described above. Readers will be tempted to enquire if there is a simpler way of obtaining a precise high temperature alloy component with complex internal passageways. As internal machining of a solid turbine blade is not possible, the detail could only be achieved by splitting the blade in half, machine matching detail into both pieces and then attach the two parts. Whilst this may be feasible, the industry worldwide has adopted and adapted investment casting to provide its requirements. Alloys have also undergone continuous development, but in doing so their pouring temperatures have risen and this has put further demands on the associated ceramics in their processing. Metal temperatures around 1800K (and held for many minutes in making single crystal castings) are not uncommon.

3.1 Selection of ceramic raw materials

The following factors have to be taken into consideration:

(a) Cost
(b) Refractoriness
(c) Stability
(d) Thermal expansion

(e) Strength particularly at elevated temperature
(f) Texture and surface finish
(g) Permeability and pore size
(h) Thermal conductivity
(i) Thermal shock resistance
(j) Dimensional stability and accuracy

4.Cost

Though not a technical factor, this is a necessary consideration, as most non-oxide materials were considered to be too expensive and probably unstable or reactive in the subsequent investment casting environment, the search for suitable materials focussed on materials already used in metallurgical applications.

Processing from raw material to finished article also had to anticipate cost bearing in mind high production quantities and the need for dimensional accuracy without extensive finishing costs ,but that set of circumstances does permit high initial tooling and equipment investment.

5. Refractoriness

Table 1 summarises melting point data on oxide materials as currently available. Choice of the correct materials for an application is essential if distortion, slumping or vitrification (leading to degradation of dimensions, permeability and thermal shock resistance) are to be avoided.

6. Stability

Hydration is an undesirable characteristic and precludes the use, of calcium oxide for instance, and magnesium oxide (unless dead burnt or fused) from general application. Similarly, for high temperature applications, low vapour pressures are required especially if vacuum conditions prevail. Possibility of reactions with other materials also become important at the elevated temperatures of casting molten alloy. As there is a need for compatibility, thermodynamic reasoning can confirm practical observations (e.g. in alloy melting and casting) and will highlight the reactions which could take place in new operations or with new materials.The common "tool" used is the concept of free energy. In practice it has to be assumed that the secondary constituents of nickel, cobalt and iron alloys could include the elements Al, B, C, Cr, Cu, Mo,Nb, Si, S, Ta, V, W and Zr. Some of these would only be present in minor amounts. Furthermore, there are certain elements which are not permitted to contaminate the alloys as they can cause unacceptable creep.

7. Thermal expansion

The linear coefficients of thermal expansion of ceramic materials listed in Table 1 all lie in the range of near zero to 18×10^{-6} per degree and is much lower than most metallic alloys (see Fig.2).

This is obviously important when there is mismatch between two refractory materials which are used in conjunction with each other. Differential strains can occur between the core and the shell on heating or cooling. Furthermore abrupt changes in expansion occur with phase changes on heating or cooling: the changes occurring with silica (e.g. the cristobolite transformation at around 250K) are well known. Particle size can also influence expansion and therefore control needs to be exercised in order to avoid strains and variation in other properties such as permeability,strength and solubility.

8.Strength

Strength of the finished product must be adequate to withstand finishing operations and inspection by engineering techniques and to avoid handling scrap by both supplier and user. However, high strength, such as with structural ceramics, is neither needed nor desirable as, for instance, the core must not unduly resist the differential contraction between hot solid alloy and the core as the casting cools down. Some compressive

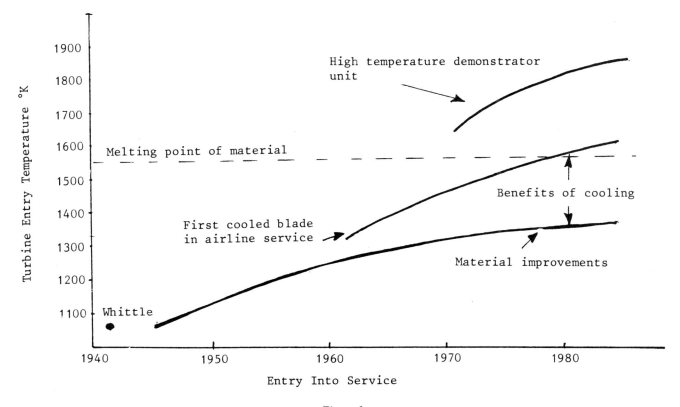

Figure 1

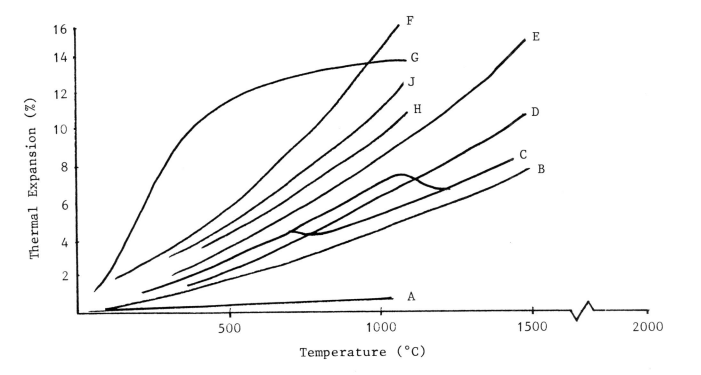

Figure 2

the differential contraction between hot solid alloy and the core as the casting cools down. Some compressive yielding of the core is required to avoid hot tearing of the casting, which must have a high order of integrity in this application. The above considerations lead to the conclusion that a lightly sintered product could have sufficient strength and therefore be porous with sufficient permeability so as to allow ready penetration of leaching agents to dissolve the core in due course. Though required strengths are now known and monitored for quality control purposes, practical experience in handling and "engineering instinct" had to be applied at early stages of the development. Experience subsequently showed that strengths of the order of 30 MN/ m^2 proved to be adequate for many formulations whose particle size distribution provided the required permeability for leaching and release of gasses from the casting process.

9. Texture and surface finish

These are a function of particle size,shape and firing conditions. However, there is obviously a conflict between the need for a range of particle sizes including some coarse ones to provide a sufficiently permeable material and the need for a fine surface finish to give the desired finish inside the casting. It was therefore decided to provide a range of sizes to give a compromise between packing density and the possibility of sufficient fine particles reaching the surface. This admittedly was empirically estimated in the first instance and refined in the light of experience and development.Typically a particle size around 250 µm was found to be satisfactory but subsequently a range of distribution sizes were needed for the range of designs which arose with time.

10. Permeability and pore size

 Figure 3 relates the influence of particle size on the important parameters of leaching rate, strength and firing shrinkage of the ceramic core and Fig. 4 shows the effect of the addition of coarser material. In order to give the best opportunity of obtaining close control of dimensions it is obvious that minimum firing shrinkage is desirable.On the other hand there is a need for high permeability to enhance leaching of the core by chemicals and to readily release gasses which can evolve from certain alloys with comparatively high carbon contents. A typical level of permeability is between 0.05 - 0.2 Darcy (1 Darcy = flow in ml/s through 1cm^3 with a pressure differential of 1 bar between opposite faces using liquid with a viscosity of 1 centipoise).

11. Thermal conductivity

The values for thermal conductivity are well documented for pore free ceramics but the following formula can be used to derive that for porous media. $Km = Cc(1-P)$ where Km is the thermal conductivity of the porous material, P, is the fractional porosity and Cc is the conductivity of dense material. It is well known that materials such as beryllia have "metal like"conductivities whilst fused silica is low.The concern with this characteristic is however in relation to its influence on thermal shock.

12. Thermal shock resistance

The following factors influence this behaviour:

Thermal shock resistance (TS) = $\dfrac{sK}{tE}$ (1 - P)

where s = strength of the material,
K = thermal conductivity,
t = thermal expansion,
E = Young's modulus,
p = Poisson's ratio

From the above it is evident that materials with high thermal conductivity, low modulus (porous materials are more flexible than their solid counterpart), low expansion and high strength, give the best thermal shock resistance. Since there is a high risk of severe thermal shock in service this is a most important consideration.

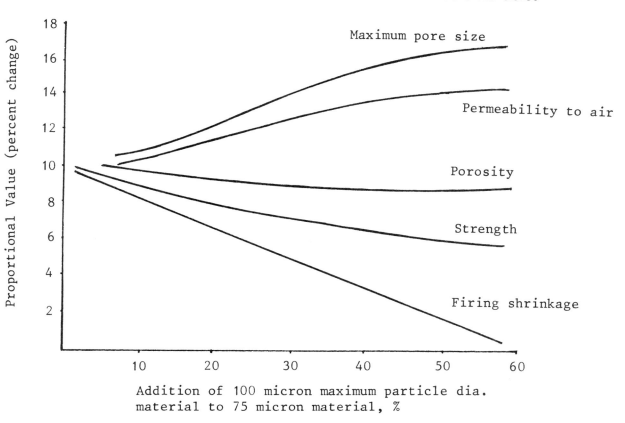

Figure 3

Table 1

Material	Common name	Melting point (°C)
ThO_2	Thoria	3,267
HfO_2	Hafnia	2,897
MgO	Magnesia	2,800
$BaO.ZrO_2$	Barium zirconate	2,700
$SrO.ZrO_2$	Strontium zirconate	2,700
ZrO_2	Zirconia	2,677
CaO	Calcia	2,600
BeO	Beryllia	2,550
$ZrO_2.SiO_2$	Zircon	2,420
$CaO.ZrO_2$	Calcium zirconate	2,345
$MgO.Al_2O_3$	Magnesia spinel	2,135
$2\ CaO.SiO_2$	Calcium orthosilicate	2,120
$MgO.ZrO_2$	Magnesium zirconate	2,120
Al_2O_3	Alumina	2,015
$3\ CaO.SiO_2$	Calcium silicate	1,900
$2\ MgO.SiO_2$	Forsterite	1,885
$Al_2O_3.TiO_2$	Aluminium titanate	1,855
TiO_2	Titania	1,840
$3\ Al_2O_3.2\ SiO_2$	Mullite	1,830
SiO_2	Silica	1,723

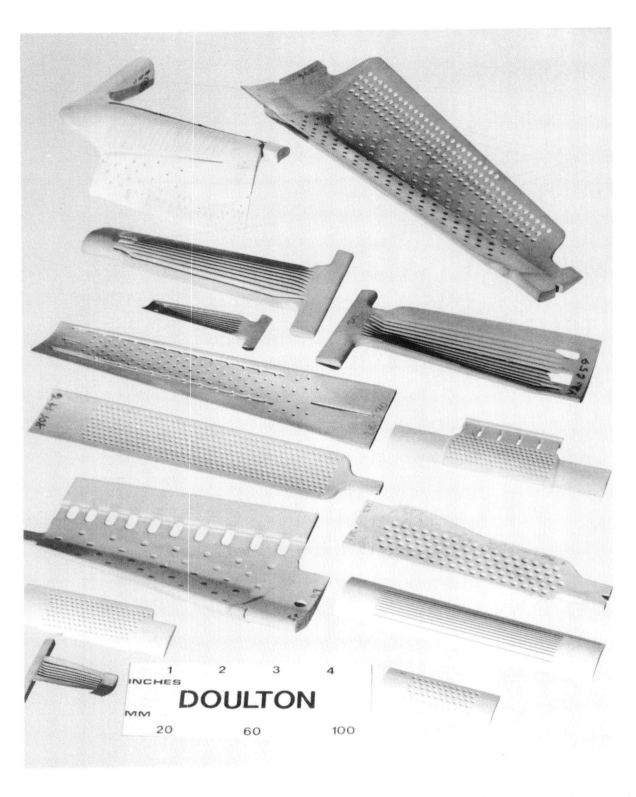

Figure 4

13. Dimensional stability and accuracy

All of the above requirements are vital to the successful production of gas turbine components. The dimensional tolerances set by the industry, require "as cast" accuracy of the order of 0.2% and surface finish better than 25 μm.

Since the ceramic core will be cycled in temperature during the casting process from room to 1800K it is vital that distortion from asymmetric expansion is minimised.

13.1 Final selection of the material

Under the heading *Technical Requiremements-Ceramic Core Material and manufacture*, factors to be taken into consideration were listed and subsequently discussed. Conclusions reached are summarised as follows:

Cost - though the product performs a valuable function, it is used only once. The amount of raw material is not likely to be of the first order of importance. It is also important that the basic material shall be available from a number of sources in the event that overseas manufacture takes place and so it is preferable that the basic material is also used for other purposes.

Refractoriness - there is a relatively wide choice from this aspect. Of the more commonly available materials however, zircon, is attractive, but it is not readily soluble for the removal stage and there is a hysteresis effect in its thermal expansion and contraction. However, this "defect" was not considered to be significant in a construction where particles are only in contact rather than in homogeneous solid form, i.e as a permeable material.

Stability - of prime importance is the selection of material which does not react with molten alloy constituents and study of practice in the foundry industry coupled with data from free energies of elements suggested that fused silica and zircon would be acceptable. Of great importance is the solubility of silica in molten caustic soda or more slowly in aqueous solution. At room temperature hydrofluoric acid reacts strongly with silica BUT it is a particularly hazardous material.

Thermal expansion - resistance to thermal shock is another priority. In an earlier text it was shown that low coefficients of thermal expansion was of major significance in this respect. Matching of the ceramic core material expansion was to that of the shell is also important, and as materials such as zircon and quartz are commonly used for this purpose, priority was given to examining the following important aspects of those materials.

Strength (particularly at elevated temperature) - since the melting point of zircon is well above that of the pouring temperature of alloys, compositions containing this oxide will be satisfactory provided it can be fabricated sufficiently strongly. As zircon has such a high melting point, it has to be bonded by another ceramic whose melting point is lower, using such ceramics as a "high temperature glue" and as a minor constituent. The strength of such a construction is also dependent on the sizes and shape of particles bonded together. Furthermore the resultant body has to be permeable for subsequent leaching after the casting is made. Another important factor is the need for sufficient high temperature strength to withstand the mechanical pressure of alloy hitting the core, as it is not possible to ensure that flow of the alloy will be equal on both sides of the core. Practical trials with test pieces indicated that a strength of approximately 30 MN/m² would survive for the designs called for initially.

Texture and surface finish - it was not possible to predict nor design the material formulation for this requirement as a priority over the needs of those parameters of greater importance i.e. strength and permeability and it was assumed that finer fraction particles would be present on the surface. For that reason some adjustment was made later in the development to get nearer to that particular target.

Permeability and pore size - calculation of the rate of leaching was another factor left to subsequent experience: similarly, suitability for releasing gasses during casting was determined by practical trials in foundries.

Thermal conductivity and thermal shock resistance -these factors are fundamental to the materials selected and for those reasons zircons and silica were favourite candidates; silica is one of the few options for solubility in solutions which do not attack nimonic alloys.

Dimensional stability and accuracy - high melting points, low coefficients of expansion and non-reactivity with molten alloys are characteristics of the materials selected; there are reasonable grounds therefore to expect good stability at high temperature. Accuracy is a function of the shaping process and this where the greatest problems were foreseen as traditional ceramic processes did not appear to meet requirements of complex shaping at a high level of accuracy i.e. without subsequent intricate machining.

Summary of material considerations - from the above it will be seen that the requirements of the end product are demanding. It is therefore not surprising that there is not much choice when all the factors are taken into consideration. The decision was therefore to sinter zirconia particles of the desired size using silica as the bonding agent and which provided the means of subsequent dissolution.

14. A new shaping process

There are two basic requirements i.e. complex shape coincidental with close tolerances as shaped.

The ceramics industry uses slip casting for complex shapes BUT the presence of a large liquid phase (water) results in a size reduction from mould dimension to fired piece, even for a porous structure of the order of 10%. Clearly process variations of only 1% would take the product out of tolerance called for i.e. within 0.2%. The elimination of the bulk of the liquid phase means that a "dry pressing" route would reduce shrinkage, but such a process can only form simple shapes with unacceptable variations in density (which would cause distortion when sintered). Furthermore initial experiments resulted in high tool wear from the abrasive particles. Though means were devised by tool design to obviate this difficulty, the anticipated trend towards cores with slots and holes,meant that a different shaping process was required to produce artefacts such as those in Fig. 4.

The above circumstances suggested a process with the following characteristics:

1. Mobility of a mix of ceramic particles of various sizes to be provided by a thermoplastic binder.
2. Shape to be formed by metal dies.
3. Rheology of the moulding compound to be capable of reproducing fine detail and thick and thin sections in the same artefact.
4. Rapid solidification of the moulding compound whilst it is in the die.
5. The resultant artefact in the green form to be readily handleable without damage or distortion.
6. Minimum size shrinkage within the moulding stage and such that total process shrinkage should not exceed 1%.
7. Subsequent ready and total removal of the temporary binder, preferably by a simple heating process and in such a manner that the ceramic artefact is not distorted during the *binding stage."
8. Finishing operations to be limited to simple removal of "flash": drawing tolerances to be met by the shaping process.
9. Die life to be 50,000 shots before major re-cut.
10. The whole shopfloor process to be suitable for unskilled labour.
11. Shot time per moulding not to exceed 1 minute.

The above specification therefore suggests an injection moulding process; which in 1962 was relatively unknown when applied to ceramics.

The key to the above requirements is clearly that of the binder system which preferably is also self-releasing from the die faces. There are of course many thermoplastics but in the interest of low die shrinkage, those with low melting points are preferable. They must also be stiff enough when filled with ceramic powder to be handleable at room temperature and must have a low viscosity when heated to a relatively low injection temperature. After examining various candidate polymers, a moulding compound based on polyethylene glycol of high molecular weight was successfully injected at temperatures less than 100° C. A mould release agent such as stearic acid was incorporated and other "plastic" additives adjusted the rheology of the moulding compound in the light of experience. Initial problems included separation of the plastic liquid phase during moulding, the sizing of injection gates and release of air from the die cavity during injection which can be relieved by venting appropriate points.

15. The Manufacturing Process

15.1 Moulding compound from constituents

Manufacture of the moulding compound can take place either in heated "Z" blade mixers or in rollmills, but in order to minimise ceramic particle size degradation the "Z" blade mixer is probably less destructive and less likely to contaminate the ceramic with wear material. (This latter factor is of vital importance as a tight specification on contaminants was in force from the aerospace industry.) Furthermore certain metal contaminants can act as fluxes during the subsequent firing cycle and therefore cause excess sintering of the artefact, reducing its permeability below the desired level. After ensuring homogeneity of the warm mixing,the compound is released onto trays for cooling, after which it is passed to a Hammermill or other suitable crushing device in order to granulate for feeding to the moulding machines. Appropriate quality control procedures are applied such as making trial mouldings in the form of test bars. These tests include all the checks on properties required of the end product and acceptable material is then released for factory use.

15.2 The injection moulding process

There are certain requirements of the moulding die i.e. the investment casting metal contractions and the ceramic process shrinkages have to be allowed for in dimensions achieved. Water cooling of the die is also desirable in order to reduce the process cycle and under certain circumstances heating of parts of the die is advantageous in order to encourage flow of material into fine passageways. It is also preferable to have a hardened or hardsurface die. The gates may also be constructed from inserts of particularly hard metal to ensure mating of the nozzle of the injector and the die entrance in the long term.

It is possible to utilise either screw or piston injection machines but whilst screw machines efficiently homogenise the mix in the barrel,they are much more expensive to maintain. Piston machines are relatively simple as replaceable piston tips can be set aside as inexpensive spares. There are features needed for ceramic injection moulding to proceed in an economic production manner but it is possible to make product with standard equipment for experimental purposes.

After setting up the die, trials will determine the temperature settings required in the barrel and the tool, according to the efficiency of filling the cavity in the shortest time. Defects may not always be detected at the moulding stage - a test firing of the product may reveal the presence of excessive porosity in sections distant from the injection point. This is a matter of trial and error. It is important to ensure integrity in this respect as otherwise there is a possibility of mechanical failure of the core when molten metal "hits" it. This of course would result in a closed passageway in the casting, which may be quite difficult to detect as the barrier may only be a few μm in thickness. Nevertheless its presence would defeat the intentions of the designer and present potential hazards to the user! To guarantee this quality, it is good practice to X-ray first off fired components to ensure continuity of cavity. There is much debate as to responsibility for inspection but there is much to be said for making the injection moulder carry out initial measurements of his or her production and it became practice for certain measurements to be made by them on each shot. Each moulding is then placed in the receptacle used for the sintering stage. The long established technique is to "bed" the component in a refractory powder whose fusion point is much in excess of that applied to the product. This ensures support of the ceramic powder particles at the stage at which the temporary binder has disappeared and before sintering of the particles has taken place.This important technique became part of the disclosure in the patents granted.

15.3 The sintering process

The product has now been embedded in a refractory container (sagger) and is ready for sintering. There is a choice of firing in an oxidising atmosphere either by electricity or gas. First the temporary binder has to be eliminated by gradual heating to vapourise the binder and in such a way that melting followed by volatilisation does not distort the ceramic from its shape. Different melting points and different volatilisation temperatures of the binder constituents will assist this important requirement of a successful technique. The proprietary nature of the formulations determine the efficiency of this stage. Binder removal takes place first by distillation of volatile constituents of the hydrocarbon mixture into gas scrubbing towers (in order to be environmentally secure). At about 500°C a carbon residue remains and at this stage the ceramic core is strong enough to be handled if it is desired to carry out the sintering in a different furnace. Normal practice is however to leave the components in the original furnace to continue the heat treatment to approximately 1200 °C, dependent on the particular ceramic composition. The carbon residue has now been completely oxidised. The whole cycle may take 50h dependent on the cross-section of the ceramic being fired. After cooling down the cores are removed from their saggers and finishing operations undertaken.

15.4 Finishing and Inspection

As stated earlier in this Chapter, one objective of the near net shaping project is to minimise finishing by machining. It will also be obvious to readers that the geometry and detail of gas turbine cores is such that it is not possible, for instance, to reposition any of the many small holes or slots as shown in Fig. 5.Dimensions have to be achieved "as made"— otherwise one would have to make only a basic aerofoil form and then machine all detail into the fired part. That would be a Herculean task — akin to making a mechanical watch in ceramic using diamond cutting tools! Finishing, therefore, consists of viewing parts under a magnifying glass, using optical or precision dial gauges set up specifically for each particular design. After elimination of defective parts, finishing is the removal of flash from the parting lines of the die, using diamond coated files and drills.This calls for skill, though attempts have been made to use image recognition techniques driving robotic devices to substitute for the human hand and eye. Process control is exercised on all materials and subsequent processes such as after grinding silica to powder.The powders are then sieved to extract the desired particles; the required particles are then reblended and the unwanted particles are rejected. The exact nature of the "sievecuts" are of a proprietary nature and therefore not disclosed. Chemical and physical composition of ceramic and polymer materials are measured before materials are released for production. Test bars are made from approved material and checked for compliance with the properties listed in Table 2 which also relates the various compositions for use with various alloys. Satisfactory batches of material are subsequently released by the Laboratory to the Factory for manufacture. Certificates relating material to batches used in products are also made available to customers as part of their process control procedures.

16. Conclusion

The above development was carried out by a mixture of classical research techniques and "common sense" to short-cut some of the alternatives which could have been followed. Consequently, the time lapse between decision to pursue ceramic injection moulding and the successful production of a commercial product was approximately 18 months and it involved a team of specially recruited technologists to supplement the existing ceramic expertise.

The same basic process has also been used to fabricate fully dense engineering ceramics of complex shape; there are greater difficulties with such dense materials as powders are much finer and for instance it is therefore more difficult to burn out the binder. The search continues for more tolerant systems using binders containing materials which sublime. Other processes developed elsewhere meanwhile are based on waxes; others contain water in an attempt to reduce the binder burnout time. The success of injection moulding of ceramics has undoubtedly acted as a catalyst to encourage the injection moulding of metal powders either for reasons of metallurgical significance or because near net shaping of complex forms is more economic.

In the author's opinion, the most important factors in achieving a objectives were the thorough examination of requirements of the aerospace industry, the characterising of ceramic and polymer materials, willingness

Table 2

Material Code	Nominal Composition	Cold M.o.R. MN/m2	Hot M.o.R. MN/m2	Thermal Expansion (%) at 600°C	Thermal Expansion (%) at 1000°C	Darcy Permeability	Bulk Density g/cc	Apparent Porosity (%)	Water Absorption (%)	Leachability mins/mm	Alloy Compatibility
LC4	Silica Based	5.5	13 at 1100°C	0.12	0.15	~0.05	1.55	30	20	9	Nickel based alloys
LC11	Silica Based	8.6	13 at 1100°C	0.09	0.20	>0.1	1.50	35	23	9	Nickel based alloys and particularly air cast cobalt based alloys which are prone to gassing problems with LC4
LC21	Zircon and Silica	7.5	ND	0.13	0.21	~0.09	2.20	36	16	6	Low and medium carbon steel, stainless steel and air cast cobalt based alloys with carbon content up to approx. 0.2%
MD	Zircon and Silica	11.0	26 at 1450°C	0.25	0.25	~0.06	1.70	34	20	12	DS and SC applications*
ME	Silica	12.4	33 at 1450°C	0.22	0.23	~0.065	1.60	30	19	12	DS and SC applications

* Directional solidification and single crystal

to "technology transfer" process concepts from other industries (viz. injection moulding of plastics), and the recruitment of precision engineering specialists to supplement their ceramic counterparts. The process* has now been in commercial operation for over 25 years and though continuously refined, it is still basically that which was conceived in the original R and D project.

17. References

1. S. Byworth, "Design and development of high temperature turbines", Rolls Royce Magazine, June 1986.

2. E. M. Briscoe, "Preformed Cores-their Use, Manufacture and Benefits", in European Investment Casters Conference, Madrid,October 1965.

3. E. M. Briscoe, "Ceramics in the Investment Casting Industry", in First World Conference of Investment Casters, London May 1966.

4. E. M. Briscoe, "Injection moulding for near net shapes", Chartered Mechanical Engineer, January 1986.

5. E. M. Briscoe, "A new era for engineering ceramics?", The Royal Society of Arts Journal, November 1984.

6. "Metal, Ceramic and cemented carbide injection moulding", First European Conference, I.B.C.Technical Services, London, December 1988. Technical Literature, Fairey Industrial Ceramics, Stone Staffs, 1989.

7. R. Morrell, Handbook of properties of technical and engineering ceramics, National Physical Laboratory, 1988.

8. Modern Materials in Manufacturing Industry. Report of a working party. The Fellowship of Engineering, May 1983.

*British Patent Number 1006518 January 1964, awarded to Doulton and Company, exploited by Fairey

Case Study 11
Dimensional Precision in PM Parts:
Coated powder mixing technology

A. LAWLEY
Department of Materials Engineering, Drexel University, Philadelphia, PA 19104, USA

Powder metallurgy (PM), in particular pressing and sintering, is the preferred fabrication method for the production of complex shaped parts. The PM advantage over casting, working or machining is primarily economic — low cost production, a high materials utilization factor, a high level of productivity, and dimensional precision in the product [1]. To maintain this competitive edge and to expand usage of PM parts, the ferrous PM industry is seeking to increase part strength and performance. This mandates more sophisticated alloy compositions, dimensional precision, and improved tolerance control (less dimensional scatter) during sintering to eliminate subsequent sizing or machining.

The conventional commercial methods of introducing alloying elements into the base iron powder are admixing or prealloying by atomization. A major drawback to admixing is the subsequent segregation of the constituent powders during handling, resulting in variations in dimensional change within the sintered part. Pre-alloyed powders are essential homogeneous with respect to the distribution of alloying elements but suffer from decreased compressibility since the alloying elements are in solid solution.

1. Introduction

Improved mechanical property levels in ferrous PM parts, in particular strength, toughness and fatigue resistance, are achieved by alloying [1, 2]. One commercial approach to alloying of the iron is atomization using water or gas to produce a pre-alloyed powder [3]. Each powder particle is essentially homogeneous with respect to chemical composition, and the extent of segregation is limited by the powder particle size. The solid solution alloying increases hardness and decreases compressibility of the iron particles which may preclude cold compaction. In the limit, highly alloyed gas atomized alloys such as high speed tool steels must be consolidated by hot isostatic pressing.

The other commercial alloying approach in ferrous PM is via the admixing of elements or master alloy powders using a double cone blender or paddle mixer [1,2]. Conventional iron-base alloys containing carbon, nickel, molybdenum and copper are prepared in this way; a schematic of admixed Fe-Cu-C powder is illustrated in Fig. 1. Frequently, alloying elements are admixed in the form of a brittle master alloy powder, for example the ferroalloys of manganese, chromium and silicon. Admixing offers flexibility with respect to the adjustment of composition and the addition of lubricants and/or binders. Typically, admixed alloy powders exhibit a high level of compressibility since solid solution alloying is delayed until the sintering step.

Admixed powders are prone to segregation and dusting during handling [4-8]. The origin of the segregation resides primarily in differences in powder density, particle size, particle shape and particle surface morphology of the constituents in the admixed alloy. A particularly vexing element is carbon (graphite) which segregates readily because of its low density compared to iron. Segregation and dusting will also occur during shipping of the powder from supplier to parts maker. As a result of segregation and or dusting, variations in chemical composition can occur from part to part in a production run — and in the extreme case within a single part.

While several factors influence the final dimensional change of a pressed and sintered PM part, variations in alloy content have a predominant effect during sintering. The influence of differences in copper and carbon content on the dimensional change of admixed Fe-2.5 w/o Cu-0.35 w/o C during sintering is shown in Fig. 2 [4]. The data show that a scatter in copper content of +0.25 % results in a dimensional change from +0.19% to 0.31% during sintering. Similarly, if the scatter in carbon content is ~0.1%, the corresponding scatter in dimensional change during sintering is from –0.18% to +0.32%. As a result of these relatively large dimensional ranges, there will be a correspondingly large scatter in the final dimensions of the sintered parts in a production run, as shown in Fig. 3.

To restate the problem, segregation and/or dusting in admixed powder alloys lead to compositional inhomogeneities from part to part which in turn decrease the extent to which tolerance can be controlled during sintering. The solution is to prevent movement of the alloy constituents after the admixing step. This has been achieved by means of coated ('sticky') powder technology. Many of the details of this approach are proprietary. There is, however, sufficient information in the open literature to discuss examples in terms of the properties of mixed powders free from segregation and dusting, and their behavior during compaction and sintering.

2. Approach

2.1 Diffusion annealing

A partial solution to the segregation problem is to admix the elemental powders and/or master alloy and then heat the powder mix in a reducing atmosphere [4]. The intent of this step is to promote chemical bonding between the base iron powder and the alloy powder particles, for example copper and nickel. By controlling the extent of diffusion, the iron powder is partially pre-alloyed — but not to the extent that compressibility is impaired. This diffusion annealing approach results in improved tolerances of as-sintered properties; consistency of powder properties and minimal segregation of the alloying element(s) are contributing factors. Commercial powder mixes prepared by admixing and diffusion annealing are sold under the trade name DISTALOY®.

The diffusion bonding technology does not solve the problem of segregation of carbon (graphite particles), and of fine ferroalloy additions containing manganese, chromium, silicon and phosphorus. These elements diffuse rapidly in iron, even at relatively low temperatures and it is not possible to exercise controlled or partial prealloying. Hardness increases via solid solution strengthening and there is a corresponding decrease in compressibility.

2.3 Coated powders

In this approach a proprietary binder is added to the mix of powders in order to coat each particle [4,8]. Graphite and the other elemental or master alloy additions bond to the coated iron particles and are not able to segregate or escape by dusting. Physically the situation is rather like the functioning of the old-style sticky paper fly catcher. The sticky paper is the analogue of the coated iron powder and the fly, adhering the the sticky paper, is the analogue of the particle of graphite, copper, or other alloying elements. The word 'sticky' is inappropriate, however, since the binder does not degrade the flow response of the powder.

3. Product

To illustrate the capability of this coated powder technology, examples are cited for the powder, compaction response and sintered properties. Material and process details for the binder addition are all essentially proprietary.

Sonobe et al. [8] prepared alloys of Fe-2 w/o Cu-1 w/o graphite and Fe-2 w/o graphite by conventional admixing and by the coated powder approach. The constituents were water atomized iron powder, electrolytic copper powder (dm = 48μm), a natural graphite (dm = 20μm) and zinc stearate as lubricant. A proprietary binder was used for the segregation-suppressed powder mix. The binder treatment gives carbon adhesion ratios* of more than 80% for both compositions, whereas the adhesion ratios were about 20% for each of the

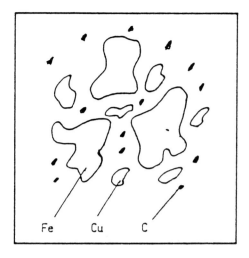

Figure 1. Conventional admixed Fe-Cu-C powder - schematic [4].

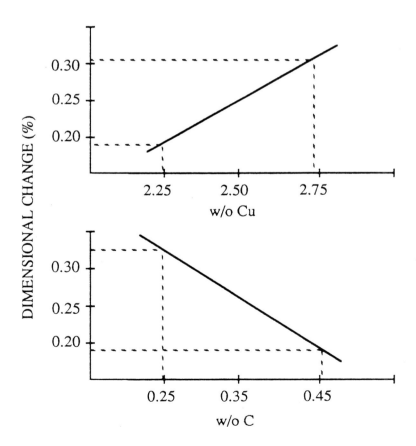

Figure 2. Dimensional change during sintering as a function of copper and carbon level; admixed Fe-2.5 w/o Cu-0.35 w/o C [4].

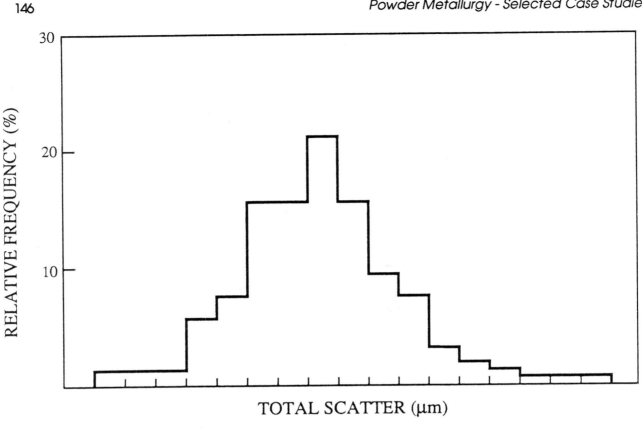

Figure 3. Relative frequency of the total scatter in sintered part dimensions; admixed Fe-2.5 w/o Cu-0.35 w/o C [4].

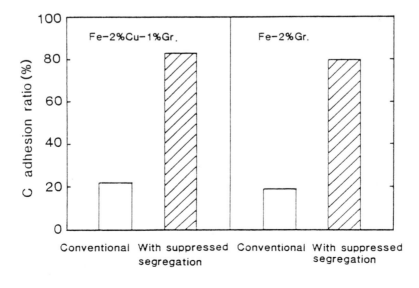

Figure 4. Carbon adhesion ratio in conventional admixed and suppressed- segregation Fe-Cu-C and Fe-C alloys [8].

conventional mixes, (Fig. 4). The extent of dusting was reduced by 90% in the bindered mix. It was also observed that concentration of graphite in the final stage of powder feeding from a hopper, characteristic of conventional admixed powders, was completely suppressed in the bonded powder mix.

Apparent densities of the two compositions in the admixed and bindered conditions are illustrated in (Fig.5). There is a beneficial increase in apparent density in the segregation-free powders. Similarly, the flow rate of the segregation-free powder mix is significantly higher (~30%) than that of the conventional admixed powder, (Fig. 6). This results in improved die-filling response in production runs. The increase in flow rate and apparent density reflects a combination of agglomeration of the fines by the binder, and the fact that the organic binder is essentially a tact-free solid at ambient temperature.

Green density is similar in both powder mixes, but the ejection forces are lower (by ~4 %) in the suppressed-segregation powder. By monitoring properties as a function of storage time for the Fe-2 w/o Cu- 1 w/o graphite alloy, it was shown that apparent density, flow rate, green density, ejection force and the carbon adhesion ratio do not change significantly after eight weeks in the bindered powder mix.

Dimensional change during sintering is compared in Fig. 7 for the Fe-2 w/o Cu-1 w/o graphite alloy. The lower dimensional change in the suppressed-segregation powder mix is attributed to the enhanced homogeneity of the graphite distribution; this suppresses diffusion of the copper into the iron powder particles with attendant growth. The standard deviation of carbon content and dimensional change decreased by 50% and 90% respectively, when the carbon adhesion ratio was increased from 22% to 80%.

Sintered compacts prepared from the segregation-suppressed mix show equivalent hardness and tensile strength, but higher toughness than the conventional powder mix [8]. The latter is attributed to the more uniform microstructure as a result of the homogeneous distribution of the graphite.

Semel has recently determined the properties of green compacts and sintered parts made via the coated powder approach, using a solid organic binder [7]. A property comparison for Fe-2 w/o Ni-0.8 w/o C (with 0.6 w/o Acrowax and 0.3 w/o zinc stearate), with and without the organic binder (~0.125 w/o) is made in Table 1. The bonded mix exhibits substantially increased resistance to compositional variations either by alloy particle migration within the mix, or by dusting from the mix; it also exhibits a much more uniform or lamellar flow response which translates into an increase in flow rate. Prior studies on binder-treated Fe-0.45 w/o P [5] and Fe-0.8 w/o C [6] gave similar trends.

The part studied was a cylindrical bushing [7]. Significant differences in mean dimensional change characteristics were exhibited by the bonded mix; otherwise response was similar to the regular admixed powder in terms of mean property values. In terms of variability, the bonded mix was statistically equivalent with respect to green and sintered dimensional change characteristics and with respect to the nickel content after sintering. Otherwise, the variability of the properties of the bonded mix was significantly improved relative to the regular admixed powder; these properties are green weight and density, sintered density, hardness, crush strength and carbon content. Full-scale production of bonded (coated powder) premixes has recently been implemented by Hoeganaes, USA under the name ANCORBOND®.

Hoganas, Sweden has also developed a blending technology to eliminate segregation and dusting in ferrous powder alloys. It is termed "Starmix" and utilizes an organic binder to 'glue' the fine graphite particles or alloying elements to the base iron powder [4]. A comparison between the standard admixed powder and the Starmix recipe demonstrates that both powder mixes have similar properties before and after sintering. The flow characteristics of the Starmix are improved and the carbon loss is lowered significantly compared to the regular mix.

* Carbon adhesion ratio = [X]/[X']
X = carbon content in -100 + 200 mesh range (C) of powder mix
X'= carbon content in total powder mix.

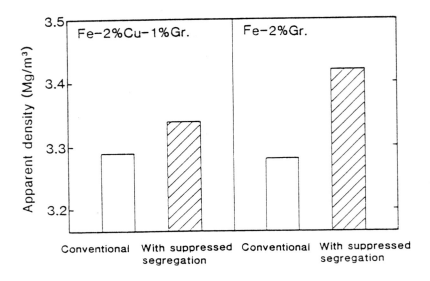

Figure 5. Apparent density for conventional admixed and suppressed-segregation Fe-Cu-C and Fe-C alloys [8].

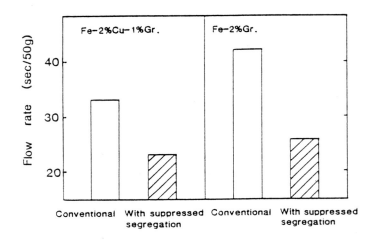

Figure 6. Flow rate of conventional admixed and suppressed-segregation Fe-Cu-C and Fe-C alloys [8].

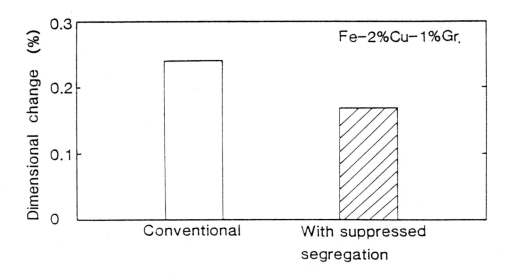

Figure 7. Dimensional change after sintering in conventional admixed and suppressed-segregation Fe-Cu-C and Fe-C alloys [8].

Table 1

Property	Bonded Mix	Regular Mix
Apparent Density (Mg/m^3)	3.11	3.04
Hall Flow (sec/50g)	31.00	38.00
Green Density (Mg/m^3)*	6.67	6.70
Green Strength (MPa)*	9.97	10.75
Dust Resistance		
Graphite (%)	96.00	35.00
Nickel (%)	85.00	31.00
Sintered Density (Mg/m^3)	6.77	6.78
Dimensional Change (%)	-0.008	-0.001
TRS (MPa)	834.00	856.00
Hardness Rb	73.00	74.00

* At 413 MPa

4. Case Studies

Two case studies are cited for production-scale runs; both pertain to the Starmix powder coating technology [4].

Two iron-base powder mixes were prepared containing 0.8 w/o P and 0.35 w/o graphite - one by conventional admixing and the other via the Starmix technology [4]. From each mix, 2000 parts were compacted and sintered (1120°C/30 min) in an endothermic atmosphere under a controlled carbon potential. The carbon content in the sintered parts from each mix is shown in Fig. 8. It is seen that in the parts made from the Starmix powder alloy, the variation in combined carbon content over the 2000-part run is about four times smaller than that in the parts pressed and sintered from the regular admixed powder. This translates into a significant improvement in the scatter in sintered part dimensions, Fig. 9. Specifically the dimensional scatter is reduced from 99μm to 45μm with the Starmix technology.

In the second case study, a large-scale production test was performed on a part at Dansk Sintermetal, Denmark [4]. The alloy examined was Fe-0.08 w/o P - 0.45% C, with an addition of 0.75 w/o zinc stearate. Parts were sintered to a density in the range 6.7 - 6.8 g/cm^3 (1120°C/30 min) in a mix of endogas and propane. Approximately 10,000 parts each were made from the standard mix and the Starmix material. Sintered part dimensions were monitored on about 300 samples from each mix, and the results are shown in Fig. 10. The improvement in dimensional tolerance (scatter) is clearly demonstrated for the Starmix powder alloy. This decreased scatter in sintered part length is attributed to the small variation in carbon content from part to part in the Starmix material, (Fig.11). The variation (scatter) in carbon content is decreased from 0.1% to 0.05% by utilizing the Starmix coated powder technology.

Conclusion

Several proprietary processes now exist which result in mixes of iron-base alloys free from segregation and dusting. These processes entail coating of the iron powder with an organic binder so that graphite and other alloying additions bond firmly to the surface of the iron powder particles. Compared to conventional admixing, this coated powder technology significantly reduces scatter in sintered dimensions, a consequence of the more uniform distribution of the alloying elements in the final part. This enhancement in tolerance control is expected to improve process efficiency and yield, and to result in a wider application of high performance PM parts, at the expense of manufacturing methods based on ingot metallurgy.

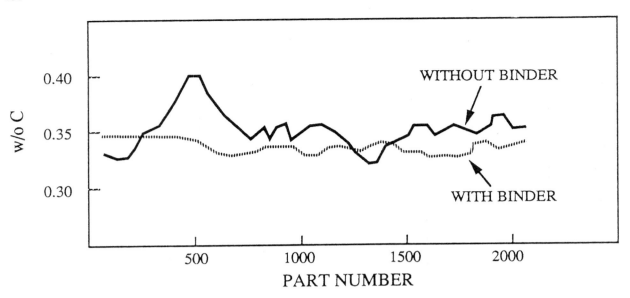

Figure 8. Carbon level in pressed and sintered parts for admixed and Starmix powders; Fe-0.8 w/o P-0. 13 w/o C [4].

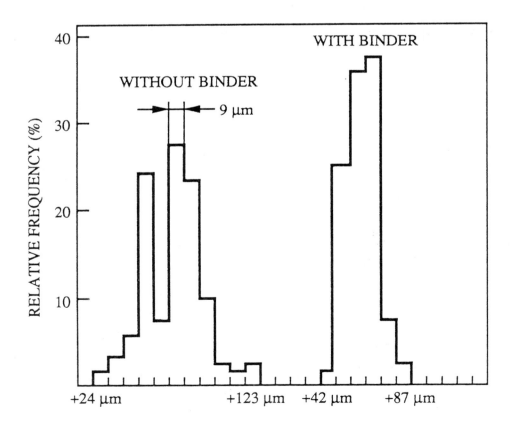

Figure 9. Scatter frequency in dimensional change during sintering of admixed and Starmix Fe-0.8 w/o P-0.13 w/o C [4]. Part length 30 mm.

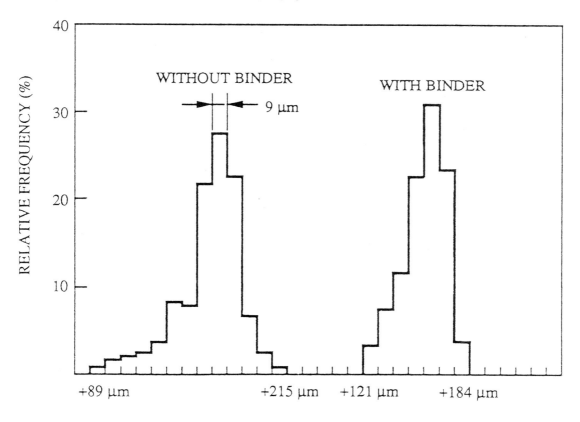

Figure 10. Relative frequency of sintered part length for admixed and Starmix Fe-0.8 w/o P-0.13 w/o C [4]. Part length 21.5 mm.

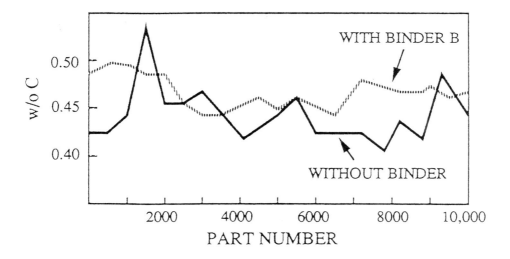

Figure 11. Carbon level in pressed and sintered parts for admixed and Starmix powders: Fe-0.8 w.o P-0.13 w/o C [4].

6. References

1. R.M. German, Powder Metallurgy Science, Metal Powder Industries Federation, Princeton, New Jersey, 1984.

2. Metals Handbook, Ninth Edition, Vol. 7., American Society for Metals, Metals Park, Ohio, 1984.

3. A. Lawley, Journal of Metals, *38*, No.8, 1986, 15, .

4. U. Engstrom, Metals Powder Report, *42*, No. 1, p. 22, 1987.

5. F.J. Semel, Progress in Powder Metallurgy, Compiled by C.L. Freeby and H. Hjort, Metal Powder Industries Federation, Princeton, New Jersey, *43*, 1987, 723.

6. F.J. Semel, Modem Developments in Powder Metallurgy. Compiled by P.U. Gummeson and D.A. Gustafson, Metal Powder Industries Federation, Princeton, New Jersey, *21*, p. 101,1988.

7. F.J. Semel, Advances in Powder Metallurgy. Compiled by T.G. Gasbarre, Jr. and W.F. Jandeska, Jr., Metal Powder Industries Federation, Princeton, New Jersey, *11*, 1989, p. 9.

8. A. Sonobe, I. Sakurada, K. Makino, T. Minegishi and S. Takajo, ibid. ,p. 39.